Praise for the #1 *New York* 

# MINDHUNTER

## by John Douglas and Mark Olshaker

"Remarkable and chilling."

—Patricia Cornwell

"A quirky, winning tale of awful crimes and awe-inspiring detective work."

—*USA Today*

"A fascinating journey into the thrill killer's psyche . . . Douglas seems to have a true gift of instinct. *Mindhunter* is gripping."

—*Dayton Daily News* (OH)

"In this . . . fascinating memoir of his twenty-five-year career with the FBI, John Douglas contends that psychopathic serial killers have a warped need to kill. . . . The key to Douglas' approach is to look for the 'signature'—as opposed to the modus operandi—of serial killers. . . . Douglas is at his best describing the terrible crimes that were committed and explaining the logic of his profiling method."

—*Houston Chronicle*

"In his spellbinding book, the legendary Douglas . . . delves into much of the gritty how-to of criminal personality 'profiling.'. . . He's downright gifted. . . . [We] defy anyone interested in psychology, detective work, or logic and puzzle-solving to put *Mindhunter* willingly aside once begun."

—*The Virginian-Pilot*

## ALSO AVAILABLE FROM
## JOHN DOUGLAS AND MARK OLSHAKER

### Nonfiction

*When a Killer Calls: A Haunting Story of Murder,
Criminal Profiling, and Justice in a Small Town*

*The Killer's Shadow: The FBI's Hunt
for a White Supremacist Serial Killer*

*The Killer Across the Table: Unlocking the Secrets of Serial Killers and
Predators with the FBI's Original Mindhunter*

*Law & Disorder: Inside the Dark Heart of Murder*

*The Cases That Haunt Us: From Jack the Ripper to JonBenet Ramsey,
the FBI's Legendary Mindhunter Sheds Light on the Mysteries
That Won't Go Away*

*Obsession: The FBI's Legendary Profiler Probes the Psyches of Killers,
Rapists, and Stalkers and Their Victims and Tells How to Fight Back*

*Journey into Darkness: The FBI's Premier Investigator Penetrates the
Minds and Motives of the Most Terrifying Serial Killers*

*Unabomber: On the Trail of America's Most-Wanted Serial Killer*

*Mindhunter: Inside the FBI's Elite Serial Crime Unit*

### Fiction

*Broken Wings*

## JOHN DOUGLAS

*Sexual Homicide: Patterns and Motives* (with Ann W. Burgess and Robert K. Ressler)

*John Douglas's Guide to Careers in the FBI*

*Anyone You Want Me to Be: A True Story of Sex and Death on the Internet* (with Stephen Singular)

*John Douglas's Guide to Landing a Career in Law Enforcement*

*Crime Classification Manual: A Standard System for Investigating and Classifying Violent Crimes* (with Ann W. Burgess, Allen G. Burgess, and Robert K. Ressler)

*Inside the Mind of BTK* (with Johnny Dodd)

## MARK OLSHAKER

*Nonfiction*

*The Instant Image: Edwin Land and the Polaroid Experience*

*Virus Hunter: Thirty Years of Battling Hot Viruses Around the World* (with C. J. Peters)

*Deadliest Enemy: Our War Against Killer Germs* (with Michael Osterholm)

*Fiction*

*Einstein's Brain*

*Blood Race*

*Unnatural Causes*

*The Edge*

# THE
# ANATOMY
# OF MOTIVE

*The FBI's Legendary Mindhunter Explores the Key
to Understanding and Catching Violent Criminals*

# JOHN DOUGLAS
# AND MARK OLSHAKER

GALLERY BOOKS

New York  London  Toronto  Sydney  New Delhi

G

Gallery Books
An Imprint of Simon & Schuster, LLC
1230 Avenue of the Americas
New York, NY 10020

This Gallery Books trade paperback edition December 2024

GALLERY BOOKS and colophon are registered trademarks
of Simon & Schuster, LLC

Simon & Schuster: Celebrating 100 Years of Publishing in 2024

For information about special discounts for bulk purchases,
please contact Simon & Schuster Special Sales at 1-866-506-1949
or business@simonandschuster.com.

The Simon & Schuster Speakers Bureau can bring authors
to your live event. For more information or to book an event,
contact the Simon & Schuster Speakers Bureau at 1-866-248-3049
or visit our website at www.simonspeakers.com.

Interior design by Ritika Karnik

Manufactured in the United States of America

10  9  8  7  6  5  4  3  2  1

Library of Congress Cataloging-in-Publication Data is available.

ISBN 978-1-6680-4940-2
ISBN 978-0-6848-5779-4 (ebook)

*For Dolores Douglas, Thelma Olshaker, and Molly Clemente*
*with love*

# AUTHORS' NOTE

As always, our deepest and most profound gratitude go out to the "first team" that made this book possible: our visionary, sensitive, and nurturing editor, Lisa Drew; her assistant, Jake Klisivitch; our research director, Ann Hennigan, who shaped and organized the entire book; our agent, manager, and confidant, Jay Acton; and Mark's wife, Carolyn, our in-house counsel and Mindhunters chief of staff.

It's about time we gave special thanks to Scribner publisher Susan Moldow, who suggested this book theme to us, was critical in the development process, supported and guided us at every step, and has always kept the faith. Publishers like her are rare, and we feel extremely fortunate to have come into her orbit.

Thanks also to our many friends and colleagues in law enforcement, forensic analysis, victims' rights, and the related fields. Your work is vital and your inspiration enormous.

To Bobby Acton, keep on plugging. You're the next generation of Mindhunters, and we need you out there.

To Sean Lee Hennigan, your obvious love, good humor, and unfailingly sunny disposition have been a constant source of strength and encouragement.

Finally, we'd like to take a moment to remember Suzanne Collins, Stephanie Schmidt, Destiny Souza, and all the rest of our angels. And if we're worthy, we hope they'll put in a good word for us.

—*John Douglas and Mark Olshaker,*
*February 1999*

*The key to the period appeared to be that the mind had become aware of itself. . . . The young men were born with knives in their brain, a tendency to introversion, self-dissection, anatomizing of motives.*

—RALPH WALDO EMERSON,
*Life and Letters in New England*

# DUNBLANE

*Why did he do it?*

I just happen to be in Scotland when I hear about the massacre.

It's the morning of Wednesday, March 13, 1996, and I'm in a television studio in Glasgow as part of a promotional tour for my book *Mindhunter,* at the invitation of our British publisher. For the last hour I've been interviewed about criminal profiling on the ITV television program *This Morning* by a very personable team of cohosts named Richard Madeley and Judy Finnigan. How did I begin in the field? they ask. How did I learn what I know, and whom did I learn it from? How did my Investigative Support Unit in Quantico, Virginia, go about creating and using a profile of an unknown subject or UNSUB, as he is known in FBI and law enforcement circles? Throughout the tour I've been really pumped up by the Brits' fascination with the subject and the interest they've shown in my career of studying and hunting killers, rapists, bombers—men whose evil and depraved acts challenge the bounds of the human imagination. Fortunately for the people of the United Kingdom, their society is not nearly as violent as ours in the United States but they come by their fascination understandably. The first known serial killer—Jack the Ripper—terrorized the East End of London in a grisly mystery that's remained unsolved for more than a hundred years. On this tour, interviewers still ask me if the killer could be profiled and the case closed. I tell them that it would be difficult to come up with the Ripper's specific identity at this late date, but that even after a century we can very legitimately profile the UNSUB and say with reasonable assurance the *type of individual* he was. In fact, I tell them, I've done it several times in the Ripper murders—both in training exercises at Quantico and on a live international television broadcast with Peter Ustinov some years ago.

I'm back in the TV station's greenroom when the producer comes in. I assume she's going to thank me for appearing, but when I look at her she's grim, and her voice is urgent.

"John, can you come back on the show here?"

I've just done an hour—what more could they possibly want? "Why?" I ask. "What's happened?"

"There's been a horrible murder in Dunblane."

I'd never even heard of the place. It turns out to be a traditionally peaceful village of about 7,300 people, midway between Glasgow and Edinburgh, that goes back to the Middle Ages. I've got about five minutes before the producer wants me back on, and she quickly hands me the wire service copy.

It says there's been a mass killing of children at the Dunblane Primary School. Reports were frantic and details sketchy, but it appears that a gunman walked into the school at about 9:30 in the morning and began shooting four-, five-, and six-year-olds in the playground. There'd been multiple gunshots, and some of the children had definitely been killed. Others were injured, their teacher fatally wounded. The news reports didn't have a name or age, but apparently the killer had more than one weapon with him—high-caliber military-type weapons, it seemed.

From these brief news flashes, it sounds like a scene of utter and appalling horror. For a father of three—even with all I've seen—it's difficult not to become sick at the thought of small children being massacred on the playground of their own school.

This is all the information we have when we come back on the air a few minutes later, still reeling from the news. The story is broadcast, and Richard Madeley turns to me and says something like, "Well, John, what do we have here?"

"Well, first of all, you're dealing with a mass murderer," I tell them, then explain how that's different from serial murderers and spree killers. A serial killer is hunting human beings for the sexual thrill it gives him and will do it over and over again, believing he can outwit and outmaneuver the police, never expecting to be caught. The spree killer kills a number of victims at different locations in a short period of hours or days. But a mass killer is playing an endgame strategy. Once he commits himself to his course of action, he does not expect to come out of it alive. He will generally either kill himself after he's "made his statement" or commit what we call "suicide by cop"—forcing a confrontation in which the police or SWAT team will have no choice but to open fire. I expect that later reports will say that this individual died at the scene. These killers are such inadequate people, such losers, that they know they cannot get away and won't give others the satisfaction of controlling them or bringing them to justice.

But what kind of person would do this? Judy Finnigan wants to know, genuinely bewildered.

"Well," I respond, "the first thing you have to understand is the motive, and the key to that is in the victimology." Who has he chosen as his victims, and why? Are they victims of opportunity, or was a careful and deliberate choice made?

"Generally speaking, mass murderers are white males, ranging from their mid-to-late thirties to their mid-to-late forties. In your country you don't have that large a percentage of blacks, so the white-male guess is a pretty good one. But even in our country, where we have many more blacks, it's still going to be a white male, and he'll be an asocial loner. That's what this gunman is going to turn out to be."

But these things don't happen in a vacuum. I know very well that even though we have few details at this point, a pattern is going to emerge as soon as we know more, and I already feel I can say what that pattern is going to be. The identity of the person who's responsible for this crime, I state, should not come as any surprise to his community. This is someone who's had a history of turmoil in this locale. And because it's a school that is the target, there must have been some problem in his relationship with the children in the school, with the school itself, or with the parents. There must be something related.

"In this kind of case," I say, "you would know that there has to be a reason why this subject would pick schoolkids—something in his life connecting schoolchildren and himself. And he'll pick a place he's familiar with, where he feels comfortable."

Children are sometimes victims in a mass murder, but normally they will be either incidental victims (such as when someone shoots up a fast-food restaurant) or members of a targeted family. This was a different type of crime altogether, and its perpetrator, I predict, will adhere to a defined pattern of behavior.

Leading up to the crime, these people are very, very frustrated; very, very angry. You would look for this one in Dunblane to have written letters—perhaps to the school principal or headmaster, the local newspaper, or some municipal authority. These types are much more comfortable with the written form of communication—and so they'll express themselves in diaries, express the hate or anger they feel about whatever it is that's bothering them. When they feel they are not getting satisfaction, they may escalate and address their grievances at an even higher level. In the United States, it could be to the president. In Britain, it might be to the queen or prime minister. Then they reach a point in their lives when they feel no one is paying attention. So they take it upon themselves to perpetrate this type of crime.

I tell my television hosts that this crime appears to me to be a kind of revenge. Because the victims were very young children, I suspect it was retaliation for some perceived wrong—real or imagined—perpetrated against the killer. The children themselves were too young to have been targeted individually, too young for the guy to conceive that any of them had personally wronged him. The main target was not the teacher, though. Had that been the case, he would have shot her, then left. She was probably heroically defending the children and he eliminated her merely to get to his primary prey. In my mind, it is as if innocence itself is the target—as if he has decided to take something very precious from either their parents, the school officials, or both.

He will turn out to be single, I say, without any significant relationships with women in his own age range. He will have had something to do with young children, either as a teacher himself or, more likely, as a scoutmaster or volunteer of some sort. This is the only sort of sexualized relationship he would feel comfortable with; he couldn't relate to his own peers, or they to him. He may be homosexual and prefer boys to girls, but not necessarily, since the victims are so far prepubescent. But parents or teachers will have become suspicious or wary of him, enough so that he's been removed from his position in charge of young children. He will think this is unfair, uncalled for; after all, all he is doing is giving them love and attention. That's what his letters will have been about: complaining that his reputation has been damaged.

When no one will listen, he realizes he has nothing of importance left in his life. And if these precious innocents are taken away from him, then he will take them away from those who are causing him this grief. He will take it upon himself to punish the authority figures, his own peers. And it doesn't matter whether the boys and girls in the Dunblane Primary School this morning were the specific focus of his grievance or not. The entire community is to blame, his entire peer group is at fault. No parents or school leaders trust him, so they are all deserving of his wrath. This is a retaliation. This is what we classify as a personal cause homicide. Most likely, too, there was a specific precipitating stressor to cause him to act when he did.

This is not someone who ever blended into the community. So often, when a serial killer in the United States is apprehended, neighbors, acquaintances, or coworkers will express shock, saying that he was the last person in the world they would have suspected of being a vicious murderer. He seemed so charming, or he seemed so ordinary. He seemed to get on so well with his wife or girlfriend.

Not this guy. Mass murderers are different from serial ones. Those around him thought of him as weird or strange. They've had an uncomfortable feeling about him that they might not even have been able to place or articulate. In the United States, I wouldn't be able to attach much significance to the choice of weapon or weapons. There, guns are all too easy to obtain, so the killer could either be a gun nut or someone who just recently procured the firearms for this one intended purpose. Here in Britain, though, guns and rifles are much more tightly controlled. If he wasn't in the military or a specialized wing of the police force, he would have to be a member of a gun club of some sort to have access to these weapons. And given his "odd" personality, this preoccupation with guns should have raised some red flags in itself. This guy was a pressure cooker waiting to explode, and these innocent children paid the price.

I'd already left Scotland by the time the definitive information was made public.

Sixteen children, ages four to six, died that morning, fifteen at the scene and one at the hospital. So had their teacher, forty-five-year-old Gwen Mayor, who courageously tried to stop the attacker as he entered the school and headed for the children's exercise class in the gymnasium—not the playground as we originally understood. Twelve other children were injured. Only one escaped unscathed, and two others, by the grace of God, were out sick that day. The killer had tried to get to the school during a time when hundreds of students were in the gym for the morning assembly, but he had received incorrect information when he asked a student about the schedule; so when he arrived, only one class was present. He had four guns with him, including two revolvers and two nine-millimeter semiautomatics. Headmaster Ronald Taylor called in the emergency and was credited with keeping the others in the seven-hundred-pupil school calm and safe as gunshots echoed throughout the building. The massacre took three minutes in total.

The gunman, Thomas Watt Hamilton, forty-three years of age, white, and unmarried, was a former scoutmaster said to be obsessed with young boys and bitter over the community's rejection of him. He'd become a Scout leader back in July of 1973, but there had been complaints about his behavior and he was asked to leave the organization in March of the following year. His repeated attempts to get back in were unsuccessful. In addition to young boys, his other primary interest was guns. He was a member of a local gun club and held the appropriate permits to fire them under the club's auspices.

Neighbors described the tall, balding Hamilton as private, a loner. Some compared him to Mr. Spock on *Star Trek,* and all thought he was weird. According to their reports, he was invariably dressed in a white shirt and parka with a flat cap covering his receding hairline. He'd originally run a do-it-yourself shop called "Wood Craft," then decided to become a professional photographer. Two female neighbors described the walls of his two-bedroom house in the Braehead district of nearby Stirling as being full of color photographs of scantily clad young boys.

When he couldn't get back into organized scouting, Hamilton formed his own boys' club, called the Stirling Rovers, and took groups of eight- to twelve-year-olds on outings and day trips, during which he would take extensive pictures, home movies, and, later, videos. One of the two neighbors was once invited in to watch a home movie of young boys frolicking in their swimsuits.

In 1988, he tried yet again to get back into the Scouts, with the same lack of success. Between 1993 and 1994, local police requested information on Hamilton from scouting organizations after spotting him in a gay red-light district. Around the same time, he sent letters to Dunblane parents, denying rumors that he molested young boys. In the weeks before the massacre, he had been turned down as a volunteer at Dunblane Primary School. He wrote to the media to complain about the police and Dunblane teachers spreading lies about him, and he wrote to the queen that the Scouts had damaged his reputation.

All in all, my profile stood up in every significant detail. Several Scottish newspapers ran headlines such as *G-man shares insight into mind of a maniac* and *Train Police to Spot Potential Killers, Says Expert.*

So how was I able to do this? How was I able to peg a man I knew nothing about except his final explosive act, in a place many thousands of miles from where I've lived and worked? Is it because I have a psychic gift when it comes to crime and criminals? I wish I did, but no, I don't and never have. It's because of my two decades' experience in the FBI dealing directly with the experts themselves—the killers and other violent offenders—hunting and profiling them. It's all in what I learned along the way.

And it's because behavior reflects personality. If you've studied this segment of the population as long and as intensively as I have, you come to realize that even though every crime is unique, behavior fits into certain patterns. Why should it not be surprising for a man like Thomas Watt Hamilton to become a mass murderer of children, but highly surprising for him to become, say, a serial killer or bomber, even though those two categories often involve antisocial loners as well?

If you've seen enough and experienced enough to be able to pick out the significant pieces of those patterns, then you can begin to figure out what's going on and, more important, answer the question *Why?* That, then, should lead to the ultimate answer: *Who?* That's what every detective and FBI agent want to know. That's what every novelist and reader want to know. What makes people commit the crimes they commit in the way they commit them?

It's like the old staple of 1930s gangster movies: Why does one person become a criminal and the other a priest? Or from my perspective, why does one become a serial killer, another a rapist, another an assassin, another a bomber, another a poisoner, and yet still another a child molester? And within these crime categories, why does each commit his atrocities in the precise way he does? The answer lies in one fundamental question that applies to every one of them:

*Why did he do it?*

The *who?* follows directly from there.

That's the mystery we have to solve.

# CHAPTER ONE

# WHAT I LEARNED FROM THE BAD GUYS

*WHO done it? And WHY?*

That's what we all want to know.

Let's look at two relatively simple, straightforward crimes. On the surface they appear very similar, but they're really very different. They even happened near each other, and in one of them I was the victim.

It wasn't long after I retired from the FBI, while we were redoing our house.

We're practically camping out, sleeping on the floor for weeks. I joke to my wife and kids that they're starting to get a sense of how the Manson family lived. Most of our furniture and nearly all of our possessions are being stored in the garage. Finally, when it's time to do the floors, we have to move out into a nearby motel.

One night the FBI gets a call from the local police; they're trying to track down Special Agent John Douglas. When they find me, a detective gets on the phone and says, "We found some of your property during an arrest here."

I say, "What property? What are you talking about?"

He says, "Well, we don't have all of it that was taken. We found a wooden box with the FBI seal on it."

"Yeah, that's mine," I confirm. It contained a special-presentation Smith & Wesson .357 magnum with my credential number engraved on it, commemorating the fiftieth anniversary of FBI agents carrying service weapons. A number of special agents had them. "You have the gun?" I ask anxiously.

"No," he says. "The gun's not here."

Oh shit, I'm thinking. Even though it was a commemorative piece, it was still capable of firing. Readers of *Mindhunter* may recall that shortly after I began my Bureau career as a street agent in Detroit, I lost my Smith & Wesson Model 10 revolver—had it stolen right out of the glove compartment of my Volkswagen Beetle. This was one of the worst things you could do as a new agent, especially while J. Edgar Hoover was still alive. And now, here I am, retired after what I think is a distinguished twenty-five-year career, and I'm still unwittingly supplying weapons to the enemy!

I didn't even know anything was missing. I ask the name of the suspects, and two out of three immediately ring a bell: they're the teenage sons of two of the men working on my house. One I don't know much about, but the other is a nineteen-year-old college freshman who'd been a standout high school athlete. I'm surprised, disappointed, and pissed off.

The cops ask me to go home and inventory what's missing. In addition to the gun, the missing items include a TV, a stereo, that kind of thing. Even if the suspects hadn't been caught, we'd know these were small-time amateurs from what they took. The arrest came after the police figured out a pattern: all of the people reporting similar types of burglaries knew one another. These three were stealing only from places they knew and felt comfortable in. When the cops executed a search warrant on the apartment they shared, they found much of the stolen stuff.

The motive: they wanted to furnish their apartment.

As I said, I was angry, but not as angry as the father of the nineteen-year-old.

He tore into his son. "Are you nuts! Not only is this man my client, he's an FBI agent. He's licensed to carry a gun and knows how to use it. What if he came home at night while you were there? You could have gotten yourself killed!"

"I wasn't really thinking," the young man sheepishly replied. The oldest of the three was the ringleader, and it was clear to me that this guy just went along.

When the cops questioned him, he swore that they'd gotten worried about my .357 and thrown it into the river. The rest of the property was returned. He pleaded guilty, made restitution, and, I think, got the crap scared out of him.

From a criminal-profiling perspective like mine, when you're investigating a break-in, the first thing you ask, as the police did here, is, what was taken?

If it's the normal stuff—cash, credit cards, and jewelry on one level, TVs, stereos, and VCRs on another level—then you've got a straight criminal enterprise burglary, and the only thing you're going to be able to do is determine the sophistication and experience of the burglar based on his choice of target and the loot taken. If you haven't already picked him up, you're not going to catch him until he surfaces in connection with another theft, as happened in my case.

Contrast this, though, with another breaking and entering, which took place only a few miles away.

In that case, a woman reported that her apartment had been broken into, and when police questioned her about what was taken, all she could determine was missing was some of her underwear. Shortly before this, there had been several incidences of women in the same garden apartment complex suspecting that a Peeping Tom had been staring into their windows. On some of the occasions in which the cops came out to investigate, they found evidence that someone had been masturbating just outside the windows in question.

Two cases of breaking and entering. The first offender (or in that case, offenders) took a gun and some valuable property. The second one didn't. And yet, while neither one of these crimes makes us happy, most of us are going to realize instinctively that the second is more dangerous. But how do we know this?

Because of motive. And how do we know from his motive—even though we haven't apprehended him and learned his identity and personal details—that he poses the greater danger? Because of the research we've done and our experience with other similar types of offenders.

A criminal enterprise burglar—someone who steals with a profit motive in mind, or in our case, simply because he wants merchandise someone else owns—is either going to persist in his unlawful pursuit or he isn't. I didn't feel this kid would. He'd faced the consequences of getting caught, and that clearly was not the turn he wanted his life to take.

On the other hand, police all too often dismiss panty thieves, or fetish burglars, as nuisance offenders—and all too often they're not. This second guy didn't take women's underwear to fence it, or because he couldn't afford to buy any of his own. Clearly his motive had to do with the sexual images it conveyed and the charge it aroused. The motive had to do with fantasy. And if we stop to consider that the evidence suggests this guy has already graduated from voyeurism to breaking and entering and theft—a far-higher-risk enterprise—there is no reason to assume he is going to be satisfied at this level. A fetish burglar is not likely to stop on his own.

Sometimes nearly identical crimes, such as burglaries, are actually the result of vastly different motivations on the part of the offenders. Recognizing these motivations is key to understanding the crime and the criminal and to evaluating the danger to society. Consider the case of one burglar I came across in my career. We'll call him Dwight. At sixteen, he, too, was arrested for burglary, and the motive was clearly the desire for money. But Dwight had also been arrested recently for assault. In fact, his first arrest came at age ten, for breaking and entering. By the time he was fourteen, his rap sheet included more B&E charges, as well as aggravated assault and grand theft–auto. He stole his first car before he was even old enough to be eligible for a learner's permit, much less a driver's license. Sent to a juvenile facility, he was consistently judged a behavior problem. Therapists and counselors described him as hostile, aggressive, impulsive, lacking both self-control and any sense of remorse. He repeatedly blamed others for his own problems and wrongdoing. He admitted using both alcohol and marijuana. He was labeled an antisocial personality.

Whereas "my" burglar came from a stable two-parent home with a mother and father who were horrified to learn of their son's crime and got involved immediately in getting him back on track, Dwight's home life was considerably more problematic. He had been left by his mother with her parents, who formally adopted him when he was four months old. The mother kept one son with her but for some reason left Dwight behind. His grandfather was in the Air Force, so they moved around a good deal; but when Dwight was nine his grandparents separated, and he stayed with his grandmother, which left him with no male role model.

He had frequent trouble in school and was suspended several times from junior high. Sadly, in his case, time would bear out a prediction many could have made from observing him early on— after years of run-ins with the law, he was ultimately sentenced to death for a horrific rape-murder.

Similar burglaries, but vastly different perpetrators. One did it because it seemed easy and he didn't think much about it. The other did it because he felt that no one else mattered.

It was sometime early in 1978 when it occurred to me that the only way to figure out what had happened at a crime scene was to understand what had gone on inside the head of the principal actor in that drama: the offender. And the only way to find that out, so we could apply the knowledge to other scenes and other crimes, was to ask him. Amazingly, with all the research that had been done in criminology, no one had attempted that before in any but the most casual and haphazard way.

I was a thirty-two-year-old instructor in the FBI Academy's Behavioral Science Unit, pulled back to Quantico after tours as a street agent in Detroit and Milwaukee. I was teaching applied criminal psychology both to new agents and to National Academy fellows. The new agents generally weren't much of a problem for me; they were younger and knew less than I did. But the NA fellows were another story. These were all experienced upper-level police officials and detectives from around the United States and a number of foreign countries, picked by their own departments for eleven weeks of advanced training at Quantico. I'd be lying if I said I wasn't intimidated by the prospect of purporting to speak with the authority of the Federal Bureau of Investigation, standing up in front of seasoned men and women who'd been on the job a lot longer and worked many more cases than I had. As a defense mechanism, before I covered a given case I started by asking the class if anyone had any firsthand experience with it. That way I'd invite him or her to give us the facts so I wouldn't stick my foot in my mouth.

But then the question was, what can I tell these people that they don't already know?

First, I thought, if we could give the law enforcement community some insight into the process, the internal logic, of *how* violent offenders actually decide to commit crimes and *why* they come up with their choice of crimes—*where* the motive comes from—then we could provide a valuable tool in pointing investigators toward what for them must be the ultimate question: *Who?*

Stated as simply as possible: *Why? + How? = Who.*

How? Why? Where? Who? These are the questions pursued by novelists and psychiatrists, by Dostoyevsky and Freud, the stuff both of *Crime and Punishment* and of *Beyond the Pleasure Principle.* These are the questions asked by philosophers and theologians, by social workers evaluating cases, by judges in sentencing hearings. In fact, they compose the central issue of what we call, for want of a better phrase, the human condition.

But we had to come to grips with these questions from our own perspective, in terms that would be *useful* to us in the business of law enforcement and crime detection. Technically speaking, a prosecutor doesn't need to demonstrate a motive to get a conviction, as long as he has compelling evidence that amounts to convincing proof. But in actual practice, most prosecutors will tell you that unless they can show a jury a logical motive, they're not going to get an appropriate verdict, such as murder instead of manslaughter.

Whether or not you come right out and say it, the study of applied criminal psychology all gets down to that key question: Why do criminals commit the crimes they do the way they do?

This was the mystery I felt we had to solve.

I was doing a lot of "road schools" at the time, partnered with Robert Ressler, a somewhat more experienced instructor who'd been a military police officer before becoming an FBI special agent. The road school was just what it sounded like. Instructors from Quantico would go out and teach local departments and sheriff's offices a compressed, weeklong version of the courses we taught at the Academy. They would take the weekend off, then teach somewhere else the following week before heading home with a suitcase full of laundry.

Being on the road gave us the perfect opportunity to try out my idea of getting incarcerated violent criminals to talk to us. Wherever I was going to be, I'd find out which state or federal prison might be nearby, then see who was in residence there who might be interesting.

Altogether, over the next several years, my associates and I interviewed more than fifty violent offenders in American prisons and penitentiaries, including the thirty-six sexually motivated killers we included in a landmark study funded by the National Institute of Justice, ultimately published in 1988 as the book *Sexual Homicide: Patterns and Motives*. Coauthor on that study was Dr. Ann Burgess, professor of psychiatric nursing at the University of Pennsylvania, who worked with us practically from the beginning, helping to organize, analyze, and make sense of the voluminous amount of information we collected. Ann also developed the parameters and rigorous standards that helped us transform our anecdotal forays into this heart of darkness into a real and useful study.

We didn't take notes during the interviews, so as soon as we left the prison we raced back to the hotel to debrief and fill in all the empty spaces on the questionnaire. Some of it we'd been able to fill in ahead of time just by examining the case file and studying the subject's record. But the key details—the ones that made the difference to us—were those we had to get right from the subject himself.

At the beginning, all I was trying to do was to get these people to talk to me, to ask them the questions I hoped would help us learn more about real applied criminal psychology, not in an academic sense but in a way that would help in the field, in finding real offenders and solving real cases.

Even now, this many years later, there is a lot of surprise and wonder that so many hardened inmates (most in for long sentences, with little to gain) not only agreed to talk to us but came clean about so much of their personal life, development, and evolution as violent criminals. Why did they agree to talk? I think there were a number of reasons, depending on the individual in question: curiosity, boredom, remorse, or an opportunity to emotionally relive predatory crimes that remained, for some, among the most satisfying experiences of their lives. My own personal feeling is that we appealed to the egos of some men who were pretty ego-driven; they had a lot of time on their hands and didn't see much apparent interest in their lives or exploits coming from anyone else in the outside world.

Not everyone was emotionally suited to carry out this kind of research. Though you'd have to steep yourself in the details of the hideous crimes, you couldn't show that you were appalled or come off as judgmental; otherwise you'd get nothing. You had to be a good listener and you had to be a good actor—to know how to play the game.

As to why so many agreed to get so personal with us, exposing so many raw nerves, I think that had to do with the depth and thoroughness with which we approached each interview. By the time a man is incarcerated for a violent crime, he's usually faced a number of interview situations: interrogation by detectives, questioning by lawyers, evaluation before sentencing, interviews with psychiatrists or psychologists in prison. And in all but the first situation, where interrogators are looking to pounce on any inconsistencies or indications of untruth, what we're really talking about is self-reporting: the offender telling the interviewer not what's really going on in his own mind but what he thinks he needs to get across for his own advantage or benefit.

We did two things differently. First, we'd immerse ourselves in the complete case file so we couldn't be fooled or misled by the subject about what he'd done and the way he'd done it. Along with the crime details, we'd go over psychiatric reports and prison evaluations, IQ tests, anything available on the subject. The only way you're going to be able to get to the truth with one of these offenders is to be able to say, for instance, "Wait a minute! How can you say you had some affection and sympathy for the victim when you stabbed her twenty-seven times, way past the point needed to kill her?" And to be able to do that, you have to know the facts of the crime backward and forward.

The second factor that made a difference was our commitment to spending as much time in the interview as it would take to move through the small talk, the bullshit, and the phony sentimentality to wear the subject down so that we could find out what was actually going on in his mind. Sometimes they would come right out and tell us. Sometimes we'd have to figure it out from clues they'd give us. But the more we heard, the more we could correlate and the more we understood.

Who were the men we went after? There were the "celebrity criminals," like Charles Manson, as well as Sara Jane Moore and Manson follower Lynette "Squeaky" Fromme, both of whom attempted to change the course of American history by trying to kill President Gerald Ford. We talked to Arthur Bremer, who, having stalked President Richard Nixon with the hope of assassinating him, finally gave up in frustration and turned his obsessive energies to presidential candidate George Wallace in 1972, managing not to kill the Alabama governor but condemn him to a lifetime of paralysis and pain. And we met with David Berkowitz, the so-called Son of Sam ".44 Caliber Killer," who terrorized New York City for a year until he was apprehended in July of 1977. We spoke to Richard Speck, the lowlife thief who made national

headlines in 1966 when he broke into a Chicago town house occupied by a group of student nurses and murdered eight of them.

But there were also many others not as well known, though
every bit as vicious, who taught us at least as much about the inner
workings of personalities whose main goals in life are to kill and
to hurt—or as I've stated many times in my career, to *manipulate,*
*dominate,* and *control.* These were men like Ed Kemper, who killed
his hated mother in her own bed and cut off her head. Before he
got up the courage to do that, he took out his anger and frustration on his grandparents and, years later, six young women around
the campus of the University of California at Santa Cruz. Jerome
Brudos had had a fetish over women's shoes since childhood before he, the married father of two in Oregon, killed four women
and cut off their feet and breasts, after dressing them in his own
collection of female clothing. Richard Marquette graduated from
attempted rape, aggravated assault, and robbery to the murder and
dismemberment of a woman he met in a Portland, Oregon, bar.
Paroled after twelve years, he killed and dissected two more women
before being captured. As grisly as their crimes were, all of these
men—and they were all men; women rarely commit this type of
crime—had something to teach us if only we could figure out how
to interpret their words and actions.

Now it's one thing to decide you're going to try to interview
these guys, but it's quite another to go face-to-face with them. Ed
Kemper is six feet nine and well over three hundred pounds. If
he wanted to—and at one point he suggested that he might—he
could have twisted our heads off and set them down on the table
for the guard to find. When we went to interview Arthur Bremer
in the Baltimore City Penitentiary, we had to walk a gauntlet
through an open yard where violent prisoners roamed freely, a
scene that reminded me of Dante's *Inferno.* And before we were

let into any of these correctional establishments, we had to give up our service revolvers and sign waivers that we would not hold the prison liable if any harm should befall us. If we were taken hostage, we were on our own. As Ed Kemper put it, he was in for life, so what more could they do to him if he killed one of us—take away his dessert? Whatever punishment might be exacted would be a small price to pay compared with the prestige among his fellow inmates for having murdered an FBI agent.

So, though we didn't exactly know what we'd be getting out of the project when we began, we definitely had an idea of what we'd be getting into if we undertook it.

We adjusted and perfected our own M.O. as we went along. We learned that if we dressed down, the subject was likely to relax with us faster. I could often tell I was about to get what I needed from an offender when he would start talking about the crime and a look would come into his eyes as if he were in a trance, as if he were having an out-of-body experience. The crime—what he did to another person, the way he exerted power and control—was the most intense, stimulating, and memorable experience of his life. By reliving it this way, he was reliving the peak sensation and bringing me with him inside his mind.

The more we learned, the better we got. We discovered, for instance, that assassin types tend to be paranoid and don't like eye contact. The grandiose types, like Manson, want to dominate you, so you position yourself below them (Manson sat on a table), where they can talk down to you. Some just want sympathy. As I said, you have to put your own emotions on hold and play the game. We would commiserate with guys who would bemoan the fact that their lives were ruined, tears streaming down their faces—ruined, in their minds, not because of what they did but because they were caught. That taught us a lot, too.

The interviews revealed some interesting and, we thought,

telling commonalities, commonalities that surfaced in my later dealings with violent offenders I profiled, and helped catch, interrogate, and prosecute. My theory was that recognizing the basic elements most have in common was the first step. The next would be to understand how their differences in personality, criminal sophistication, and *motive* led one individual to become a mugger, for example, and another a mass killer. First, I had to learn what qualities and experiences they shared: where they came from, literally and figuratively.

All of them, on one level or another, came from dysfunctional backgrounds. Sometimes this was overt: physical and/or sexual abuse; alcoholic parents or guardians; being shuttled—unwanted—from one foster home to another. In other cases it was more subtle: the absence of a loving or nurturing atmosphere; inconsistent or nonexistent discipline; a kid who, for whatever reason, never adjusted or fit in. Ed Kemper's parents fought violently throughout his youth, until they divorced, after which he was ridiculed and dominated by an alcoholic mother who made him sleep in the locked basement when he reached puberty, claiming she was afraid of what he would do to his sister. David Berkowitz was born illegitimate and told by his adoptive parents that his mother died giving birth to him. He always felt guilty and responsible. When he later learned his birth mother and sister were alive, he went to see them and found they wanted nothing to do with him. He was devastated and began blossoming into the serial killer he became.

When later, at the FBI Academy, we began studying the backgrounds of other violent and serial criminals, we found they all tended to conform to the models we constructed from the prison interview project. Albert DeSalvo, the early 1960s "Boston Strangler," had as a role model an alcoholic father who broke Albert's mother's fingers in anger. The man regularly beat him and his six brothers and sisters, and brought home prostitutes. John Wayne Gacy, the Chicago-area builder who dressed as a clown to entertain sick children in the hospital when he was not raping and murdering boys and young men—more than thirty—was regularly beaten and belittled by his own alcoholic father. I could go on and on with these examples.

Why one boy grows up to be a rapist or killer, another grows up to be a bomber or extortionist, and another who seems to have just as bad a background grows up to be an admirable, contributing member of society is a mystery we'll learn more about as we go along. But we did find that in addition to unstable, abusive, or deprived family situations, which understandably produced a severe lack of self-worth and self-confidence, most convicted sexual predators had relatively high IQs, much higher than you would expect to find in the general criminal population.

The prison interviews also revealed equally significant differences in what might appear to be, on the surface, a similar type of crime—think again of the very different burglars described at the beginning of this chapter.

Here's another example: the rape and murder of young women in our society is all too common, and all rapists would appear to be angry, aggressive psychopaths. On one level, I would certainly not disagree with this appraisal. But it doesn't tell us much about *why* the offender committed the particular crime, and it doesn't help us very much in trying to profile his personality. So let's start looking at the *behavioral clues* we find at the scene.

First, what was the state of the body when it was found? I don't mean the state of decomposition (although that can tell us a lot, too), but what did the killer do with and to the corpse? If the cause of death was stabbing and there were a lot of concentrated knife wounds—what we refer to as "overkill"—particularly around the face, then I know the chances are very good the killer knew the victim well; the crime was a personal cause. And that points us toward motive—toward *Why?* If the body is wrapped up in a sheet or blanket, say, or obviously cared for after death, that's going to suggest that the killer had some tender feelings toward the victim, maybe even remorse. On the other hand, if the body is mutilated and/or left in plain sight, or casually dumped by the side of a road, that tells me the killer had contempt for the victim, maybe even a disdain for women in general.

How do I know all this? Not because as a profiler I'm some kind of psychic, but because the offenders themselves told us. And after we'd heard the same thing a few times over, *we* could start telling *them*. If a rape-murder victim was left lying on the floor, covered by a sheet, we knew that wasn't an attempt to hide the body, at least not by a sane offender. It was a feeble attempt to give that victim some dignity, or to physically hide her from the sight of someone who did not feel good about what he'd just done. We'd simply heard that truth from enough killers who'd covered their victims' bodies.

I had a recent experience that confirmed our ability to "predict" what the killer was thinking. I'd been retired from the FBI for a couple of years and I was back in a large Eastern state penitentiary, interviewing a convicted killer on behalf of the state parole board. The board wanted my opinion on whether the subject was a suitable candidate for parole. As far as I'm concerned—and I told my clients this—that means only one thing: Is he likely to commit another violent act if he's let out? I spent many hours with the guy, wearing down his resistance, making him more and more vulnerable to the truth, trying to find out to my own satisfaction (a) whether he had any sense of the moral dimension of what he'd done, and genuine contrition for it; and (b) whether he still found overwhelming emotional satisfaction in manipulating, dominating, controlling, and exerting life-or-death power over another person. Each thing he told me fit into a pattern I had heard many times before from many other men in his situation, men whose thinking, crimes, and motivations I had studied for more than two decades. And so, when I made my recommendation to the parole board, I was very confident I was giving them solid information. When people in the field of criminology or forensic psychology tell you they can't predict future violence, what they really mean is that *they* can't predict future violence, because they haven't done the direct study and don't have the direct experience. I don't claim I can tell you whether each and every previously violent predator is going to strike again if given the chance, but I can sure as hell tell you whether parole is a risk worth taking or not.

Most violent offenders, we found after some study, had two factors warring within them. One was a feeling of superiority, grandiosity: societal mores were not meant for them; they were too smart or too clever to have to start at the bottom and work their way up, or to live by the normal rules that govern a relationship. The other, equally strong feeling was of inadequacy, of not being able to measure up, of knowing they were losers no matter what they did. And since the first feeling generally made them unwilling to study, work, pay their dues, whatever you want to call it, they often were, in fact, inadequately prepared for a job or a relationship that would give a normal person genuine satisfaction. This just reinforced their outsider status.

What motivates many, if not most, of these guys, then, is a desire for power and control that comes from a background where they felt powerless and out of control. And while most abused or neglected children develop coping skills and strategies to overcome a difficult upbringing, the ones who don't often grow into angry, hostile, frustrated adults and become violent offenders. No one denies that the emotional scars and baggage remain with most people who've been abused as children. But a kid who channels his frustration, hurt, and anger into, say, competitive sports—becoming an outstanding high school athlete with a scrapbook full of local press clippings and yearbook photos documenting his accomplishments—is going to turn out a much stronger, healthier adult than one who doesn't develop such an outlet, one who attempts to soothe his negative feelings by making others hurt, too, torturing small animals before moving on to adult crimes that provide much more gruesome subject matter for his scrapbook. Being able to manipulate, dominate, and control a victim, to decide whether that victim lives or dies, or how that victim dies, temporarily counteracts, for some, their feelings of inadequacy and speaks to the other side of the psychological equation. It makes them feel grandiose and superior, as they believe they are entitled to feel. In other words, raping and murdering sets the world right with them.

You will undoubtedly notice that I am confining myself here to characterizations of men. By definition, this is sexist, but by definition, men are the problem. Both the FBI behavioral science divisions and (even more so) Ann Burgess and her associates have studied women who come from the same kinds of abusive and neglectful backgrounds as the men in our prison profiles. But for whatever complex reasons, women do not manifest their frustrations and emotional injuries in the same aggressive ways. They may become self-destructive, resorting to drug or excessive alcohol use, gravitating toward abusive men who will inflict more of the punishment they're used to and subconsciously feel they deserve, possibly going into prostitution or attempting suicide. They may even abuse their own children. But with very, very few exceptions they do not become predators as men do, and they do not take out emotional and sexual rage on strangers. Some of this may spring from inherent differences in the "hardwiring" of male and female brains—or from the predominant hormonal influence of estrogen instead of testosterone. But women are not the predators and they are not the problem. Of course, while most of what we say about development and motive relates to men, the better women understand these processes and issues, the better they will be able to recognize these behaviors and combat them.

I must make one point here, about a concept that runs throughout my law enforcement career and my writing. Essentially all the men in our study can be said to have mental problems of one sort or another. Based on what they've done, you might even be moved to call them crazy. But "crazy" is a subjective term. "Insanity" is a legal term with a specific legal definition. From the perspective of the men and women of my Investigative Support Unit at Quantico, the crucial word is "choice." With the exception of a very few truly insane (and generally delusional) individuals, these men choose to do what they do. They may obsess about hurting women. They may be motivated to act out their obsessions. But in fact, they don't *have* to behave in this manner. They are not *compelled*. They choose to do it because it makes them feel good. I deeply sympathize with a man who's been beaten or sexually abused or deprived of love as a child. I understand why he may have deep psychological problems as an adult. But I do not accept that he is compelled as a result of this background to hunt, hurt, or kill others, particularly women and children. We can argue whether or not we are responsible for what we *are*, but in the overwhelming majority of cases we are certainly responsible for what we *do*.

So, where does this violent behavior come from? After interviewing a large number of serial predatory criminals, we were able to compile what we called a Sexual Homicide Motivational Model, organized according to the influences, both environmental and emotional, that seemed to determine the developmental course these men took throughout their lives and criminal careers: the factors that commonly contributed toward a *motive* to commit violent acts. In each instance we recorded how many of our subjects were affected by the various factors, and who practiced the various resulting behaviors. For example, an astounding 50 percent described having their first rape fantasy between the ages of twelve and fourteen! From this fact alone we can see the critical importance of some kind of meaningful early intervention if we are going to have any chance not only of saving these kids but, even more important, of protecting ourselves and our loved ones from the destruction they'll wreak if not stopped.

Many children display traits that may be interpreted as antisocial, and the vast majority of them grow up to be, as the cliché goes, decent, law-abiding people. What we were looking for in our interviews were *patterns of behavior* we could correlate with the end results of our subjects' crimes. We found that the men we studied seemed to realize early on, sometimes even as very young children, that the power to manipulate others gave them a sense of control that they felt was so lacking in their lives.

The next developmental stage after this power recognition is fantasy, and we found that this becomes tremendously important in understanding the development of the sexual predator. First there is the fantasy of overcoming the problems of his life: the pain and the failure. This, of course, involves becoming successful and getting back at the people the subject believes have hurt, slighted, or not properly respected him. And along with this comes sexual fantasies. One of the things we clearly established was that in any sexually related predatory crime, the fantasy always precedes the acting out. So if someone's already fantasizing about rape at age twelve, you can imagine where this might lead him.

Remember, too, that the fact that a particular crime might not appear on its surface to be sexual does not mean it is not based on sexual fantasy. Arson and bombing—where there is no direct physical relationship between offender and victim—are nonetheless often perverse sexual manifestations. David Berkowitz, who stalked lovers' lane areas of New York City looking for couples parked in cars to blow away with his .44 caliber semiautomatic, told me that on nights when he could not find the appropriate victims of opportunity, he would return to the locations of his previous crimes and masturbate, recalling the sexual charge and feeling of supreme power he'd had as he pulled the trigger of his large Charter Arms Bulldog.

The sexual fantasies that interview subjects recalled from adolescence ran the gamut, but it was notable how many involved violence, sadomasochism, bondage, and other domination-and-control-related scenarios. As early indicative behaviors, 79 percent of the men in our study reported what they described as compulsive masturbation, 72 percent said they were active Peeping Toms (or voyeurs), and 81 percent described active and regular involvement with pornography.

Whenever the subject of pornography is raised, the issue of cause and effect inevitably arises. Shortly before his 1989 execution in Florida, Theodore "Ted" Bundy granted an interview in which he seemed to blame all of his problems (that is, abducting and killing beautiful young women throughout the country, from Washington State to Florida) on his pervasive involvement with pornography. Does exposure to pornography, especially violent pornography, motivate a male to commit violent or sexually aggressive acts? Or are those already motivated in that direction just naturally attracted to this material? There is no simple or foolproof answer to this question, but I can make some confident generalizations from my experience with and study of violent predators.

First, do I believe that *but for the pornography,* Ted Bundy would not have become a serial killer? The answer is an emphatic "No!" This is just one more manifestation of guys like Bundy trying to shove blame for their actions onto someone or something else. Bundy did what he did because he *wanted to,* because it gave him satisfaction and made him feel better than anything else in life did. And I'm not projecting. That's something we got from interviewing many men like him.

So, what I'm saying is that pornography—even the most violent, women-hating, sadomasochistic pornography—does not ever turn normal men into violent sexual predators. But what we have found is that individuals already prone to that sort of thinking and fantasy—the type of men we interviewed in our study—did have their passions inflamed by this kind of pornographic material and did tend to get some of their ideas from it. We learned this originally from what the interviewees told us, and later confirmed it by correlating scenarios offenders actually performed with material we discovered they had been reading. I don't think I know any normal men who have not perused girlie magazines or other mild forms of pornography at some point in their formative years—and I do know a large number of fine upstanding citizens—so, clearly they were and are able to handle the influence. Likewise, the old saying goes that 90 percent of men will admit to having masturbated and the other 10 percent are liars. But the red flags should go up when we see certain obsessional preoccupations, practically to the exclusion of all other satisfactions.

What then follows, according to the experience of many of our subjects, are the various ways of acting out their obsessions. None was as universally popular with our subjects as compulsive masturbation, voyeurism, and involvement with pornography—except fetishism. According to the *DSM-IV*—the American Psychiatric Association's *Diagnostic and Statistical Manual of Mental*

*Disorders,* Fourth Edition—fetishism involves the arousal of fantasies, sexual urges, or other behaviors from nonliving or nonhuman objects. And for a budding killer, this is where, developmentally, things start getting dangerous.

Fetishism is classified in psychiatric circles as a paraphilia, or disorder of sexual aim. There is a wide variety of paraphilias, some harmless and essentially matters of preference, some harmful or potentially deadly—such as pedophilia (which involves sexual activity with children) and sexual sadism. Most paraphilias occur along a continuum, and fetishism is a good example. Probably the most common fetish item in our society would be women's undergarments.

Seventy-two percent of our interviewees had a preoccupation with fetishism of some kind during their formative years. Now again, we're dealing on a continuum here. I think it's probably safe to say that a significantly large percentage of the normal American male population is turned on by black lace panties and (if they're of a certain age) fishnet stockings. According to psychiatric experts such as my friend and colleague Dr. Park Dietz, whether you are similarly affected by more prosaic items such as pantyhose will depend on the time, circumstances, and specific associations of the dawn of your own sexual awareness and coming of age.

Again, what is important to keep in mind in our examination of criminal motivation is the emphasis, preoccupation, and overall pattern of the sexual thinking or behavior. In other words, does it turn you on for the moment, or consume your life? And while a lace-panty fetish may not be all that unusual, a foot fetish is somewhat rarer. In and of itself, it is harmless. But then you look at a guy like Jerome Brudos, mentioned earlier—who killed women, cut off their feet, and used them to display his own collection of ladies' shoes—and you realize these fantasies can have a real psychopathological base. The distinction between the motivations behind a harmless childhood or teenage interest in and appreciation for feet and the motivations of a Jerome Brudos is one of the key topics we're going to explore in this book.

Among the other behaviors and interests our interviewees detailed were indecent exposure, making obscene phone calls, and sexual contact with animals. All occurred in roughly around 25 percent of the subjects. Cross-dressing, prostitution, and frottage (sexually rubbing up against strangers in public) occurred in between 10 and 20 percent. Again, going back to our continuum, none of these behaviors is particularly significant in and of itself. But they are all significant in what they indicate to us about the development and motivation of the violent predator.

Together with these sexual interests and actions, we see the externalized ways that these people begin handling their stressors. Unlike better-adapted men—and almost all women, who, as we've noted, tend to internalize their own problems and frustrations—the male who is going to grow into a violent or predator personality becomes aggressive to his peers. He gets involved in antisocial acts such as burglary, arson, theft from his parents or other family members, mistreating animals, and cheating in school. Despite his intelligence level, he is likely to drop out of high school and use drugs or alcohol to manage his stress. He will act impulsively without considering the implications of his actions, either for himself or for others. And he will feel a growing sense of isolation from his peers and from society in general, so that any way he decides to lash out will be justified in his own mind.

So, what's the difference between the kid who robbed my garage and a young, developing, future predator? It takes only one stupid experience for some kids to be scared straight, but along the way, our second guy discovers that his aggressive behavior leaves him in an increased state of arousal: he finds his behavior pleasing and fulfilling, which is why, instead of feeling shame and remorse over his deeds, he looks for ways to enhance them. This is what we term the "feedback filter." He sets about to practice more of the acts that leave him feeling powerful and satisfied, sorting out the factors or actions that get in the way of the experience. He discovers expanded areas and situations where he can practice his domination and control of others. And he learns from his own experience, perfecting his technique to avoid detection or punishment. He learns how to become a success at what he does. The more success and satisfaction he has, the tighter that feedback loop becomes.

This is why the fetishes and other paraphilias we mentioned earlier become increasingly dangerous. As the subject learns more and more about what makes him feel good, the paraphilias will escalate. The young man whose particular thing is voyeurism may move on to fetish burglary of things belonging to women he spies on. Once he becomes comfortable with breaking and entering and knows how to get away with it, he may then escalate to rape. Depending on the circumstances, if, for example, he realizes he could be identified by his victim if he doesn't take preventive action, rape can end in murder. And if he then finds that killing gives him an even greater arousal and an increased sense of power and satisfaction, he's entered a new dimension of control, and the murders very well might continue. This is similar to what we saw with Jerome Brudos.

I am by no means implying that every Peeping Tom (or even most) ends up as a serial killer. But I am saying that if you study the most violent of the sexual predators, as we have, you will find in virtually all cases an escalation from relatively innocent beginnings.

What other clues, then, do we have to work with? Just as we try to figure out why an adult offender commits a particular crime, we need to understand the motive of young, developing antisocial offenders.

There are three youthful behaviors that together make up what has come to be known as the homicidal triad: enuresis (bed-wetting) beyond an appropriate age, fire starting, and cruelty to animals and/or smaller children. Again, not every boy who displays these traits is going to grow up to be a killer, but the combination of the three was so prominent in our study subjects that we began recommending that a pattern (rather than isolated incidences) of any two of them should raise a warning flag for parents and teachers.

You have to look at the entire package. If you're looking at a six- or seven-year-old who's regularly out on the sidewalk burning ants with a magnifying glass, and the kid comes from an otherwise well-functioning family situation and is not manifesting any other symptoms, you probably don't have a problem that can't be handled with simple parental intervention. Or if he's wetting the bed regularly but has no other alarming behaviors, he should be evaluated for a physiological condition; and if that proves negative, then work on the problem on its own terms. But if you've got these two factors and he's hanging around predominantly younger kids and bullying them or taunting them, if he's aggressive with his own siblings, or if he doesn't socialize with anyone, plays with fire, and graduates from ants to dogs or cats or hamsters, then you've got a real issue; you've got the beginnings of sociopathic behavior that isn't likely to correct itself on its own. This is unlikely to be "a phase."

Teachers will be able to add to the picture. Aside from bullying and disruptive behavior in school, they will describe him as intelligent but say he just doesn't seem to care. Maybe he's a smart aleck; he's not motivated. The fact is that he is motivated, but not in the direction the teacher would like to see.

When I do interviews or speak before various community groups around the country and I say that it's my experience that serial killers are made rather than born, I'm often asked about whether certain children simply are "born to kill." In other words, are there "bad seeds"? Are they just plain evil? That's more of a theological question, which I'm not really equipped to answer, but it is unquestionably true that some kids, from as early as you can observe them, are far more aggressive than others, have far poorer impulse control, are noticeably antisocial. That doesn't mean they're doomed to become criminals. But our studies and the work of leading psychological researchers throughout the country and much of the world do show that if you start out with a kid predisposed like this, throw him into a severely dysfunctional environment, and then don't do anything to intervene, you are pretty likely to come up with a violence-prone adult. This may also be one of the reasons why we frequently see two or more boys in a given family and only one of them grows up to be a predator or other type of lawbreaker. Three kids may have had the same influences, but one was born more vulnerable than the other two.

I want to pause here to repeat myself because it is very, very important. The fact that I can explain some behavior does not mean I excuse it. We may understand the influences that led someone to a life of crime and violence, but he's not compelled to hurt people. No background of deprivation or abuse causes an individual to be unable to resist these kinds of temptations, and virtually no one is born with impulse control so impaired that he must give in to every temptation. If he were, he'd be a very easy offender to catch—whereas the people I've hunted in my career have been very difficult to bring to justice. No one I've come across in my nearly three decades in law enforcement can recall a single case of an offender so compelled to commit a violent crime that he knowingly did so while a uniformed police officer was present. This is such an article of faith that it has been dubbed the "policeman at the elbow" principle.

Think back to the example of Dwight, the career criminal from our robbery scenario in the beginning of this chapter. Perhaps no one could predict that he would end up facing execution for brutalizing another person and taking a life, but you're probably reading this saying something to the effect of, sure, that one's obvious. He was just a time bomb waiting to go off.

And yet, he was allowed to go off. No combination of early intervention, therapy, incarceration, or other behavior modification that he received was enough to derail him from what seems in retrospect to have been an inevitable course. This is an easy one to figure out. Some of them will get more subtle as we go along.

Now, just as early childhood indicators can predict trouble, there are also certain adult behaviors—not in and of themselves necessarily criminal—that should set off warning buzzers just as clearly as Dwight's early criminal activities. Let me tell you about several cases—all of which involved the same fetish item—and show how an experienced profiler can use them to understand motivating force and predict the likelihood of predatory criminal activity.

One of the enduring icons of American society in the second half of the twentieth century is the Barbie doll. Having raised two daughters, I'm accustomed to seeing Barbies strewn around the house in all forms of attire or lack thereof, and all stages of repair and disrepair.

Generations of girls have grown up with Barbie and Ken and their various friends. No big deal. It's when this potent symbol of style, glamour, and beautiful womanhood comes into less innocent hands that I get interested from a professional standpoint.

In the late 1980s, a photo lab contacted the FBI after processing a series of photos of a man in his late twenties or early thirties dressed in camouflage gear, posing in the woods on the tailgate of his sport utility vehicle with a Barbie doll he'd made up to look tortured and abused. His face is blackened and he has a furry white husky next to him. In later photos in the series, blond and brunette Barbies are decapitated, with blood painted on them. The guy did not have a criminal record and broke no laws by mutilating a doll, but I said this was someone to watch. The fact that he had gone to such effort to make these pictures told me this was an important aspect of his life. The fact that he was an adult playing with dolls told me he wasn't very well adjusted or assimilated into a peer environment. And the fact that he owned a vehicle and hunting equipment told me he had the mobility, financial means, and weaponry to do some damage. At this point, he was only playacting. I would not expect him to have committed any serious crimes against women yet. It's common sense: you don't go from raping and murdering to staging sadistic scenes with dolls.

But remember, we said the fantasy always precedes the predatory act. A time could easily come when the dolls would no longer satisfy him. He'd yearn for, fantasize about, an actual experience. And when the opportunity presented itself, he might take advantage of it. Say, for example, he was out in the woods just finishing one of his photo sessions, highly aroused, and two attractive female campers happened to wander by. On impulse, a guy like this could suddenly turn his fantasy into reality. Since he has a camera, he'd probably even photograph his crime and see how close he came to his doll scenario.

This one worried me. I felt he was seriously motivated. But there was really nothing law enforcement could do about him. What I did suggest to the local police was that they keep him in the back of their minds so that if other crimes occurred along the escalation route we outlined earlier, he would be a good suspect.

Ideally, they could pick him up and take him out of circulation before he was responsible for anything really serious.

Another guy, whom we found sticking hundreds of pins into naked Barbies on the grounds of a Midwestern mental hospital, was certainly no better adjusted than the first guy, but I said he'd be less dangerous. There was no effort to personalize the doll he was torturing, and to me, his actions represented a guy who had more serious problems dealing with adult women his own age. He may have had the same hostility as the first guy, but not nearly the sophistication or the means to do damage, as long as he was kept at the hospital and watched. Like certain types of arsonists and bombers that we'll get into later on, this guy was a coward and a loner. He didn't even have a dog!

What's the difference in motive between these two? The second guy is taking out his anger and frustration about the way he is by punishing a fetish representative of what he aspires to but can never have. (Had he done the same thing to a baby doll rather than a mature-woman doll, I would have come to a very different conclusion.) The first guy, however, even though he hasn't acted on his fantasies yet, is actually trying to get back for some real or perceived wrong by a woman, or women in general. In his mind, he is destroying all females. His will toward manipulation, domination, and control, if allowed free rein, could easily result in murder.

Here's another example. In the mid-1980s, I was called in on an extortion case in the South that had been brought to the FBI. A single mother of two young children had received two letters requesting—alternately demanding and begging—that she take seventy-two black-and-white nude photographs of herself and deliver the rolls to a designated location at a shopping mall. If she didn't comply with the demands, her children would be killed.

After analyzing the letter, I thought the extortionist would be a pretty inadequate guy, and with this type, there's usually a follow-up of some kind to see whether she's going to go along with his demands and deliver the pictures. He could also personalize her a little bit more by actually seeing her. So, I told the locals, he's going to come up with some ruse to come to her house, like asking for directions.

If he was asking for seventy-two photographs and specifying black-and-white, I also told them, the chances were he was going to develop them himself in his own darkroom.

It happens that while two agents are interviewing this woman, a laundry truck pulls up in front of her house. The agents look out the window and notice this guy in a uniform with his name on the shirt staring in. Since I'd told them to be on the lookout for the extortionist to stop by, they asked him inside. Flustered, confronted with the FBI agents before him, he spontaneously confessed.

When they executed a search warrant of his house—he lived alone—they found the darkroom and several series of photographs of women in various stages of undress, mostly taken through windows of unknowing victims. But there was another series of black-and-white prints, from a camera mounted on a tripod. In them, the guy himself is tormenting a rather heavy-set teenage girl with a knife. Throughout the series, he becomes more "threatening" and she appears in progressive stages of undress. In the final scene, she is lying naked on the bed and he is straddling her, with his hand raised back as if to slap her.

As alarming as this sounds—and, on one level, is—it is apparent from the stiffness of the poses and the wooden expressions on both the man's and the woman's face that this series is posed. I suspected immediately he'd given the hapless girl money to act out the fantasy sequence with him.

It turned out he had chosen his extortion victim after observing her and following her home from a local shopping mall. This guy is clearly another inadequate loser, and not the type who is going to plan to rape and murder an actual victim—or even approach young children. But he can still be dangerous. The fantasy aspect is strong, and we can see the evolution we know we should worry about. First he was content to peep and take photos of unsuspecting women in their own houses. When that was no longer enough, he acted out tableaux of his fantasy with a compliant partner. Then he began extorting noncompliant ones. Let's say he then goes for breaking and entering, maybe in search of fetish souvenirs—lingerie, perhaps, or even photographs the woman's husband or boyfriend has taken of her. And let's say she happens to come upon him in the act. He'll be thrown by this, embarrassed and confused. He's trapped. He'll know he has to do something to deal with the problem. He's also got a detailed fantasy scenario already in his mind. Hell, it's already captured in film, albeit with a paid actor. I don't have to spell out the potential danger any more clearly than that.

Finally, some cases are so bizarre you're left shaking your head in wonderment before you pull your senses together enough to interpret and evaluate what you've seen.

One night, two police officers in a cruiser stop next to a couple making out in a car by the side of the road.

"What's wrong, Officer?" the man asks.

"You shouldn't be doing that here," one of the officers answers sternly.

"What do you mean?" the man says indignantly. "You should check out the guy we passed down the road. We were going to park there until we looked in his car. He was screwing a chicken!"

"What?" the officer stammers. He and his partner follow the couple's direction and find this guy in the car. Sure enough, he's having sex with a chicken, as anatomically improbable as that sounds. Not only that, he's videotaping the act!

When he spots the cops, he immediately tries to cover things up, but the cops bust him.

The reason I know this to be true is that I've seen the tape. So have a lot of people by this time. Whether it's right or not, artifacts like this one tend to take on lives of their own. And you can imagine how police audiences, with all the horrible things they see, will treat this one.

But as ridiculous as it seems, this isn't a laughing matter. Watching this tape, I do not believe this individual is passionate about chickens. He's talking as if he's having degrading, forced sex with a woman. I submit that if this were a readily achievable goal for him, he wouldn't be using this feathered surrogate. Clearly this guy is weird, he may even be nuts, and the cops have no choice but to treat this as a nuisance offense. The best they could get him on would be cruelty to animals and indecent exposure. But he is clearly motivated by fantasy, and I wonder how long it will be before the chicken, like the Barbie dolls for the other offender, will no longer be enough.

In my unit at Quantico, we were often called in to analyze and assist in solving "motiveless crimes." While we were eager to help, we tried to make clear our belief that there is, in fact, no such thing. Every crime has a motive. It's our job to learn enough about what goes on inside the heads of the men who commit these types of crimes so that the *Why?* is clear enough to lead us to the *Who?*

# CHAPTER TWO

# PLAYING WITH FIRE

It comes as no surprise that children with violent, antisocial tendencies often mistreat animals or smaller children. It might not even be surprising that these kids can be late bed-wetters, since everything we know about them suggests an underlying frustration with their lack of control. It's the third part of the homicidal triad that presents the most intriguing challenge to our knowledge of the criminal mind. What is it about fire starting that captures the imaginations of so many future predators? Each individual is going to be different, and an eight-year-old kid pulling the handle on a fire alarm box is probably not giving us the same message as that same kid doing it at sixteen, even though the motivation appears to be similar. But early in my career I knew that if we were really going to understand these people, we had to come to grips with why this was such a significant part of their developmental process.

I first started hearing the fire-starting stories early in our prison interview program.

David Berkowitz, the self-proclaimed Son of Sam, set more than two thousand fires throughout New York City before he evolved into a serial killer. This fact is documented in his own personal diaries. He was what we call a fetish arsonist and what the police call a nuisance arsonist, because he would set fires in trash cans, or vacant trash-strewn lots, or abandoned buildings, primarily in Queens and Brooklyn, then watch as the fire department responded. So complete and meticulous were his records that he even wrote down the type of equipment called in to fight each fire, and atmospheric conditions such as whether there was any wind to fan the flames.

Often, while watching the fire—Berkowitz told us when we interviewed him in Attica—he would stand to the side and masturbate; this indicates that arson very often is a sexually based crime. He talked a lot about masturbation, and I asked him if he had "a problem with masturbation," a question that would make its way into our questionnaire.

"Yes," he replied.

"To this day?" I asked.

"Yes, to this day." Numerous times a day. He said he could never satisfy himself, even though he could achieve multiple orgasms while masturbating.

So, right away I start flashing back on everything that's happened since I entered this prison conference room. The first thing I did was shake his hand! I can't wait until I can go out and wash mine, though I know I have several hours of interviewing ahead of me.

As I began to understand the relationship between setting fires and self-arousal, I used to advise detectives to have a crime scene photographer take crowd photos at suspicious blazes and then study them afterward. If you found a guy jerking off, with a transfixed look on his face, there was an excellent chance he was your arsonist.

One time I mentioned this to some detectives from the NYPD.

"That may work in other parts of the country, Douglas," one of them said to me, "but here in New York, this is the big time! You go to practically any good-sized fire and look at the crowd, you're going to find several masturbators, some urinators, who the hell knows what else!"

Regardless of location, though, arson is the crime with which so many dangerous offenders begin their criminal career that this is where we need to begin.

Like the overtly sexual crimes of rape and rape-murder that many offenders evolve to, arson is often an attempt to gain control and power and attain a feeling of success in their lives. Look at all the people an arsonist gets to manipulate and control: the victims of the fire, firefighters, police and other figures of authority, the media, and even the community in general.

In 1980, I was over in England teaching a course in profiling at Bramshill Police Staff College, about an hour's drive from London. Bramshill is the British equivalent of the FBI Academy in Quantico, which, coincidentally, is about an hour's drive from Washington. (In English fashion, though, it all struck me as much more formal than Quantico. The students all wore their respective uniforms or detectives' business suits in class.) Much of the material we covered was based on cases the participants themselves had worked on, and one was particularly fascinating in that it confirmed many of the conclusions I was coming to about the early development, evolution, and motivations of serial arsonists.

Peter George Dinsdale was born in 1960 into some pretty dreary and unhappy circumstances. His mother was a prostitute, and he was an epileptic with a deformed right arm. At first he lived with her mother, until, three years later, his own won custody back for herself and her common-law husband. But that didn't work out very well. Peter set fire to a shopping center at age nine, and in a later confession said that he would light a fire every time he got a "tingling" in his fingers. When he was thirteen he set a fire in which one victim died. Four years later, he targeted a retirement home, and eleven elderly men perished.

Other details of his personality fit right in. He once got into an argument with an old man who accused him of disturbing his pigeons. Dinsdale came back and strangled all the birds, then set fire to the man as he slept in an armchair, burning him to death. Typical of the strong fantasy element in many of these guys' lives, when he was nineteen, Dinsdale changed his name to Bruce Lee in honor of the martial arts movie star he idolized. The next year he torched a house in Hull, killing a mother and her three sons. Lee was picked up in the massive manhunt that followed that crime. He pleaded guilty to a long list of manslaughter charges and was confined indefinitely to a mental institution.

When questioned about his motive, Lee replied, "I am devoted to fire. Fire is my master, and that is why I cause these fires."

Perhaps even more telling was what the prosecutor assigned to the case said about him: "The sad fact is that this is his only real accomplishment in life."

One of our most interesting serial arson cases took place in the early 1990s in Seattle.

Gus Gary was an agent from the Bureau of Alcohol, Tobacco and Firearms (ATF) who worked with my Investigative Support Unit. He had an office within our windowless suite, sixty feet belowground, at the Academy. Once the profiling program was well-established and respected for helping to solve violent crimes such as murder, rape, and kidnapping—particularly linked, or serial, violent crimes—I wanted to expand outward and start bringing other investigative agencies like Secret Service and ATF into our orbit.

ATF special arson investigator Dane Whetsel had attended a serial arson course, and when a case came to him in the Seattle area that he thought might be helped by profiling, he forwarded the crime scene information to Gus, who then brought it before the unit. Whetsel himself had been brought in by the fire department in Lynnwood, Washington, a suburban community on the north side of Seattle, when two churches went up in flames early one Sunday morning. Whetsel was a former defense lawyer and an extremely savvy investigator.

What we're hoping is that we can use profiling to figure out where the arsonist might strike next. Or if we can't do that, maybe we can come up with a proactive technique to flush him out or force him to make a mistake. Gus Gary immediately knew we were dealing with a sophisticated, experienced operator.

The first incident known to be part of this guy's series was on August 6, 1992, when fire was set to several homes under construction. Investigators later determined that they had been ignited by a pocket lighter set to tar paper. When the fire department responded, the arsonist lit three more fires, to jerk them around and again make them go where he "told" them to.

Three days later, August 9, was when the two churches went up—first the Lynnwood Alliance Church, then the Trinity Lutheran Church. That same morning, another house under construction burned. That was when Whetsel joined the case. A little more than two weeks later, two more churches burned in three days. On Labor Day, an office building was set on fire. After a few more fires, with targets ranging from a bakery to a lumber company, on September 19, the arsonist struck at an occupied residence as a family slept inside. Both parents, a nine-year-old, and an infant were able to escape just in time. This was just one of four occupied homes targeted that night.

This case was complicated because of the range of targets. If someone is specifically torching predominantly black Baptist churches, while you don't necessarily have the real, underlying motive, you've certainly got the apparent motive, and you can use your profile to start narrowing down suspects. But here we were dealing with almost every kind of building you could think of, and most alarming, there seemed to be a progression, an evolution, in his work.

Generally, by the time detectives or arson investigators pick up on the linkage between several fires, the UNSUB is well into his series. Certainly, we figure, he will have set other fires as a child or teen that no one knows about or connects.

Then, on September 22, the stakes changed further. When the Four Freedoms House retirement home went up in flames, three elderly women died. This fire was initially ruled accidental, but when we looked at the pattern of fires and saw that there were two other probable arsons that same night, we couldn't rule out that the Four Freedoms fire was intentional. If that was true and it was the same UNSUB, we were no longer dealing with a destroyer of property; we were hunting for a killer.

Since the Four Freedoms House fire had not been ruled an arson, police couldn't be sure this UNSUB had caused any deaths yet, but the property damage was already in the tens of millions of dollars. As the case wore on, a special investigative group was established, headed up by Whetsel and Seattle Fire Department lieutenant Randy Litchfield. It was made up of police and fire department personnel from several jurisdictions, and called the Sno-King Arson Task Force, since most of the fires had occurred in Snohomish and King counties. The task force instituted a toll-free tip line, and they even got a police helicopter up with infrared thermal-imaging equipment, trying to spot the arsonist while he was actually at work. The task force gave him the code name Specter and offered a $25,000 reward for information leading to his arrest.

The suspicion that Four Freedoms might be a related arson was encouraged when the Anderson Retirement Home burned less than a week later, on September 28. Fortunately, a sprinkler system kept the fire from getting out of control, and the investigating team finally got some physical clues to work with. Evidence there suggested that the arsonist removed a window screen, climbed through, and lit a bedspread. There were two fingerprints on the screen, but they didn't match anything on file.

The stepped-up pace continued through October, November, and December. In October another home in Lynnwood started burning as a family with seven children slept inside, then six more fires erupted the same night within Snohomish County Fire District Number 1. Around 3 A.M., neighbors of ninety-three-year-old Helen Allen saw her house in flames, broke in, and got her out safely. Altogether, twelve fires had been set within a four-hour period.

But there was another potential breakthrough that night. A couple in a car noticed a well-dressed man get out of a sedan and walk between two houses while talking into a cellular phone. He returned and drove off, and a couple of minutes later, flames broke out. The couple called the fire department, then reported the man's physical description to detectives. Lieutenant Litchfield realized that the suspect was not using a mobile telephone at all, but listening to a police scanner.

November 2 saw fires at another residence and two more warehouses. That same night a man walking home from a bar noticed a car (which police determined from his description to be a Chrysler-made vehicle) make a sharp U-turn and duck into a side street. A few minutes later, he saw fire engines arrive at the scene. The witness stated that the car appeared to be new and had temporary tags and a Chrysler advertising card in the window.

Under Dane Whetsel's direction, detectives followed up on every Chrysler dealership in the area and any advertising agency that might have made up the card. Nothing panned out.

Another possible sighting occurred on November 17 when a woman in a phone booth almost a hundred miles southeast of Seattle noted a man near a vacant building. As in the previous sightings, soon smoke and flames began billowing out and the man quickly left. She called the police, who immediately put out a description of the man's car that a police officer in nearby Cle Elum picked up. He saw such a car pull into an Exxon station. The driver was well-dressed, though, and didn't strike the officer as looking like an arsonist. Another witness, Bonnie Spurrier, saw a man get out of a car and stand near her as she was watching firefighters battle a blaze. His demeanor was suspicious, and she gave investigators a description that led to a sketch.

Late in November a fire was set in the garage of an elderly couple's home. And in December there was a blaze at a boat-storage facility. The couple who ran it lived upstairs and barely escaped. The geographical range of the fires was more than thirty miles, all the way down to Tacoma. Neighborhood watch groups were set up. People were urged to report any suspicious activity.

The local investigators had come up with some interesting and significant findings. Nearly all the fires believed to be part of the series were lit between waist and chest height, instead of right on the ground or floor. Also, none of the fires was set during bad weather. Both of these facts led investigators to conclude that the offender liked to keep clean. Witnesses had given detectives descriptions of generic American cars leaving the scenes. Since the cars could easily have been fleet vehicles, there was some thought that the UNSUB might be a traveling salesman.

When Dane Whetsel contacted Quantico and asked Gus Gary and the unit to get involved, we brought the series up at one of our regular case consultations, where we get as many of the agents as we can around a table to listen to the presentation, ask questions, critique the lead agent's analysis, and share their own ideas. As with any other set of serial crimes, you try to figure out what the pattern means—in other words, what can we say about the evolution of the offenses?

The first thing you look at in an arson series is whether the targets were occupied, or whether the offender would have reason to believe they were when he set each fire. If he's targeting un-occupied buildings, you've got more of a nuisance-type offender, regardless of the cost of the damage. If he evolves from nonoccu-pied structures to occupied ones, though, then he's just like any other type of escalating predator. In all likelihood he's nonspecific on victims; if he had a specific victim or series of victims in mind, he wouldn't have stayed with the nuisance stuff very long. Anyone who sets fire to a building that he can reasonably expect to be in-habited at the time is displaying a general level of anger and hos-tility against society, either for perceived injuries of some sort or simply for not paying proper attention. Arson, like bombing and various other forms of terrorism, is the crime of a coward. It is perpetrated by a person (typically a man) who wants to strike out but does not have the courage—or even the interpersonal skills, for that matter—to face his intended victim nose-to-nose. And in the case of arson, especially, that victim is usually a faceless, sexless cipher in his mind rather than a living, breathing human being.

We speak of these criminals as internalizers, as opposed to externalizers. Both begin with the fantasy. The externalizer acts on it directly. For the internalizer—the arsonist, the bomber—it re-mains one step removed. The internalizer is the loner, the asocial who has to put emotional and physical distance between himself and everyone else. Just so you know and understand that there are no simple or absolute formulas in this business, an internalizer can be a rapist or a one-on-one killer. But if he is, the victim is going to be someone obviously smaller, weaker, and/or more vulnerable than he is—someone he doesn't have to deal with on a challenging or even equal basis. The other possibility is that he'll choose his victim and the circumstances of the crime very carefully so that he can launch a "blitz-style" attack, neutralizing the victim or rendering her unconscious or defenseless before he has to deal with her as a human being. I've often said that all predatory criminals are cowards on one important level. But the internalizers are among the most cowardly of all.

By setting several fires in one night, we concluded, the Seattle UNSUB was taunting the authorities with his own superiority. As we analyzed it, part of the pattern was to wait until the fire engines left a station to respond to a call; then he would immediately set his next fire near the now-empty station.

What's happening is that he's getting caught up in the media, starting to believe in his own power, a power that in every other aspect of life he completely lacks. Since in most cases he will not personalize potential victims, setting fires in which there is likely to be a loss of life is an escalation of the power drive. He doesn't hate these people, but he finds he's getting off on the power over life and death. The fires are going to get bigger and more spectacular, and he's getting more dangerous with every "success" he enjoys.

Whenever you have a series of escalating crimes, whether you're talking about rape, murder, bombing, or arson, you look to the early crimes to make some determination of where this guy might live. This certainly helps you limit your investigation.

When they're starting out, the offenders will operate within their own "comfort zone," which usually means close to where they live or work. They have to feel comfortable that they know the geography, know the escape routes, can blend in on the street, get back to the refuge of home or someplace else that's safe, and have confidence that they can talk their way out of a jam if necessary. If they continue to be successful, then they start to feel they know what they're doing and they can get more elaborate. Their self-confidence and obsession with their own power grow, and they can venture farther and farther from their own zone of confidence. That's why analysis of the early crimes is so important.

The local ATF investigator noted that, especially in these early fires, the UNSUB used materials he found at the scene, building a tepee out of whatever combustible objects were lying around and igniting them with his lighter. The investigator referred to this as the arsonist's "signature," a trait you would know or recognize him by. But in our parlance at Quantico, we would refer to this as "modus operandi." The modus operandi, or M.O., is just what it sounds like—the means by which the crime is carried out—and as such, it's dynamic. It evolves as the offender learns more and gets better at what he's doing. If you rob a bank at gunpoint, the gun is part of your M.O. True signature, on the other hand, is the aspect of the crime that emotionally fulfills the offender, and so it remains relatively the same. Torture, for example, is almost always a signature. No matter what crime an offender is committing, he doesn't need to torture a victim to pull it off. He does so because of a sadistic emotional need. So, if an offender uses a gun to capture a victim so that he can torture her, you've got both an M.O. and a signature. It's important to understand the distinction between the two because they come up over and over again in what we do. M.O. changes as the offender becomes more experienced and proficient. But signature is a critical clue in coming up with the UNSUB's personality and motive.

A signature for an arsonist would be a particular target or set of targets, but the Seattle offender didn't seem to have any, so that aspect didn't give us any leads. If, in addition to setting fires, he'd clearly urinated on the floor, or taken a dump, or displayed a pattern of vandalism, or obviously burglarized—particularly if he'd stolen fetish items—any of those would be a signature element that could help us out. The only thing we really had to go on here was the number of cases and the escalation of power manifestations.

But we were pretty confident about the profile we could construct, based on Gus Gary's analysis and our experience with other types of serial criminals. The witnesses had pegged him as a white male in his twenties or thirties, and this came as no surprise. Arson is primarily a crime of white men. You just don't see many blacks, Hispanics, or Asians doing it, at least in this country. Based on the evolutionary process, this guy would be in his late twenties to mid-thirties to have become this sophisticated an arsonist. And he would have a long-standing interest in fires, going back to early childhood, where you'd first see him setting small nuisance fires close to home. As a child he would also have displayed cruelty to animals and/or other children and possibly have been a late bed-wetter. The police scanner was not a surprise. He'd be a police or fire department buff and probably entertained the thought of becoming a professional, but couldn't cut it or washed out for one reason or another, compounding his frustration with his life. You often see guys of this type applying to be volunteer firemen or working as auxiliary cops—anything like that which gives them some identity and authority. He'll be an emotional loner whose relationships with women have not worked out. This would also go back to childhood. In school, he would have had few friends, and his classmates would have described him as an oddball. Teachers would describe him as a disruptive influence and an underachiever who never lived up to his potential.

As a partial compensation for his low self-esteem, he would be very concerned about his personal appearance and would always want to put up a good front. If that front were ever pierced or cracked, he could easily come apart. Those with whom he worked or socialized would notice him sometimes going into a rage with very little provocation. He would be quick to blame others and never see, or be willing to admit, that anything was his own fault. We would expect to see an interest in rough-style pornography, especially having to do with bondage and other forms of control.

If the witness descriptions were in any way accurate, then the UNSUB has a good job with which he can buy nice clothes. He has a new car, and he's mobile and resourceful. He's not one of life's pathetic losers, so his big problem is his own self-perception. Regardless of the actual externals of his life, he feels in control only when he's marshaling the resources of the region and capturing the public fear. The efficiency and organization of the arsons would suggest that he's probably scouting out the sites during the day, then coming back to quickly set the fires at night. This would be another supporting argument for a salesman-like job because he'd be mobile but unaccountable for his time during the day. He could miss no work and arouse no suspicions, but still do the amount of scouting necessary to set more than a hundred fires.

There probably was a triggering trauma leading to this round of fire starting, we concluded; and the two most common events are loss of job or loss of love. As far as current behavior, those around him might notice a tremendous preoccupation with press reports and media accounts of the fires. This goes hand in hand with the desire to manipulate and control authority and public facilities. The media attention is a validation for him. But it will also cause him stress. In the past he would have turned to drug or alcohol abuse, and there could be a return to those habits now. And now that the task force is geared up and the investigative heat is definitely on, he may look for an excuse to leave town, which might not be too hard to pull off, since, again, there's both forensic and behavioral evidence to suggest that he might be a traveling salesman. Not only were there eyewitness accounts of a salesman's type of vehicle, but serial offenders often get themselves into professions where they can drive long distances on their own. We found from our research that driving like that, particularly at night, is closely akin in their minds to hunting. And as the investigation intensified, those around the UNSUB would see his emotional condition deteriorate noticeably.

So the task force now had a good understanding of the arsonist's M.O., a vague possible sketch, a general description of his car, and the profile Gus delivered from Quantico. Then, as the next step, Gus and I met in my office to decide what to advise them to do with that profile information.

One of the most important uses of a profile is to aid local police in limiting and refining their suspect list so they can direct their resources where they might do the most good. But another key use of a profile in certain circumstances is to go proactive, to let the public become your partner in crime solving. As we will see, particularly with regard to bombers, these guys almost inevitably have to display some sort of behavior to those close to them that will indicate their involvement with the crime. If you can only get those people to be aware of what they've seen, know how to interpret it, and be willing to come forward, you can solve your case and put an end to the series of crimes.

That's what we thought they should do in Seattle. On January 27, 1993, the Sno-King Arson Task Force held a news conference in which they released the composite sketch and elements of the behavioral profile.

"He has no self-esteem," Dane Whetsel declared. "He may come from a dysfunctional family. There's some indication that he may be mentally ill, such as schizophrenia, however it may be as simple as a deep-seated emotional problem." Whetsel added, "He gains a great deal of enthusiasm and thrill from setting these fires."

The news conference went on to suggest that a triggering emotional trauma probably occurred sometime in late July. "Someone may know this person. Come forward," Randy Litchfield said.

Ben Keller, a twenty-one-year-old student at Seattle Pacific University, happened to watch the news on television, and the longer he watched, the more his alarm grew. Both the sketch and the behavioral profile sounded an awful lot like his older brother, Paul Kenneth Keller, a traveling salesman for their father's local advertising agency. He called his sister, Ruth Wacker, the next day. She also worked at the agency; her husband, Preston, happened to be deputy sheriff of Snohomish County. Ben suggested that she pull Paul's gasoline charge receipts and see if there happened to be one from Cle Elum for the previous November 17.

*Yes* was Ruth's alarming response.

The same day, their parents, George and Margaret Keller, were reading the report of the news conference in the *Everett Herald*. The headline on the story read, *Officials: Someone Knows This Person*. They also were troubled by their son Paul's resemblance to the police sketch, and even more troubled by his resemblance to the behavioral profile. He was twenty-seven years of age and divorced. In July of 1992 he had indeed experienced a severe emotional blow when he'd filed for bankruptcy, an act that George characterized as "personally devastating." Paul maintained a neat appearance, had been interested in fires since early youth, had twice been rejected as a volunteer fireman, and knew the locations of all the fire stations in the Seattle metropolitan area.

George Keller courageously went to the Everett Fire Department that same day and talked to Investigator Warren Burns. This is exactly the kind of thing we hoped would happen and proves that there's almost always someone out there who has the information needed to complete the puzzle. Burns, in turn, contacted the Sno-King Task Force and got the elder Keller in touch with Whetsel and Litchfield. In a statement to investigators that I was given to read, George Keller recounted the reasons for his concerns and told investigators that Paul had numerous emotional problems as a child and was caught setting fire to a vacant house in the neighborhood when he was about eight or nine. He had been caught shoplifting, bullied his brother and sister, and got into screaming fits with his parents. He worked as a bookkeeper for an Everett company until about five or six years before. He'd been fired after the desk where he worked caught fire under suspicious circumstances. And the matter of the automobile was cleared up. Paul did drive a new Chrysler-made vehicle, but it was a Dodge, not a Chrysler. The eyewitness who recalled the Chrysler advertising card had been mistaken. In fact, Keller Advertising had created the window card and leased the vehicle from one of their clients.

George Keller and the investigators didn't let on anything to Paul. But the task force began an intensive scrutiny of Paul as a suspect, with George's full and admirable cooperation. Checks of Paul's cellular phone records showed him in the vicinity of a number of the fires. When the witness saw him speaking into what looked to be a phone but police thought was a scanner, we thought he probably had both in his hands. Paul also told his father he'd watched some of the house fires as they burned. All of these had been classified as suspicious in origin.

The information George Keller gave the task force was extremely useful, as well as fascinating to us back in Quantico. He said that about a year before, the family business bought an expensive camera, which Paul asked to use for his personal projects—mainly driving all over the state of Washington to take pictures of his twin passions, old trains and modern fire and emergency services. He used to show the pictures to his father, but once details of the hunt for the arsonist became public, he stopped. George said he thought that was very uncharacteristic of his son.

Paul was an aggressive driver who put a lot of wear and tear on his vehicles and frequently earned himself traffic and speeding tickets. In addition to his hobby of seeking out fire stations and listening to emergency broadcasts on a police scanner, he kept a fireman's yellow turnout coat in his trunk. When he picked up a good fire on his scanner, George said, Paul would drop everything and race to the scene. Several of his friends and family members reported seeing him at various fires, and in at least one case, he almost struck someone with his car in an attempt to quickly maneuver closer to the show.

The description George Keller provided of Paul could almost have been our profile, it fit so perfectly into our developmental models. He described his son as suffering from extremely low self-esteem despite his obvious intelligence. Paul dressed well, both professionally and casually, and groomed his hair and mustache to the point of obsessiveness, but often neglected such basic hygiene as brushing his teeth.

He was acutely sensitive to anything that might tarnish his public image, and if anything happened that made him seem less than perfect, he could fly into an instantaneous rage, with verbal abuse directed at anyone who happened to be nearby. Then, just as quickly, he could shift emotional gears and become utterly charming. Despite his problems with handling frustration, he could be sensitive and tender, particularly with elderly people. He sang in his church's choir.

From an early age, Paul was a convincing liar. He was a hyperactive child who often displayed what his father characterized as inappropriate behavior at times, such as laughing when another child fell down and hurt himself. He would continually torment his younger brother and sister and took satisfaction in hurting them. One time he spread golf balls across the floor and then got year-old Ben to walk across them. Ben broke his leg and had to be in a partial body cast for a long time. George would often come home to find Margaret in tears over her inability to control Paul. No form of discipline or punishment seemed to have any effect. It was as though he was totally oblivious to his own behavioral problems. Instead, he constantly accused his parents of siding with Ruth and Ben. Though George felt Paul improved somewhat over the years, he still found his son argumentative and demeaning with his siblings. Everyone else was wrong, never him.

Throughout school, Paul was a loner without any real friends. George did not recall a single girlfriend from high school. Despite his intelligence, his academic record was poor. He was disruptive in class and openly ridiculed his classmates. On one occasion he used a pencil to stab in the back a student who was sitting at the desk in front of him.

Despairing at their son's behavior, the Kellers tried counseling, but with no effect. They sent him to a Boys' Farm program for troubled youth, but he had to leave after a severe food allergy reaction.

His fire setting began at the age of eight or nine. The cruelty to his siblings and other children began even earlier. Those are two prongs of the homicidal triad. Other details were equally as interesting and predictable from a profiling perspective. Paul had no interest in college, and after high school he got a job with a security company in north Seattle. He was very proud of his uniform and his car with flashing light bars. But he lost the job, and subsequent ones, because he couldn't get along with his coworkers. It was after this that he took the position as a bookkeeper with the Light Rider Canopy Company, where his desk mysteriously caught on fire.

Paul met his future wife at church during the summer of 1989 and determined to marry her, despite the fact that he didn't have much experience with women. Her uncle worked for the Everett Fire Department. But shortly after the honeymoon, Paul told his father he had made a mistake. After two years, they were divorced and he once again felt very lonely.

George hired him for the family business, and he was a successful salesman, but his frequent outbursts continued to be a problem. It got so bad that in August 1992, George wrote him a note saying that if he didn't get counseling for his anger, he would lose his job. Margaret backed George and told Paul so during a very confrontational telephone call. This could have been an exacerbating stressor in the string of arsons. The timing was certainly right.

Now, with this type of profile and personal history, we have to ask ourselves the central question of this book, *Why?* Mr. and Mrs. Keller seemed to be fine, concerned, and loving parents, and indeed, two of their three children turned out very well. If we look closely at Paul's background, though, we do find one early trauma that could have had influence on his later course.

Shortly after he was born, at Everett General Hospital, Margaret's mother noticed that the baby was covered with blood. His umbilical cord had detached prematurely and he had hemorrhaged. Emergency surgery saved his life, but his later hyperactivity was thought to have resulted from this. Treatment by specialists over the years and various forms of medication had had little effect.

Could this medical emergency be the key to Paul Keller's overwhelming need for control in his life, resulting in his hostile attitude and antisocial behavior? I don't know. No one does, but it's an issue we continue to confront and speculate about. What is clear is that despite his parents' best efforts, this kid did not fit into his environment and could not control his anger and frustration. Certainly he had some problems with impulse control, but just as certainly, he made the choices to do the things he did. I think it's important to note his father's observation that he could turn on a dime from abusive to charming. The reason he behaved as he did and committed the acts he did—the motive, if you will—was that they gave him a level of satisfaction and deliverance from his frustrations and anger that nothing else would.

The confidential investigation into Paul Keller's life revealed other details that fit into the profile of this type of offender. He had been spending a lot of time and money at bars, massage parlors, and adult video stores, drinking heavily and using marijuana—which contributed to his personally devastating bankruptcy. But despite all of this and the consistent developmental history, investigators didn't have much in the way of solid evidence toward a conviction. Short of a confession, prosecutors would have a real problem. So we helped the task force investigators with a strategy we thought might lead in that direction.

As we predicted, George and Margaret Keller had noticed their son's emotional state deteriorate to the point that they were afraid he might try to hurt or kill himself. Also, as we predicted, on February 5, 1993, he told his father he was considering going to California to visit a woman he knew there. The investigators had to move.

Members of the Sno-King Arson Task Force arrested Paul Keller around 6:30 on the morning of February 6, 1993, at his residence in Lynnwood. Though they thought he was good for nearly a hundred fires, they arrested him for the three with the best evidence: a warehouse and a residence on November 2, 1992, and another warehouse on New Year's Day.

They brought him back to task force headquarters in a police convoy, sirens blaring. In other words, they made him feel important on a level he would understand. Inside the building, county fire chief Rick Eastman met him wearing his full dress uniform, the one he usually put on only for official funerals. As I'd often advised in the past, the interrogation location had been dressed or staged for maximum effect. They'd set up bulletin boards with the police sketch, next to which they'd put Paul's picture and a sign that said, IDENTIFIED.

But the key element we advised was to have Paul's father on site. If there was any authority figure in Paul's life, it was George. George met his son in the interrogation room and hugged him. Then he said something to the effect of, "It's all over now, son. They know what happened, so you have to tell the truth." We figured that if Keller didn't feel he had to keep the truth from his father any longer, he'd be more comfortable confessing it to the investigators.

The next stage was for those investigators to express their admiration at how brilliant he had been—what a master arsonist—underscoring the effect of the police motorcade. And the strategy worked. At first he admitted to a few of the scores of fires on the task force's list. Then gradually, over the course of several more hours, he gave details for more and more of them. During the confession, he said he wasn't proud of what he'd done and asked not to be sent to prison. He blamed the influence of alcohol and some of the owners of the torched properties for leaving combustible materials lying around. You can imagine what I thought of that one; it's like a rapist excusing himself by saying his victim was asking for it.

"I'm not the guy they should be putting in jail," Keller said during his confession. "I mean, dock my insurance or something to pay it back."

A month later, Paul Kenneth Keller formally pleaded guilty to thirty-two counts of arson, admitted setting an additional forty-five fires, and was sentenced to seventy-five years in prison by Snohomish County Superior Court judge Kathryn Trumbull. Later, when he was tied to the Four Freedoms House fire, in which three women died, he was sentenced to an additional (but concurrent) ninety-nine years in King County Superior Court by Judge Jim Bates.

"The one thing that stands out is that Paul Keller is not safe to be at large," said Craig Peterson, one of the prosecutors. I just wish everyone in a position to do something would get it as Peterson did—that as important as the concepts of both punishment and rehabilitation might seem, the most important consideration is to get guys like this off the street.

As he was sentenced for the first set of fires, Paul Keller finally went at least partway toward accepting responsibility for what he'd done when he read aloud a letter of apology.

"I do not negate any of my actions, or their serious nature," he stated to his victims. "But in reading some of your statements, I hear you feel I was out to harm and kill. Nothing could be further from the truth. My conflicts are now being diagnosed and discovered." He goes on to say, "A life of disappointment in myself, not you, led to my actions."

Then later: "To the fire department and police agencies, I also ask for your forgiveness. Dozens, if not hundreds of you knew me as a man whose care for and interest in the fire and EMS fields were legitimate. I never tried to twist these interests into a perversion. I am so sorry at the risk you had to take and the costs incurred. It is also very painful to lose so many valued friends. To those of you who have remained my steadfast friends, I thank you for looking past circumstances and into my heart."

As I said, he takes some responsibility and shows some insight. But when he says he didn't try to harm and kill, what he's really telling us is that he depersonalized his potential victims so much that their possible death wasn't even an issue to him, even when he set fire to a home where elderly people were present. If he were a different kind of predator, one with somewhat more self-confidence and less personal cowardice, I could see him being even more destructive—say, by depersonalizing a female rape victim so that he could then mutilate and kill her without connecting to her as a human being. By the same token, if he'd had different life experiences, such as a technical or military background, he might have graduated from setting fires to making and planting bombs. If he'd become a good shot like David Berkowitz, a powerful handgun might have been his weapon of choice rather than a simple cigarette lighter.

And as far as accepting responsibility, during an interview he gave to independent television producer Brian Halquist, Keller claimed that at the age of twelve he had been abused sexually by a volunteer firefighter, as if that would explain or excuse his crimes. It is important here to note that his father stated that Paul's fire starting began at age eight or nine.

George Keller, one of the real heroes of this story, accepted the $25,000 reward money and immediately turned it over to Pastor Richard Rouse of the Trinity Lutheran Church in Lynnwood, one of the churches Paul burned. "I have lost my son. I have lost hundreds of thousands of dollars from my business," George stated at a news conference. "I have paid a price to do what was right."

And my hat goes off to him that he did.

Just as an individual's background, education, and vocational experiences may be reflected in the type of crime he commits, so his personality is reflected in the particulars of the specific crime he chooses. For example, we can classify and analyze arson just as we do rape.

The inadequate, nuisance-type arsonist would correlate to what we classify as the power-reassurance rapist, a sexually and socially inadequate offender who rapes to convince himself of his own power and self-worth and often feels guilty about the assault immediately afterward. He may even apologize to his victim before leaving the scene. On the other hand, an arsonist who sets fire to a populated apartment house and takes pleasure and satisfaction in watching people jumping out of windows and fleeing for their lives would correspond to the power-assertive rapist, who, as the term suggests, assaults because he enjoys the power and control over other people. He would be a very violent rapist who would enjoy watching his victim cry and suffer.

As with any other violent crime, the details of the arson lead you to the motive and, therefore, the personality type of the offender. Keep in mind, however, that any nuisance arsonist can escalate if his life situation or emotional state deteriorates. It's the fantasy that comes first, which is why both rapists and arsonists usually start out as Peeping Toms.

I've found that investigators and others in and around law enforcement frequently confuse the terms "motive" and "intent." Intent refers simply to the deliberateness of the act—consciously choosing to commit the crime. Motive is the offender's reason for setting the fire, and there are eight basic arson motives that we encounter frequently: fraud; pyromania; crime concealment; vanity; spite or revenge; civil disorder; political or revolutionary activity; and the simple mischief of juveniles and adolescents playing with fire.

Each of these motives will represent offenders with distinct profile elements.

*Fraud* arson is the type most often committed by a professional—someone who makes his illicit living by creating fires that are supposed to appear to be accidental. Fraud arson is most commonly done for insurance money, and the motive is clear: monetary profit. Other fraud arsons have equally trans-

ing manner. A forty-five-year-old man was arrested on charges of murder, kidnapping, sexual assault, arson, and insurance fraud after setting fire to his house trailer in an effort to fake his own death and thereby collect life insurance money *and* evade justice for sexual assaults on children. He moved to another state and changed his identity. It was another man who died in the trailer fire.

There are two main categories of what we call *vanity arson*. The first is "profit vanity," which is also a form of indirect fraud. A watchman wants a pay raise that will increase the profile of his job. A fireman wants longer or better shifts. The second form is "hero vanity," and it is often related to forms of pyromania. A police officer or firefighter wants to appear heroic. A private citizen wishes to gain attention. A young man wants to impress his girlfriend by saving her from a burning building so he sets the fire to stage the act. A babysitter wants to save a child and so creates the situation to make that happen. As you might suspect, these people are often amenable to treatment, much more so than those who set fires for the more traditional motives of manipulation, domination, and control.

*Arson for spite or revenge,* initiated by hatred, jealousy, or other uncontrolled emotions, may be the most deadly of all types of intentional fire starting. It usually takes place during darkness, and there may be large life or property loss. Love and/or sex often appear as motivating factors, to keep a lover from running around or to get even with an ex-lover. The target is often a place of public assembly, such as a bar, tavern, lounge, or disco. More than in most crimes, we see spite and revenge arsons frequently being the work of women or gays. This is not because they are more prone to setting fires, but because they are less prone to settle scores using a knife or a gun. So if they are going to commit violence for spite or revenge, they are more likely to let fire do it for them.

Other motives for spite/revenge arsons include labor disputes, religious or ethnic antagonisms, and racial bigotry, such as the firebombing of black churches in the South.

An example of a spite arson would be a woman setting fire to her soon-to-be-ex-husband's car and belongings. There was a case not long ago in Detroit in which an eighteen-year-old woman copied a scene from the movie *Waiting to Exhale.* She discovered through a conversation at a beauty salon that her boyfriend was cheating on her and set fire to his late-model Chevy Monte Carlo. When questioned about it, she told police that the movie scene came to mind in which Angela Bassett's character, Bernadine, piled her husband's belongings into his BMW and set them on fire after he left her. Where the fire is set, who the victim is—all of this needs to be studied very carefully.

*Civil disorder and political arson* may have an individual of-fender or a mob reacting under the emotional heat and pressure of the moment. In this case, the destruction of property is used as a weapon of social protest or a demonstration of group strength. Race riots, ghetto riots, war protest marches, and anarchist activ-ities all fall under this heading. More than in any other type of arson, here the power of suggestion is a critical factor. A crowd gets worked up and a snowball effect is created. Often other motives factor into the equation. What appears to be a political arson might actually cover up spite and revenge, looting, or other vandalism. These crimes may be difficult to solve because of the problem of pinning them on a single individual and the fact that groups not involved often claim public credit to further their own motives.

As far as *arson by juveniles or adolescents* is concerned, there is a natural curiosity about fire displayed by both sexes, generally showing up between the ages of four and twelve. The younger the fire setter, the more likely the fire results from this curiosity, rather than malevolent or criminal intent. One of the tip-offs is that these curiosity fires are usually seen in bedroom closets, under beds, in basement or attic crawl spaces, under porches, in alleys—in other words, not places intended to create a public scene. And in these cases we need family counseling or professional help rather than prosecution or punishment. Of course, we look at the entire pattern of behavior to help determine motive. The older the fire starter, the more serious the problem is, and that gets into many of the other motives, such as revenge, vanity, or concealment of other crimes. Vandalism as a motive for arson can be seen in all ages, from young children up through mature adults, but in children it often arises out of sheer boredom. Our two greatest forensic considerations in youthful arson are the sophistication of the crime and the behavior pattern of the suspect. And again, we certainly look to the target itself. If it is a building that the offender, even a youthful offender, might reasonably expect to be inhabited, so that people will be hurt by his actions, then you've got serious personality and law enforcement problems to deal with.

One of our goals in the behavioral sciences and criminal investigative analysis units at Quantico was to transform criminal psychology from an arcane academic discipline, bogged down by technical terminology of use only to psychiatrists and other therapists, into something that would be practical and useful for police officers, detectives, and other law enforcement professionals. And one of the important insights that emerged from the serial offender interviews and study was the classification of offenders into categories—organized, disorganized, or mixed—based on general attributes of M.O., crime scene conditions, pre- and postoffense behavior, and the like. This is just as applicable to arsonists as it is to burglars, rapists, murderers, and other violent predators.

The motive for the organized arsonist is most likely to be

profit, or concealment of other crimes, or the fact that he is a professional "torch." The disorganized arsonist, generally younger and less sophisticated, will be a loner who feels rejected; he may be abusing alcohol or drugs, will have few friends, and tends to set fires near home, in his own comfort zone. Such factors as planning, complexity of staging or cover-up, and methodology will all speak to the UNSUB's level of organization.

Back in 1983, my unit in Quantico got a request to consult on a string of fires in Hartford, Connecticut. In one week in August of that year, someone set fire to both the Emanuel and Young Israel synagogues and the home of Young Israel's rabbi, Solomon Krupka, in West Hartford. The phone records for Young Israel showed that someone placed a large number of long-distance calls from there to topless bars in Dallas, Texas.

I had an intense caseload then, and so I assigned Special Agents Dave Icove and Blaine McIlwain to work with me. They were both new to the unit. Dave had just come in from Tennessee, where he'd developed a computer program called AIMS (Arson Information Management System).

After the first string of Hartford arsons, on August 17, fire engulfed the home of Connecticut state legislator Joan Kemler, an active member of Emanuel. The fire was set around 5:45 A.M. on Yom Kippur, the most solemn Jewish holy day. Given the religious connection between all four targets and the timing of the last fire, local authorities and many citizens in the West Hartford community assumed the arsons were hate crimes, with anti-Semitism as the motive.

I wasn't so sure.

Late in September, Hartford police investigated a note found at the back door of a Jewish family's home, reading, "This Jew house is next," in words cut out of magazines and newspapers. But there was no fire and the M.O. was completely different from in the previous crimes, so we all determined this to be the work of a cowardly copycat who was just demonstrating his religious bigotry by using someone else's actions.

The fire at Young Israel was a small one, started with matches in a trash pail. Then the UNSUB set fire to curtains in the main chapel. At Emanuel, curtains had also been set on fire, and three of their Torah scrolls kept in the sanctuary in a sacred ark had been burned. At the rabbi's home, gasoline had been poured on the back door and the back step and lit with matches. At the Kemler residence, empty soda bottles found outside had been filled with gasoline and the concrete foundation doused and again lit with matches.

Despite the obviously hostile, antisocial, and upsetting nature of the series, these were not sophisticated crimes and didn't seem intended to do a lot of damage. Rather, they looked like an attempt to get attention by a youngish offender. So I thought it very important to focus on the first crime, because that would be within the UNSUB's comfort zone.

Dave Icove constructed a map with dots on the locations of all the cases, and when he finished, we all studied it and concluded that the guy was probably an inadequate type living somewhere close to the center of the case dots. We believed he'd be in his late teens or early twenties, socially withdrawn, living with his mother or both parents. He probably wouldn't have a prior criminal record.

We didn't consider this one a very difficult case. Our best guess, and this wasn't a particularly popular one under the circumstances, was that the UNSUB would turn out to be a member of the first synagogue torched. The fact that someone this unsophisticated would feel comfortable enough to make all those phone calls from a synagogue told us that he must not feel threatened staying there for some length of time. And Blaine's written profile noted that the UNSUB appeared to burn the Torah scrolls from right to left. This odd fact suggested that the offender might be well-versed in Hebrew, which, unlike Western languages, is written and read right to left. It wasn't a hate crime per se. What it seemed like was a young person acting out against authority. When investigators talked to the rabbi about it, he said he knew someone who lived just about at the central point of Dave's map.

His name was Barry Dov Schuss. He was seventeen years of age and a member of Young Israel synagogue, from an orthodox religious family. He offered no resistance and surrendered voluntarily on December 14, 1983, facing four counts of second-degree arson. He took full responsibility but couldn't explain why he had set the fires. At the time of his arrest, he was a psychiatric patient at a local hospital. He pleaded guilty to two counts of second-degree arson and two counts of third-degree arson—a reduction in two of the counts because at the time the fires were set the synagogues were not occupied. Schuss was sentenced to fourteen years in prison plus five years' probation, though the judge suspended the jail time on the condition that he receive in-patient treatment at a private psychiatric hospital. In this case, I agree with the sentence. With help, this kid is not the kind who's going to go on to a life of crime. What this type really needs is to get his life sorted out, because the person he's most dangerous to is likely himself.

I try to be as hopeful as my experience allows me to be.

In 1986, I was contacted by Detective Sergeant Ray Mondragon of the Clovis, New Mexico, Police Department about having Quantico help in the prosecution of a twenty-four-year-old man named Edward Lee Adams for the rape and murder of an eighty-one-year-old woman earlier that year. Adams was also accused of setting the woman's house on fire after the attack. His trial was scheduled for the following month.

Any rape or murder is horrible, brutal, and disgusting by its very nature, and I'd do anything I could to help bring the culprit to justice. Mondragon had taken courses at Quantico, including one that I taught, which is how he knew about me and the unit's work. In those days, I was program manager of profiling and consultation for the Behavioral Science Unit. I was interested in this case for a couple of other reasons. Even though I'm from Long Island, New York, I happen to have spent four years of my life in and around Clovis, first at Cannon Air Force Base when I was in the service, then at Eastern New Mexico State University in Portales. It was there in New Mexico that I met the FBI agent who got me interested in pursuing a career in the Bureau. And the arson aspect of the case, apparently committed in the context of another crime, interested me. I wanted to learn all I could about this, so I assigned the case to myself.

Normally, the main thing the prosecution wanted from me or my people was an answer to the question *Why?* This might not seem as important once the subject is caught, but it is a very important consideration when prosecuting a case in court. Juries often have a difficult time convincing themselves that someone committed a particularly heinous act if they can't figure out what the motive was. As you will see, there was good reason to think that the defense would attempt to muddy up this point.

This is what Eddie Lee Adams was charged with:

On the morning of January 31, 1986, Ola Temple, in her eighties, was raped and murdered in her home, which was then set on fire. Firefighters found the victim's body in the bedroom, on the bed, with her feet hanging over the side. Her glasses and bra were found elsewhere in the house.

At first the fire was assumed to be accidental, since Mrs. Temple was found in her bed and was known to smoke there. But here was the critical element: the medical examiner found that the level of carbon monoxide in her blood was so low, she had to have been dead before the fire started. It was later determined from a postmortem examination that she died from manual strangulation (though the defense put forth the proposition that she actually died of a heart attack). In addition to a broken neck and a damaged larynx, she suffered three broken ribs, and there was clear evidence of vaginal sexual assault.

Adams was targeted as a suspect from descriptions of witnesses who saw him walking in the vicinity of the Temple home. Also, his name had recently been brought to police attention when they were notified of his parole from prison on an earlier, similar-type rape. A search warrant of his residence turned up incriminating physical evidence, including a cigarette butt that was Mrs. Temple's brand but not Adams's. Cuts to his lip corresponded to wounds she would have inflicted trying to defend herself against the attack.

Although he confessed to the crime, Adams found a way to deny full responsibility as he had with the previous rape. In the first case, he had tried to claim that the woman raped him; in the Temple case, he argued that he hadn't meant to kill her, and her wounds were inflicted as he tried performing CPR when he noticed she wasn't breathing.

I look for patterns of behavior, so first I wanted to know the details of Adams's prior conviction.

On July 30, 1978, at 10:30 A.M., sixteen-year-old Adams broke into the home of a forty-seven-year-old woman and raped and robbed her. According to the victim's account, which to me is the single most important element of any behavioral analysis, Adams seized her from behind, ordered her, "Be quiet or I'll kill you," then carried her into the bedroom and removed her clothing. On the bed, he placed a pillow over her head as he raped her both vaginally and anally. He told her to perform oral sex, but she refused. At some point he asked for keys to one of the cars parked outside the house, which she said she didn't have. He also demanded money, and she said she'd give him what she had if he would leave. He went to her purse in another bedroom and took money before returning and telling her again that he would kill her. He pressed his fist against her throat but was distracted by a noise outside. As he left again to check on the sound, she ran to the other bedroom, where she kept a gun. When he saw the weapon, he fled.

In this first case, too, Adams was arrested after witnesses placed him near the scene; he matched the description given by the victim, and she identified him when he was picked up by the police. He told them the woman let him into her home, then pulled a gun on him, forcing him to have sex with her before giving him money from her purse. She sustained her injuries, he said, when he grabbed the hand holding the gun and choked her, then released her when she dropped it. He said he then ran out of the house, dropping the money as he left. He later confessed to a version of events that agreed with the victim's statement, pleading guilty to criminal sexual assault and aggravated burglary.

I knew from my research that offenders don't start out with crimes like these two. And when I looked into Adams's background, the familiar dysfunctional profile emerged: split home, separation at one time or another from both parents, a grandmother who couldn't control him, and a long, sordid rap sheet beginning at an early age and gradually escalating in seriousness. This wasn't the kind of guy I wanted out on the street.

So I flew out to Albuquerque, rented a car, and drove about two hundred miles to get to the district courthouse in the town of Tucumcari. I met with District Attorney David Bonem and his prosecution team, letting them know what to expect and how to bring out Adams's real personality for the jury in case he decided to testify.

The other strategic role I was there to play was that of expert witness in the event the defense called a psychiatrist or psychologist to the stand to mitigate Adams's culpability or intent. If that happened, I would be called to testify as to Adams's true motive in the crime, based on the behavioral evidence and what I felt the previous rape said about him.

At the end of the five-day trial, Adams was found guilty on seven counts: criminal sexual penetration, arson, tampering with evidence, aggravated burglary, robbery, kidnapping, and first-degree murder. The jury had to deliberate for only about an hour and a half. As it turned out, no psychiatrist was called to testify, so there was nothing for me to rebut. When the defense saw what Bonem was planning on using me for, they apparently dropped that plan of attack. But the penalty phase became very interesting.

Why did Adams do the things he did to this woman? How likely was he to do it again if he ever hit the streets? Was there a pattern he was likely to continue? Was this a crime of criminal sophistication or a misguided breaking and entering that went bad because the offender couldn't even control an elderly woman? These were some of the questions before District Court judge Reuben E. Nieves.

The prosecution was going for the death penalty, which in New Mexico meant that they had to show "aggravating circumstances." Bonem wanted to bring in the details of Adams's earlier conviction and call in the victim to testify. Since Adams admitted being involved in that crime, that woman never had to testify against him. The defense strongly objected to having her do so here, maintaining that the earlier incident had no bearing on this crime, which Adams still asserted was an unintentional death. So

Judge Nieves held an in camera session in his chambers with the attorneys and Adams. It was there that I was able to give my analysis. If I could convince the judge that the two crimes were related and represented a pattern that might also point to future behavior, then—we figured—the previous victim might be allowed to tell her story. Adams was this big, mean-looking guy, and I recall him sneering at me the entire time we were in there.

The defense wanted to argue that their client felt remorse for what had happened and could be rehabilitated, which the prosecution and I were having none of. As far as I was concerned, this brought up forensic psychologist Dr. Stanton Samenow's question of how you expect to *rehabilitate* an individual who has never been *habilitated* in the first place. Adams had killed Ola Temple just *one week* after being released from prison for the earlier crime. Listening to the testimony at trial, I theorized that in attacking the elderly victim, Adams was symbolically acting out against his grandmother, who he felt hadn't treated him right.

Adams wasn't a tremendously bright guy. But he had criminal sophistication. These crimes were not two rape-robberies that "just happened." A look at the behavioral evidence revealed there was a well-developed M.O. in both cases. Both were morning robberies in the homes of female victims considerably older than the offender, and each was alone at the time. In both cases he conned his way in. In both he placed a pillow over the victim's face, pressed his fist across her throat to choke her, robbed money from her purse, and threatened her with death if she didn't sexually cooperate with him. Maybe you improvise all of this once; you don't improvise it twice. He had planned to kill the first victim, but circumstances got in the way when she was able to get to her gun. Mrs. Temple was less able to defend herself, which showed that he learned from the first experience in choosing her as his victim. He also knew from the previous mistake, which landed him in prison, that he had to kill this one, to leave no survivor or witness. From my experience talking to many killers about their mind-set and thought process during a crime, I knew the fact that Adams did not try to cover or disguise his face in either attack was highly significant. If a violent, power-assertive, or sadistic-type rapist embarks on the assault with no intention of killing his victim, he will often attempt to cover his face or the victim's, to prevent her being able to identify him later. Nothing like that was done in either case here, and since Adams otherwise showed strong signs of organization and control, I thought that spoke clearly to his murderous intent.

While the crime scene team examined Temple's home, the telephone rang. Detective Mondragon picked it up, but whoever was on the other end didn't say anything. He suspected it might have been the killer, a hunch that was confirmed in Adams's confession. This tells us something very important: that he monitored the situation—clearly a mark of a sophisticated, organized-type criminal.

Then we get to the arson itself. If we look at all the possible motives for setting the fire—a pyromaniacal thrill, revenge for some perceived wrong Mrs. Temple had done to him, racial hatred or resentment (Adams was black and she was white)—only one makes any sense, and that is arson to conceal another crime. The fact is, Eddie Lee Adams was criminally sophisticated enough to set fire to the house in an attempt to destroy all the evidence. But it wasn't as complete as he'd hoped. One of the reasons he made the subsequent telephone call, I believe, was to see if the coast was clear so he could go back and try to get the fire going again. Unlike other offenders we've looked at in this chapter, Adams seemed to have no emotional stake in setting fires. It was not a signature, something he needed to fulfill himself; that was what the rape and murder were about. The fire was part of a clear-cut modus operandi.

Had Adams not been arrested, had he gotten away with the Temple rape and murder, there is no question in my mind arson would have become a standard part of his M.O. in future rapes and murders, and there is no question in my mind, looking at the behavioral evidence and his criminal developmental pattern, that there would have been future rapes and murders. His first victim was a middle-aged Hispanic woman. The second was an elderly white woman. He had no particular victim of preference. He was simply a predator who had to act out his aggression against women in general—whoever happened to be available.

After hearing the arguments on both sides, Judge Nieves was sufficiently convinced of the relevance of the first crime in establishing a pattern of behavior and intent, and he ruled the first victim could testify before the jury for their consideration of sentencing recommendations.

It was an extremely emotional session. The woman sobbed so hard upon recalling the events of eight years before that she could hardly speak. Other listeners were crying, too. The defense did not cross-examine. Then, when Ray Mondragon was about to testify, Adams sprang to his feet and began yelling, "You didn't have to put that poor woman through that shit! Bonem, you give me the shot now," referring to the lethal injection. When his own attorneys couldn't get him to sit down and be quiet, Judge Nieves cleared the courtroom.

The jury recommended the death penalty, which the judge imposed, but the sentence stayed in effect only a month. In November 1986, outgoing governor Toney Anaya commuted the sentences of execution for all five inmates then on New Mexico's death row. Then, in February of the next year, Judge Nieves sentenced Adams to an additional twenty-eight years—four for each of the seven charges from the Temple case—because Adams is a habitual offender.

"The governor's action confirms that he shares our sense that executions are nothing so much as dramatic public spectacles of premeditated violent homicide," Henry Schwarzschild, director of the American Civil Liberties Union's anti-death-penalty project, told UPI.

I'm not going to go into a long discussion of the death penalty here, but I must pause long enough to say that regardless of your ethical opinion, calling it "premeditated violent homicide" is an action I find morally repugnant because it places the killer and his victim on the same level and therefore trivializes the critical distinction between the guilty and the innocent. We owe Mrs. Ola Temple's memory more than that. And once we lose sight of this distinction in our society, then we're really playing with fire.

I just remember that, at the time, I hoped Governor Anaya, in perpetrating this boldly political act, spent as much time thinking about motivation and intent for all five of these killers as I had for Eddie Lee Adams. But I doubted it.

## CHAPTER THREE

# MAGNUM FORCE

My former colleagues and I look at the behavioral evidence at a crime scene, in the witness statements, or in autopsy protocols, anything we can get that might lead us to helping the police in their hunting down the UNSUB. In the process, we come up with a profile that, among other things, ventures our opinion about the motive—about why this particular crime was committed. Then, if we're fortunate enough to see a perpetrator arrested, we get to compare our notion of why he did it with his stated reason. This is always an interesting exercise, since his idea and ours don't always match up very well.

It makes sense. The accused offender and his attorney aren't going to be very successful with a defense that admits he raped and killed a young child because of the intense thrill of control, power, and heightened sexuality it gave him. So if you, as the defendant, can't dispute the facts of the case, your best shot at cutting a break from the jury or sentencing judge is to try to come up with an explanation (as Eddie Lee Adams did) that puts you in a somewhat more sympathetic and understandable light. Something must have strongly *influenced* you to do the terrible thing you're accused of. But for that influence, you never would have committed such a bestial act on your own.

We're all used to hearing the bad-childhood excuse as a motivating factor in committing crime. I've often said that while an abusive or dysfunctional background can explain why you might become a dysfunctional, unhappy, or otherwise psychologically messed-up adult, it doesn't explain away, or let you off the hook for, perpetrating acts of violence against other human beings.

But there's another so-called influencing or mitigating factor that has come into fashion in the past several years, and that is the media. And it's pervasive enough—along with media influence in our society in general—that we ought to take it on in our exploration of the anatomy of motive.

Stated simply: Do people get ideas for crimes from watching television or movies and then go out and commit them? Can movies, television, books, or pornographic films or magazines transform an ordinary man into someone who will perpetrate violence against women or children? Can an abundance of violence in television programs and feature films desensitize society to the point that some among us have lost the ability to distinguish between right and wrong, proper and improper, or lose control over our impulses?

My own view, developed over many years of research and observation, is that the media can provide criminals with ideas for their crimes (both modus operandi and signature elements), may serve as an influencing factor in those already prone to violent actions, and may desensitize all of us to the real horror that is out there, but except in a few specialized types of cases, the media (and that includes pornography) do not lead otherwise good or law-abiding people to commit violent antisocial acts.

Let's look at several different examples of the relationship between the media and violent crime, using cases I used to teach at Quantico.

On June 4, 1976, an eighty-two-year-old widow named Elinor Haggart was shot and killed in her home in Miami Beach, Florida, after surprising two burglars—her neighbor Ronald Zamora, fifteen years of age, and Darrell Agrella, fourteen. Upon his arrest, Zamora, a slightly built, five-foot-three high school student and immigrant from Costa Rica, confessed twice that he shot and killed Mrs. Haggart. But in each confession he offered a different account of the events.

Neither was taped or written out, but both agreed on how the crime began. Zamora and Agrella, who were friends, needed money. They knew that Zamora's elderly next-door neighbor kept money in her house, so they broke in and found an envelope full of cash and a .32 caliber revolver. Mrs. Haggart came home, found the two boys there, and said she would call the police. They asked her not to do that. From this point on, Zamora's two confessions differ.

In the first confession, Zamora claimed that he shot her accidentally. "I don't know what happened," he said. "The gun just went off." Mortally wounded, she asked for some whiskey but fell over dead as Zamora brought it to her.

In the second account, which Sergeant Paul Rantanen of the Miami Beach PD considered to be more honest and believable, the two youths talked to Mrs. Haggart for about an hour and a half, pouring glasses of whiskey and water until they got the mixture right for her. She showed them photos of herself and her late husband, and they thought she agreed not to call the police. When she finally said she was going to call them after all, Zamora said he wrapped the gun in a pillow and shot her. What happened next, according to both confessions, was a ransacking of the house, during which Zamora and Agrella wiped their finger-prints off everything they could think of. They ran off with several of Mrs. Haggart's possessions, including two TVs.

In what was to prove an interesting irony, Zamora's trial was the first covered on television in Florida, part of a one-year experiment approved by the Florida Supreme Court. It was also the first murder trial televised anywhere in the United States. Representing Zamora was the prominent defense attorney Ellis Rubin. There wasn't any doubt that Zamora killed his neighbor, so Rubin's strategy was to argue innocence by reason of insanity—Zamora had been driven mad by too much exposure to television violence. In his opening statement to the jury, Rubin said he would show "the creation and destruction of [a] TV addict."

In what might have been a brilliant piece of PR, Rubin hoped to get actor Telly Savalas to testify on the influence his hit detective show, *Kojak,* may have had on the young offender. Savalas was subpoenaed and did not resist the subpoena, although he said he really had nothing to contribute. He was later released as a witness when it became unlikely that Circuit Court judge Paul Baker would allow him to testify. Nor was a psychologist brought in by the defense allowed on the stand when she admitted to the judge that she didn't know of any cases in which a television program actually made someone kill. In spite of that, Rubin characterized television as Zamora's "instructor, his brain-washer, his hypnotizer." He claimed his client "could not distinguish whether he was in a television play acting it out, or whether it was cold-blooded, premeditated murder."

A witness the defense did manage to get on, psychiatrist Dr. Michael Gilbert, testified that "the pulling of the trigger was in effect a conditioned response, brought on by his 'habituation' to television and his fondness for viewing violent crime shows like 'Kojak.'" Gilbert said that Savalas's character was Zamora's hero and that his mind flashed on an episode of *Kojak* after he heard gunfire and watched his victim fall. Gilbert stated that Zamora was so into *Kojak* that he tried to get his stepfather to shave his head like Savalas's.

Yolanda Zamora, the defendant's mother, testified that her son was suicidal in the weeks before the murder. She said he'd taken a psychological test that spring that showed he was. She cried on the stand, describing her son spending hours watching TV and not talking to anyone.

The prosecution called four teenage boys who testified that Zamora took them to Disney World just hours after the murder, driving them in Mrs. Haggart's car. He paid cash for the trip's expenses from the wad of several hundred dollars he had on him. The other boys said they did not know that the car and money belonged to his neighbor, or that Zamora had killed her.

Zamora was convicted of first-degree murder. Prosecutor Tom Headley didn't seek the death penalty, but Ellis Rubin did ask for leniency, contending that Zamora, overdosed on TV violence as he was, was mentally ill and suicidal. He petitioned Judge Baker to set aside the conviction and commit Zamora to a program for youthful offenders. The judge was also presented with petitions for leniency signed by many of Zamora's classmates. But Baker did not overturn the jury verdict and sentenced Zamora to life in prison for the murder, with no parole possible for the first twenty-five years, and to fifty-three years for the burglary and assault charges. At the sentencing, the judge pointed out that while the defense asked for leniency, a juvenile court that reviewed the case initially forwarded it to adult court because of the serious nature of the offenses.

Darrell Agrella pleaded no contest to second-degree murder in exchange for a life sentence without the hard twenty-five Zamora was given.

Then, in the spring of 1978, Zamora and his parents filed a $25 million civil lawsuit for damages against ABC, CBS, and NBC, claiming that the violent programs they aired "showed the impressionable teenager . . . how to kill." At the same time, the U.S. Supreme Court okayed a California suit against NBC and its San Francisco affiliate station filed by the parents of a nine-year-old girl who was sexually assaulted for days after the station aired the movie *Born Innocent,* which depicted a crime similar to the one she suffered. In September 1978, U.S. District Court judge William M. Hoeveler dismissed Zamora's suit, stating that Rubin had not shown negligence on the networks' part and that a finding for Zamora would amount to new regulation of broadcasting that would be unenforceable. (The *Born Innocent* suit would later be dismissed as well.)

Once again claiming others were to blame, with new counsel, Ronald Guralnick, Zamora petitioned for a new trial, claiming that the defense in the first trial was incompetent. But in December 1979, the bid for a new trial was denied, with Judge Frederick Barad finding that Rubin had met the "reasonably effective" standard.

Now, which elements of Zamora's crime took place because television made him a walking automaton of violence? Are there behavioral hallmarks here we can look to that will help us establish the defense's motivational claims?

Far from being unique, the basic facts of this case, sadly, aren't even very unusual. This was and is a typical crime against the elderly in American society. In profiling, our general rule of thumb is: the older the victim, the younger the offender—unless victim choice and other elements of the M.O. reveal a higher level of criminal sophistication, as with Eddie Lee Adams. When we're trying to determine the age of the UNSUB in a violent crime, we usually start at twenty-five and add or subtract years based on the degree of sophistication. With a victim in her seventies or eighties, we lower the initial age estimate into the teen years, particularly if there is a sexual component (which there was not in this case). A woman whose husband has passed away and lives alone is a prime target. She's dependent on other people to maintain her home, many of whom will be youthful, and it may be difficult for her to get out, so she keeps cash in the house. If a kid wants money, who better to steal it from than an old woman close by who offers little or no resistance?

The key point is that we have a clear and convincing motive for the initial crime, and that is greed. Ronald Zamora went to his neighbor's home at a time when he knew she was not there with the self-professed intention of stealing money and other goods. This choice itself reveals an inconsistency with the TV intoxication argument: an obsession with television violence drove him to rob an empty residence. The motive that put him at the scene had nothing at all to do with violence he may have observed on *Kojak* or any other television show. In fact, if he identified so heavily with the Kojak character that he urged his stepfather to shave his head (there were even rumors he wanted him to suck lollipops as Savalas did), he should have been fighting crime rather than perpetrating it.

But once he and his accomplice decided to break into the house for the purpose of burglary, what motivated Zamora to kill his victim? Clearly, he was surprised and panicked when she returned unexpectedly. You could make the argument that the media had desensitized him to the horror of violence and killing, and I will be the first to acknowledge that in many cases we have, as a society, become desensitized to violence. If it is all around us, then we tend to take it for granted. But that includes reports on the news, as well, and I'm certainly not saying that the news media should not report what actually happens.

The hard fact is that violence breeds violence; and that, in turn, breeds insensitivity.

So you could say that Ronald Zamora had become desensitized by what he had seen on television. But could he have become desensitized to the point that he no longer knew or understood that it was wrong to pull a trigger and blow an old lady away? Not on your life! I have seen nothing in my experience—and absolutely no data—to support this. Certainly Zamora understood robbery was wrong—he killed rather than get in trouble for doing it.

What you had here was all the ingredients for disaster: a youthful, inexperienced offender who was suddenly faced with a situation he hadn't expected, thought about, or planned for. Then you add a gun to the mix—something he knows from television will immediately produce his short-term fix—and that's what happens. If the gun hadn't been available, he might have tried to kill his victim some other way, but that would have been more difficult and time-consuming. Even with a knife he would have had to get up close and personal, something many young and "cowardly" offenders are unwilling to do. If the Ronald Zamora case teaches us any lesson, it is first of all that if we really understand what motive is all about, we cannot blame the media for hypnotizing him, and second of all that, before we start trying to ban the depiction of violence, we should work on what we depict: the violence itself. I'd far rather potential criminals had less access to handguns than to *Kojak*.

When an offender actually does get an idea to kill or hurt from the media, it's often pretty obvious. My colleague Roy Hazelwood, one of the pioneers of modern behavioral science at Quantico, was once called in on a case in Germany where an American serviceman had brutally killed his wife and child in a scenario that came straight out of a detective magazine. The reason we know this was that the magazine itself was found on top of the television, opened to the page depicting the scene of mayhem that had just been acted out. The same weapon was used, the woman's body was displayed in the same way, the entire style of the crime was replicated from this magazine.

The evidence here was clear. There can be little doubt that this crime would not have happened this way without the influence of this magazine story. But there can be almost as little doubt that had the offender not seen this magazine, he would have killed his wife and child anyway, and the crime would have been based on another magazine, a film, or something out of his own perverted imagination.

The great danger of the so-called detective magazines, in Roy's view, is what he calls "the erotization of violence"—that is, making a connection between violence and sexual arousal in the minds of antisocial and violence-prone readers. In 1986, he and Park Elliott Dietz, the nationally renowned forensic psychiatrist who has been a consultant to the Investigative Support Unit, along with psychiatrist and law professor Bruce Harry, wrote a landmark article for the *Journal of Forensic Sciences* titled "Detective Magazines: Pornography for the Sexual Sadist?" In their study, they examined the covers, interior illustrations, and story content of a wide variety of such periodicals. Their greatest criticism was that the magazines routinely and relentlessly juxtaposed conventionally erotic images (such as beautiful, scantily clad women) and written descriptions of sexual acts with images of violence and the helpless suffering of innocent victims. And the authors found a direct link between the fantasies of certain sexual predators and the photos and stories in these periodicals, which were sold at most newsstands and easily available to minors.

They were careful to note, "While there is no doubt that detective magazines provide a rich source of sexually sadistic imagery . . . the cases we have described do not prove that detective magazines 'cause' sexual sadism or sadistic offenses." But they also expressed concern that the continual juxtaposition of sexual and violent images might cause impressionable young men to begin associating the two in their own thoughts.

The article received a tremendous amount of attention within the law enforcement and forensic psychological communities and has even been credited with getting the magazine publishers to change the subject matter of many of their covers and get away from the more blatant sadomasochistic imagery. This is all a positive and hopeful development. But it's very important to remember that in cases like this, as with others we've been examining, the media don't cause the crime. What they can do is influence and heighten the details. They don't create motive in people for whom it is not there already. That comes from someplace inside, far deeper and scarier.

Here's another notorious case where the motive was already there and the media provided one of the important details.

On April 22, 1974, around 6 P.M., Dale Selby Pierre and William Andrews, two Air Force enlisted men, both nineteen years of age, robbed the Hi-Fi Shop, a stereo equipment store in Ogden, Utah, just as it was closing. They forced the two clerks, Stan Walker, twenty, and Michelle Ansley, eighteen, into the basement and tied them up. At just about that time, sixteen-year-old Cortney Naisbitt came in to thank Walker for a favor he'd done, and the two robbers forced him into the basement and tied him, too.

Rather than just grab what cash and small appliances they could, the offenders spent more than an hour loading stereo equipment into a van. They heard footsteps at the back door and hid in the basement as Orren Walker, Stan's forty-three-year-old father, came by the store to see why his son had not yet returned home; he should have closed down the store long before. Pierre surprised Orren with a gun and forced him down the stairs, where the rest of the hostages were being held. Apparently agitated, Pierre fired two shots into the basement wall, whereupon Michelle and Cortney became panicked. Michelle pleaded for her life. Stan Walker told the robbers to take what they wanted and leave; none of them would try to identify them. There is no evidence that the captives put up any resistance or posed a physical threat to the two offenders at any time during this ordeal.

Pierre told Andrews to bring something in from the van. It was a bottle wrapped in a paper bag, from which Andrews poured a blue liquid into a plastic cup. He ordered Orren Walker to have the three people lying on the floor drink it. Orren refused, and Pierre bound his hands and feet and left him lying facedown on the floor. Just then, Carol Naisbitt, Cortney's mother, fifty-two years old, came into the store looking for him. The robbers grabbed her, bound her, and placed her next to her son.

Pierre and Andrews then forced each of their prisoners to drink, propping them into sitting positions so they'd be able to swallow. Pierre told them it was vodka with a German sleeping medication in it. As soon as each victim swallowed, he or she began to cough and retch and choke violently. Seeing this, Orren feigned swallowing and imitated the distressed behavior of the others. The liquid burned the insides of the mouth and throat, and wherever it spilled, it burned the skin. Pierre tried to seal each victim's mouth with tape, but because of almost immediate blistering on their lips, the tape wouldn't hold. Not satisfied with the speed or efficiency of the poison, he went to Carol Naisbitt and shot her in the back of the head, then to her son and shot him. He fired at Orren Walker at close range but somehow missed, then shot Stan before going back to Orren and shooting at him again.

Michelle Ansley was still pleading for her life as Pierre untied her, brought her to the far end of the basement, forced her to take off her clothes, then raped her repeatedly. He then brought her back to where the others were lying, brutally placed her facedown on the floor, and shot her in the head. Not convinced that he'd managed to kill Orren Walker, Pierre tried to strangle him with a garrote he fashioned from a wire he'd cut off a stereo at the store. When that didn't kill the victim, he then stuck a pen in his ear and stomped on it with the heel of his combat boot until it punctured Orren's eardrum and pierced all the way through to his throat.

The victims were discovered shortly after 10 P.M., when Mrs. Walker and her younger son, Lynn, came to the store frantically looking for Stan and Orren. Lynn kicked in the door. They called for help, but Stan and Michelle were already dead at the scene. Carol died shortly after being taken to the emergency room. Miraculously, Orren and Cortney survived. Orren had severe internal burns and extensive ear damage. Cortney required 266 days of hospitalization. The blue liquid had been an industrial drain cleaner whose active ingredient was hydrochloric acid.

Shortly after this horrible crime, police got a call from an informant, another airman, in whom Andrews had confided a couple of months before, "One of these days I'm going to rob a hi-fi shop, and if anybody gets in the way, I'm going to kill them."

A few hours after the call, two young boys found wallets and purses belonging to the victims in a Dumpster near Pierre and Andrews's barracks at Hill Air Force Base. The detective who was called to the scene happened to have taken courses from us at Quantico and understood both the investigative techniques and the dramatic flair we sometimes advocate if we feel it might help in hunting an UNSUB. Based on what he had learned about offenders monitoring investigations, he thought there was a strong chance the UNSUBs might be in the crowd of spectators already gathered around the Dumpster.

He utilized a pair of long needle-nosed pliers to pluck potential evidence from the Dumpster without compromising it, and every time he thought he might have something, he'd wave it clearly in front of his colleagues and the crowd before inserting it into an evidence envelope. He noticed that two of the airmen watching became noticeably agitated. They walked back and forth, in and out of the barracks. Later, he told me that just from their demeanor, he thought these two might be suspects. They turned out to be Pierre and Andrews. We didn't yet have a formal name for what the detective did, but we now refer to it as proactive techniques. The detective won a Justice Department award for his work, and we at Quantico were gratified that the training he received from us had been so effective.

Pierre and Andrews were arrested, and then the police executed a search warrant on their living quarters. Under a rug, they found flyers from the Hi-Fi Shop and a rental contract for a unit in a storage facility, where police discovered the stolen merchandise and a bottle of the drain cleaner—half empty.

Dale Pierre and William Andrews were both convicted of first-degree murder and sentenced to death. A third man, Keith Roberts, received a jail sentence for his involvement in the robbery and eventually was paroled. Pierre was executed by lethal injection in August 1987, the first execution in Utah since Gary Gilmore's 1977 execution by firing squad. In fact, as Gilmore was being led down the hall to the firing squad, he is said to have shouted, "I'll see you in hell, Pierre and Andrews." Guards at Utah State Prison reported that Gilmore laughed as he said this. Pierre and Andrews did not as they listened silently.

Andrews received a number of last-minute stays of execution until he finally met his death by lethal injection on July 20, 1992. At the time of his execution he was thirty-seven years of age and had spent eighteen years on death row. A number of groups, including Amnesty International and the NAACP, had protested the imposition of the death sentence against Andrews, arguing that he was not the triggerman and that there were racial overtones to the case, since all the defendants were black and all the victims were white, as was the entire jury. They stated that whites in Utah convicted of vicious killings of blacks, such as Joseph Paul Franklin, who murdered two black men in 1981 as they jogged with white women, were not sentenced to die for their crimes.

Needless to say, I am always extremely troubled anytime we can point to an apparent inequity in the legal procedures surrounding capital murder. I would like to see the death penalty administered more fairly, more uniformly, and, frankly, more quickly. Then we wouldn't have to argue about whether someone like William Andrews—who didn't pull any triggers but administered his own "lethal ingestions" with the full intent that his victims should die—deserves the lethal injection himself. There was no ambiguity about whether Andrews and Pierre were the real offenders, so that argument against capital punishment isn't relevant here. And if we look to motive, it is clear that regardless of who the actual shooter was, both men went into this crime knowing they were going to kill whenever and whomever they had to.

"I participated in a robbery and expected it to be nothing more than a robbery," Andrews told *USA Today*. "But so many things happened. Everything got out of hand."

In fact, he and Pierre followed a movie scenario as their model. And in fact, Andrews brought the bottle of drain cleaner in from the van. What did he think they were going to use it for?

This savage case became known as the Hi-Fi murders. We taught it at the Academy, and I included it in the *Crime Classification Manual*. When interrogated, it turned out that the two offenders got the idea for the drain cleaner by watching the Clint

Eastwood *Dirty Harry* sequel *Magnum Force,* which came out the previous year. They liked it enough that they saw it two or three times.

The circumstances in the Hi-Fi murders are not all the same as in the movie scenario. The movie concerns San Francisco PD detective Harry Callahan rooting out a rogue element of motorcycle cops dispensing vigilante justice to bad guys the law can't touch but who they feel deserve to die. One of the bad guys they decide to summarily execute is a very mean and flamboyant pimp who kills a prostitute in his stable in the backseat of a taxicab as punishment for holding out money from him. His means of murder is drain cleaner, which he forces the woman to drink. Then she falls instantly dead on the floor of the cab.

According to the categories we established in the *Crime Classification Manual,* the Hi-Fi murders are indiscriminate felony homicides—homicides committed in the performance of a felony, indiscriminate because the offenders planned to kill as an element of the robbery but had no idea in advance who their victims would be. I would also say there were overtones of sadistic homicide, a separate category, because Dale Pierre seemed to get some emotional satisfaction out of inflicting pain and emotional suffering on the victims under his manipulation, domination, and control. And he viciously raped one of the victims, which had nothing at all to do with his motive of stealing property. The opportunity presented itself, so he took it. The fact that the young woman was pleading for her life likely made the act all the more satisfying to him.

On a procedural level, the crime was very well planned. We know they had been thinking about it for months; they secured a storage facility to hide the stolen goods; they chose a time of day for the robbery in which they had expectations of remaining undisturbed; and they thought they had a good idea for eliminating witnesses, from a movie they enjoyed enough to see more than once.

Were Pierre and Andrews influenced by the media in the commission of their crime? On a very specific level, they sure were. But they had already decided on this particular criminal enterprise, and now they were casting about for methodologies. In *Magnum Force,* the prostitute dies immediately and without resistance after she's forced to drink the drain cleaner. What a good idea, as far as getting rid of the witnesses! It's clean, it's easy, it doesn't risk alerting anyone with a gunshot blast, there's no blood-spatter mess to clean off your clothing. Even Dirty Harry seems to be impressed when they tell him how the hooker died.

But like so much else about the movies, real life doesn't live up to the fantasy. The real victims didn't die right away. It was messy. They choked and gagged and threw up. They made noise. Pierre had to shoot them anyway. The medical examiner determined that the drain cleaner eventually would have killed each victim who swallowed it, but it might have taken as long as twelve hours.

The point is that these two sadistic creeps would have committed this crime regardless of what they'd seen or heard. What the media influenced was the details. The media, however, did not make Dale Pierre and William Andrews into the monsters they were. If I'd been profiling this case as an unsolved crime, it would have made no difference whether I'd seen or knew about *Magnum Force* at all. The behavior speaks for itself.

Now, interestingly, if the criminals had not been caught the way they were, this was the kind of case in which we in law enforcement could have used the media proactively to influence the outcome. I don't mean by manipulating or misleading; I mean by just getting out the analysis and explaining its significance.

If we'd come to the Hi-Fi murders as an unsolved crime, it would have quickly become obvious that there was more than a single offender. It would have been virtually impossible for one person to control five others, not to mention remove heavy and bulky stereo equipment and load it into a van all by himself. Both from clues here and from our experience with other crimes of a similar nature, we would have been working on the assumption that one of the two (or possible three or four) offenders was the dominant one, calling the shots and controlling the hostages. The body of the rape victim would have told us that only one offender was involved in the vicious and sadistic sexual assault.

We would therefore construct our profile of the leader of the attack and release this information to the public via the news media. Then we would release the next piece of our theory of the crime, which was that this was a criminal enterprise that got out of hand; we understood the dynamics and were quite confident the case would be solved. But the leader let things get out of control, and he was losing control again. He is now afraid that his partner or partners will cave, and so he will turn on them before they can do that.

"You, Mr. Accomplice, should be very, very fearful as long as this guy is on the loose. The odds on your life are very, very short. Your only chance is to turn yourself, and him, in. That way, you at least get the legal process as protection, something you're not going to get from him."

Ironically, the media truly would have played a key role in this case—but it would have been in solving the crime, not in making it happen in the first place.

Some offenders, especially the more intelligent ones, can use the media to serve their own motives, needs, and desires even after they've been caught. Such an individual is Michael B. Ross.

He was born in Connecticut in 1959, where his parents ran a poultry farm. He excelled in animal sciences in high school and began at Cornell in 1977, the same university that told me my high school record wasn't good enough for me to pursue my goal of studying veterinary medicine there (they were right, by the way). After graduating in 1981, Ross worked on some farms in the Midwest for a while. On September 28, 1981, during a bicycle trip through Illinois, he kidnapped a sixteen-year-old girl and bound her before police arrived. He pled guilty to unlawful restraint and got a two-year probation and a $500 fine. He returned to Connecticut and had several more similar clashes with the law, including trying to choke into submission a woman who turned out to be an off-duty police officer.

He was eventually tagged with six murders of young women ranging in age from fourteen to twenty-three. Two trials in Connecticut resulted in guilty verdicts and sentences of 120 years and death.

What's relevant about Ross for our discussion here is that this obviously bright, articulate, and Ivy League–college-educated guy has been writing articles for publications with large circulations, putting forth his positions on such subjects of personal significance to him as redemption and forgiveness and the efficacy of the death penalty. I have no objection to anyone getting published if they can, even a convicted murderer. But it is interesting to see how his position has changed over his years on death row and how you could interpret his use of the media as increasingly self-serving.

In 1988, Ross responded to written questions submitted by the *Hartford Courant* by saying that the death penalty was not a deterrent because killers don't take it into consideration when they commit their crimes, and that, therefore, it's simply the state's "retribution." In February 1995, he wrote an article for *America,* analyzing the death penalty and essentially asserting that while it may be legal and emotionally satisfying to many, it really isn't worth the cost in money and legal resources it takes to move a convicted killer to the point of execution, and that we should just leave him in prison and use the resources elsewhere. Okay. This isn't an unusual position, and Ross is a pretty good writer who constructs cogent, logical arguments.

Then, in December of that year, he came up with a different slant on the costs of imposing or not imposing the death penalty. Associated Press writer Brigitte Greenberg reported that he wrote AP a letter, saying that he thought he ought to be executed for the greater good. "There is no need to drag the families of my victims through that gruesome and emotionally disturbing testimony," Greenberg quoted Ross's letter. "While I do not wish to die, my life is not worth the pain to the families that it would cost."

"This is what Ross wants to do," Greenberg writes:

He wants to agree that there are many aggravating factors in his case—the viciousness and senselessness of his crimes. And he wants to stipulate that there are no mitigating factors, such as mental impairment, even though he believes that mental illness—sexual sadism—led him to kill.

Finally, he wants to prevent anyone else from testifying that he was mentally ill, even though the state has in its hands the psychiatric report that the [state Supreme Court] judges cited in overturning his death sentence.

If there are only aggravating circumstances—and no mitigating ones—a death penalty would be a certainty, and Ross would be on his way to becoming the first person executed in Connecticut since 1960.

"To allow (the families) to be hurt further, just to save my worthless life, is not something I am prepared to do," Ross writes.

Even now, after Ross dismissed his public defenders and took over as his own attorney, experts agree he knows what he's doing.

In an April 5, 1996, article in the *National Catholic Reporter,* then in a very similar piece on July 7 for the *Cleveland Plain Dealer,* Ross wrote only of seeking reconciliation with the victims' families, of how he had come to accept responsibility for his own actions and asked God to give him "the strength, perseverance and moral fortitude to complete my journey before I am finally executed."

For the Catholic publication he left out the execution reference and spoke instead of becoming "one with that light."

Again, no problems here. In fact, I'd say he was getting me and thousands of others of his readers on his side by this demonstration of insight and remorse.

I have no effective way of determining Ross's motive here. I can speculate about three or four possible ones, but I don't have good evidence to support any of them. The motive could be total self-denying altruism from a man who finally sees the evil of his previous ways and wants to explain and atone. It could be that, knowing he's overwhelmingly likely to spend the rest of his life in prison, he wants to do something interesting and productive with his intellect and talents and therefore gets a large degree of ego satisfaction from his writing and fame. Or it could be that he's still trying to manipulate, dominate, and control in the only way still left open to him.

As I say, I don't know which is the real motive, or if, in fact, it may be an amalgam of all three. But in an article by Howard Swindle in the *Dallas Morning News* of April 21, 1997, Ross's position evolved into detailed explanations about his childhood, his mental condition, and the reasons he did the terrible things he did. Swindle wrote:

Today he receives monthly injections of Depo-Lupron, a chemical castration drug that reduces his testosterone and alleviates the symptoms of his sexual disorder.

Mr. Ross spends his time on death row writing articles and editorials against the death penalty: "We may be aware of the criminal acts that put an individual on death row . . ." he wrote in *The Providence Journal,* "but very few of us know of the human being whom society has condemned to death."

A little over a year later, on August 5, 1998, the Associated Press reported that the now thirty-nine-year-old Ross is no longer willing to be executed without a fight and "wants a thorough defense."

Though I deplore the length of time the capital punishment appeals process generally takes in this country, I cannot quibble with someone who has a change of heart about blaming himself for his crimes. That's between him and his conscience, if he has one. But I can't help but think that, having originally established his credibility with media pieces saying he thought he ought to be executed, what he's gotten himself in the process is a lot more interest, attention, understanding, and sympathy for his newly formed position of wanting to avoid the imposition of the death sentence. How much concern can he actually have for the families of the victims he professed to care so much about if he now uses the media not to give them closure but to save his own neck? I'm not in favor of imposing censorship in situations like this, but if I were an editor who knew the history of the media dimension of this case, I'd think long and hard about what I decided to print from Michael Ross.

As this book was being written, Michael Ross once again tried to take control over his own situation. This time it was by ingesting a potentially lethal overdose in his cell at the high-security Northern Correctional Institution in Somers, Connecticut. The fact that he was even able to obtain that concentration of pharmaceuticals speaks to his intelligence and sophistication in dealing with the system. And the message here, in my opinion, is quite clear: guys like Michael Ross always have to be calling the shots one way or another. Some of these cowards will even commit suicide immediately upon capture, as Leonard Lake, the sexual sadist who tortured and murdered young women, did when he swallowed a cyanide capsule during questioning in a San Francisco police station in June of 1985. Others, under siege and facing capture, will force what we refer to as "suicide by cop." But either way, the significance is the same: manipulation, domination, and control up to the very end.

Let's face it, we're all conditioned by the media. We all want recognition for what we've done. I've gotten a lot of publicity in my own career, and I have to admit that it was a kick every time I saw stories about myself with headlines like *FBI Supersleuth Had a Big Role in Williams Trial* (in the *Atlanta Journal and Constitution*), *FBI's Modern Sherlock Holmes* (*St. Louis Globe-Democrat*), or *Chilling Details from the FBI's John Douglas, Model for "The Silence of the Lambs" Agent* (*USA Today*).

Serial criminals are like that, too. Many of them are proud of their "accomplishments," and once they're incarcerated, they want to be known as the biggest, the baddest, and the best. The late and unlamented Ted Bundy used to get off on academics writing to him saying they wanted to study the sophisticated criminal mind. Henry Lee Lucas claimed credit for at least seventy murders he did not commit.

I interviewed a guy named Joseph Fischer, a strange, impulsively violent, alcoholic, and disorganized drifter who was in prison in New York State for three murders of women. One of them was his wife, twenty-eight years his senior, whom he just got tired of at one point. But he wanted to be known as the biggest, baddest serial killer of them all. When he was picked up by police in Dutchess County, New York, in 1979, he confessed to thirty-two murders, even though police, after a year's investigation, could tie him only to the three. He was acting the entire time I was with him, railing about what a bitch his mother was, since he thought that's how serial killers are supposed to act. Later, he even got himself on a TV documentary about serial killers, where he got to do his act and make his numerous confessions for his perceived public.

An even stranger and more flagrant example of post-arrest manipulation, domination, and control is that of Clifford Olson of Vancouver, the Canadian murderer of young women and children and self-perceived superstar of serial killers. Once under arrest, he offered a deal whereby he would give details on the locations of bodies of his still-missing victims for $10,000 each! The Royal Canadian Mounted Police were understandably outraged and first balked at this offer, but the British Columbia attorney general Allan Williams overruled them on humanitarian grounds and agreed so that the victims' families could have some closure and peace. He specified that most of the money had to go into a trust fund for Olson's son. However, some of it went right into Olson's pocket. The television set in his jail cell at Kingston Penitentiary was paid for with this ransom money. He joked at the time that he led police to an additional body for free as a good-faith gesture. Loving the limelight, Olson attempted a further deal—another twenty graves for the bargain price of a hundred grand total—but that one the Canadian authorities couldn't stomach. He pleaded guilty in January of 1982 and received eleven concurrent life sentences. Eventually his notoriety grew so large and his public statements so infuriated his victims' families that a Canadian judge ruled that he couldn't give any more interviews.

After the film *The Silence of the Lambs* came out and the media started identifying me with the Jack Crawford character, I got a call from Olson in my office at Quantico. Imitating the brilliantly evil Hannibal "the Cannibal" Lecter, whom agent Clarice Starling enlisted to give perspective on her current serial murder case, Olson was giving interviews in which he would analyze the Green River murders from the perspective of the UNSUB. Knowing the special abyss that the long-unsolved Green River case represented in my own life, a case I almost died while working on in 1983, Olson at one point told me that he was the Green River killer.

Over the course of about a year, Olson called me repeatedly, often daily. I took the calls and spent the time with him because even though I sensed right away what a tremendous bullshitter he was, this was still a good opportunity to delve into the criminal mind. I found him gregarious, manipulative, and smoothly seductive, almost the exact opposite of Joseph Fischer. I could easily see how he might successfully entice children to go off with him, or how he might even con law enforcement to do his bidding. One thing I did not detect during my numerous conversations with Olson was any sign of remorse or sorrow for all the lives he'd destroyed. Actually, it was worse than that: he used to write harassing and threatening letters to the families of some of his victims until prison authorities got wise to it and started screening his mail. Like Michael Ross, his words have appeared in numerous newspaper and magazine articles, and he wrote letters to various journalists. In some of his statements he said that if he got out of prison, he would never kill again because he knew the difference between right and wrong. In others he said that the only cure for someone like him was execution. Anything for publicity. He kept a box of tape cassettes in his cell on which he'd lovingly collected his reminiscences about each of the murders in preparation for writing his autobiography. His only fear was of being forgotten.

Writing in the Canadian magazine *MacLean's*, journalist Peter Worthington described asking him how he compared himself to Hannibal Lecter. "Peter, there is no comparison," Olson replied. "Hannibal Lecter is fictional—I'm real."

What he wanted from me, other than the phone audience, was for me to take him on a highly publicized trip out to Washington State so he could tell me about Green River and where more bodies were buried. If I'd thought there was a chance he was being straight with me, I would have taken him up on the offer in a minute and done whatever I had to to clear it with the Canadian authorities. But I'd spent enough time studying the details of the case that I knew he had no idea what he was talking about. He just wanted the attention and recognition that would make him into something he desperately wanted to be but wasn't.

Building up his own image, Olson described to me how he was kept in a Plexiglas-type cell, just like Hannibal Lecter in the movie. I inquired on my own and learned that the reason for the glass was that other prisoners hated him so much for being a child killer that they would throw feces and cups of urine at him. So much for recognition from the audience that knew him best.

There is another dimension to media influence on crime we need to get into, and that is the out-and-out criminal enterprise motive—the only category where it is entirely valid to say the offender was directly influenced by the media. Here is one of the classics.

On December 13, 1966, NBC ran a made-for-TV movie titled *Doomsday Flight*, written by six-time Emmy Award winner, television pioneer, and *Twilight Zone* creator Rod Serling. The program was an engrossing and well-written thriller about a disgruntled former airline employee who places a bomb on a passenger jet. (Interestingly, as we'll see, the UNSUB as a disgruntled airline employee was for years the working theory behind the Unabomber crimes.) The twist in Serling's story was that the bomb was altitude-sensitive and set to go off once the plane descended below four thousand feet. The pilot eventually figures out how to solve the dilemma—by landing at the Denver airport, which is even more above sea level than that. Serling got technical assistance from his older brother Robert, an accomplished writer himself who had been aviation editor for United Press International. It must also be added that Bob Serling was quite nervous about the project from the outset, writing his brother a letter that cautioned, "I hope you'll carefully ponder the possibility that somebody might get an idea from the story and actually try an aneroid bomb plot."

The show was a huge hit, one of the highest-rated television shows of the season. But within a week of the broadcast, extortion-for-ransom threats were made against Eastern Airlines, Qantas, TWA, National, Pan Am, and Northwest. Some of the airlines paid out money, but in no instances were bombs found. Actually, this was one of those cases of life imitating art imitating life. Bob had told Rod the little-publicized story of a real extortion threat against an American Airlines plane whose pilot had been ingenious and resourceful enough to divert to Stapleton, in Denver, even though the airline did not fly out of that airport at the time.

Serling, who was a friend and early mentor of my coauthor Mark Olshaker, was devastated by the effect his script had. He told reporters who flocked to interview him, "I wish to Christ I had written a stagecoach drama starring John Wayne instead." And years before his untimely death, in 1975, Serling was still haunted by *Doomsday Flight*.

The extortions committed under the inspiration of *Dooms-day Flight* would be classified as criminal enterprise—that is, the motive is money. We can comfortably say that they were carried out by criminally minded individuals; no otherwise honest person watched the show and said to himself, *What a great idea for making money—threaten the airline at its most vulnerable point and I don't even have to bother actually planting a bomb!* But we also have to say that in this case, had it not been for the influence of the program, these extortions would not have taken place. Serling's teleplay did give bad guys ideas that were not difficult to act upon. This premise was confirmed when, after a rebroadcast five years later, similar threats started again.

The lesson from experiences like those surrounding *Doomsday Flight,* and there are a number of them, is not a particularly pleasant or reassuring one. We have to realize and accept that there will always be individuals out there who will take away whatever they want from any presentation, just as there are perverts and pedophiles out there who can get the same sexual charge from looking at children in a Macy's catalogue as others of their ilk might get from the most despicable hard-core kiddie porn. The copycats who phoned in these threats could just as easily have been reacting to a news report of that American Airlines incident.

Years after the *Doomsday* broadcast, Serling had sufficient perspective on the experience to have a standard line ready for reporters who asked him about it. He told Mark, "I tell them I'm responsible to the public, but not for the public."

So are all of us in law enforcement, and I'm not about to suggest throwing out the baby of our sacred right of free expression with the dirty bathwater of certain antisocial and criminal copycats taking perverse advantage of that right. But as we'll see in the next chapter, these people present us with another dimension on motive that we can't afford to ignore.

# CHAPTER FOUR

# NAME YOUR POISON

The *Doomsday Flight* copycats were practicing only one of several forms of public terrorism or mass extortion, all with the motive of greed, that we classify under the heading of criminal enterprise. But there is another form of mass extortion that became even more significant—the crimes we refer to as product tampering. In this chapter we'll be exploring several such cases that may look like the same kind of crime on the surface but that actually involved very different types of offenders acting on very different types of motives.

Even if the M.O. in a case is the same as in some others, and even if the UNSUB is able to kill people without ever physically coming into direct contact with them, there may be details—behavioral clues to motive—that we can work with to push that UNSUB ultimately into giving himself or herself away. Part of this has to do with the way the crime is staged.

Fear of product tampering, though we may not think much about it, is practically part of our collective unconscious. When the evil queen fails in her attempt to have her huntsman assassinate Snow White, she takes matters into her own hands by poisoning an apple, then offering it to her intended victim. We'll begin here with the grandfather of all real-life product tampering cases, the one that made all of us in society feel a new kind of vulnerability, a feeling of being held hostage in our own homes. And that is the case the FBI coded as TYMURS—the Tylenol poisoning murders in Chicago.

This was my first product tampering case as a profiler, and unlike any other case I can think of, the Tylenol poisoning in some senses changed our way of life. It profoundly altered the way we, as consumers, took things for granted when we went to the store. It changed the ways companies packaged their products. And it led to laws written specifically to address this area of crime, which was deadly, though not violent in the traditional sense. Ironically, though perpetrated for a traditional motive, it is not typical or representative of extortion, because most extortionists establish their credibility without resorting to killing. This one did kill. This is also a great mystery story, since the cases remain on the books as technically unsolved.

Between September 29 and October 1, 1982, seven people in the Chicago area died mysteriously, beginning with a twelve-year-old girl who stayed home one day with the sniffles and collapsed on her bathroom floor. The epidemiology that linked the cases and recognized the pattern was accomplished by two suburban firefighters who also happened to be trained arson investigators. Philip Cappitelli of Arlington Heights and Richard Keyworth of neighboring Elk Grove Village heard of the unexplained deaths in their communities and immediately started looking into them. Without their detective work, the crisis might have gone on a lot longer and been a lot worse. Dr. Thomas Kim, chief of critical care at Northwest Community Hospital in Arlington Heights, was the one who first put the medical puzzle together and alerted the Cook County medical examiner.

The deaths turned out to be caused by potassium cyanide, a particularly rapid and effective means of poisoning. Cyanide inhibits the blood from taking oxygen from the lungs and transporting it throughout the body, so the victim quickly becomes oxygen starved. Respiration increases in a futile attempt to make up the deficit. Blood pressure drops; the body can go into convulsions and then coma. The eyes become fixed and the heart finally stops.

The only thing the victims had in common was that they'd all taken capsules from the red-and-white Extra-Strength Tylenol packaging. This was a particularly difficult challenge for law enforcement, since Tylenol is one of the most widely used nonprescription painkillers in the world. The police catalogued several lot numbers of the medicine that were involved, but it seemed clear that the contamination was carried out on individual bottles, probably on store shelves, rather than at the manufacturing level. At the time, the bottles simply had easily removable tops and a wad of cotton at the neck protecting the medicine.

As soon as word of the poisonings got out—which occurred quickly and played big, since the media picked up this story with a vengeance—a deep and pervasive sense of insecurity and vulnerability settled over the population of Chicago and, indeed, the rest of the United States as well. If you couldn't take a simple capsule for an ordinary headache without fear of being killed by it, where in life were you safe any longer? Let me also say at the outset that Johnson & Johnson, the parent company of Tylenol's manufacturer, McNeil Consumer Products, handled this crisis admirably from start to finish, with complete integrity and a clear message that their only concern was the safety of their customers, not profit or protecting the image of one of their most valuable product lines. They dispatched a team of chemists to the Chicago area to work with the state chemists and to help sample thousands of individual units of the medication. They also offered a $100,000 reward for information leading to the arrest and conviction of the killer or killers.

Rumors spread. One had it that a Palestine liberation group was behind the poisonings.

A multiagency task force was formed, including Chicago police, Illinois state police, and the FBI. Ultimately more than a hundred agents would be involved, including thirty-two from the FBI alone. Ed Hegarty, the SAC, or Special Agent in Charge, of the Chicago Field Office, contacted me at Quantico and asked me to help out with their efforts. The ASAC, or Assistant Special Agent in Charge, Tom DuHadway, was overseeing the TYMURS investigation. DuHadway was not only a fine agent but a terrific guy as well. The Bureau lost one of its great leaders when he died suddenly of a heart attack in 1991 while heading the Intelligence Division.

Because of the importance of the case, I fly out to Chicago and head straight to the field office. Hegarty was an authoritative and commanding presence, so much so that he had been given the nickname Lord Baltimore back when he headed the Baltimore Field Office. (It was not a title many people used to his face.) Anyway, Hegarty leads me into a spare office where all the case materials are piled up, indicates the desk, and says, "Well, Douglas, let's see you do your thing." That's the kind of guy Hegarty is. Then he and the other agents working the case left me alone. I think they went out to dinner while I sweat my ass off trying to decide what should go into the profile.

After going through all the photos, documents, and reports, the first question that comes to mind, the one issue I know we have to be able to answer if we're going to have a shot at catching this creep, is, "What the hell is the motive?"

The tragedies were unspeakable, but there was no discernible pattern to the victimology. The first victim, Mary Kellerman, was only twelve. Her parents found her unconscious on the bathroom floor. She died at Alexian Brothers Medical Center less than three hours later. About two hours after that, and five miles away, Adam Janus, a twenty-seven-year-old postal employee, came home and took Tylenol for muscle aches in his shoulder. He went to lie down and never got up. He died that afternoon at Northwest Community Hospital. Other family members rushed to his home to grieve together. Adam's younger brother Stanley, twenty-five, developed a headache from the stress and took two Tylenol capsules to relieve the pain. So did Theresa, his twenty-year-old wife of three months. When they both died, it became clear that health authorities were dealing with a major problem.

Mary Reiner, like Adam Janus also twenty-seven, had just gotten home from the hospital after giving birth to her fourth child a week earlier. Her life ended in the very hospital where his began. Mary MacFarland, thirty-one and the mother of two young sons, took Tylenol after complaining of a tremendous headache to her coworkers. She was rushed to the hospital late on a Wednesday night and died early the next morning. Investigators found a bottle of Extra-Strength Tylenol in her purse. And Paula Prince, a thirty-five-year-old flight attendant, was found on the bathroom floor of her apartment after she didn't show up for her flight. A receipt near her body showed that she purchased Extra-Strength Tylenol just before the bottles were removed from store shelves.

Another perplexing aspect was that the killer did not follow the usual pattern: most extortionists do something to establish their credibility, then make their demands. For example, this case would have made more sense and the motive would have been clearer if the UNSUB had sent a letter to a local newspaper, television station, or police department instructing them to look on such-and-such a shelf at such-and-such a store to find the product he'd sabotaged. Then, if they didn't meet his demands, he would start killing. This one just started killing without trying to prove himself and without making any demands.

Unlike most murders, crime scene analysis here isn't going to tell you anything directly about the offender. Even more than a bombing, you've got no specific place on which to focus. What is the crime scene—the store, the factory, the home where the victim takes the adulterated product? What is any of them going to tell you? And it's such a cowardly crime that you wouldn't expect him to contact the media and make his personality known. If he had to see the results of what he did at close range, I thought, this type would be emotionally distraught.

Despite the fact that this was early in my profiling career and I'd never done a product tampering case before, nor had I ever interviewed a convicted tamperer in prison, it seemed to me that the killer would likely fit the developmental models we'd observed for other types of cowardly predatory crimes. Whatever his specific motive was, he would generally be driven by anger in most of his attitudes and endeavors. He'd have bouts of severe depression and feelings of despair. He'd feel inadequate, helpless, hopeless, and impotent, but at the same time he'd be convinced that he was always being unfairly maligned by those around him or by society in general. There would be a long list of personal failures throughout his life, and these could include education, employment, social experiences, and relationships with women of his own age and intelligence level. I even speculated that some of his feelings of inadequacy might stem from physical ailments or disabilities. Like the arsonist, he would gravitate toward positions of authority or pseudoauthority, such as security guard, ambulance driver, auxiliary firefighter—something of that nature. But as with anything else, he'd have trouble keeping that job. Likewise, I wouldn't have been surprised to see some military background;

someone of this nature would gravitate to the Army or the Marines. And again, if there was such a military background, I would have expected to see some behavioral problems there along with episodes of psychiatric treatment.

What I believed we could say with some assurance was that the UNSUB would be a white male in his late twenties to early thirties, a depressed, nocturnal loner. Thinking about what he had done, I classified him in the assassin mold—someone who constantly thinks about killing but never lays hands on his intended victim. And I felt secure in supposing that there would be a precipitating stressor for this type of crime, just as there usually is for other predatory murders. Based on when the first crime was discovered, that stressor—loss of job, wife, girlfriend, or possibly parent—would have occurred sometime beginning around the middle of September.

So what else did we know or could we figure out?

The adulterations are not very sophisticated. Essentially, the UNSUB appears to have opened bottles on drugstore shelves, introduced the cyanide, and put the packaging back together. Therefore, I don't envision this guy as a particularly organized or methodical offender. That, at least, lets me rule out anyone high up in the McNeil or Johnson & Johnson organizations, though it still leaves a lot of regular employees who might hold a grudge for one reason or another, if revenge was the motive. The problem is, as I say in the profile, we don't know if the subject was getting back at the manufacturer, the stores that distribute the drugs, the victims themselves, or society in general. Likewise, the selection of Tylenol as the agent of distribution of the poison might or might not be significant. It could just have been that the drug was so popular that there were a lot of potential victims out there; or it could have been something as simple as the killer liked the package it came in for one reason or another. Cyanide is such an easy substance to obtain that tracing sales or purchases would be like trying to find a needle in a haystack.

I would expect this guy to revisit some of the sites, particularly once the media started picking up the story. These might include not only the stores where he planted the poisoned capsules but also the graves of some of the victims, once the press identified them. He could even go so far as to begin secretly surveilling their homes.

He'd be driving a five-year-old or older car not very well maintained. The way the crime was carried out, the way the Tylenol capsules were adulterated, all of this reflects a sloppy and distracted, rather than meticulous, personality. And I thought this would be reflected in the car he drives. But it could resemble a police-type vehicle, say a large Ford sedan, which would represent strength and power—two characteristics he seeks but does not possess.

The task force needed to investigate disgruntled employees and former employees, both of Johnson & Johnson and McNeil and of the individual drugstores targeted. But the more I thought about it, and the more I looked at the particulars surrounding the Tylenol adulteration, the more I became convinced that the motive here was general rage and resentment against a society that had wronged or ignored the killer, rather than someone with a specific grudge or grievance against the drug company or store. This guy was out for revenge against any and all people he thought had slighted him or done him wrong, and that included society in general. In all probability he would have written letters in the past to people in positions of power and prominence, specifically President Ronald Reagan and Chicago mayor Jane Byrne, but it could have been virtually anyone from the director of the FBI to the Pope. These letters would concern wrongs that he perceived had been done to him for which he achieved no recompense or satisfactory resolution. He would now feel ignored, and this gave him reason to escalate. But since he would have signed his real name to those letters, that might provide a fruitful investigative avenue to pursue.

Okay, that was the personality profile I came up with all alone in that room in the Chicago Field Office. But a lot of people in the Chicago metropolitan area would fit that mold, so it wasn't likely to lead directly to an offender. Rather, once the police developed a list of suspects, it could help them narrow and prioritize that list. But what could be helpful would be some proactive strategies that might get the UNSUB to inject himself more directly into the investigation.

I thought one personality trait the police might be able to exploit would be his curiosity. Anyone who takes the time and effort to lace Tylenol with cyanide is going to be curious about what he's been able to make happen: How have the stores that sold the poisoned Tylenol reacted? Have they changed their operating procedures? What's happened to the families of the victims? What about the drug company itself? One way or another, I felt, he would have to see for himself the influence he had finally had over other people.

One of the ways he would manifest that need would be talking to other people, maybe in bars, or with clerks in the drugstores, with police officers in their local hangouts. He's got international attention for the first time in his life, so this is a tremendous ego boost for him. He might keep a scrapbook as well as a journal or diary of his activities. If we ever got to see his personal writings, I would expect them somehow to reveal and reflect his feelings of inferiority.

I advised that it was important that the authorities keep the pressure on him by making only positive statements to the press about the status of the case. Don't say anything like, The case is at a standstill, or, It's reached a dead end. Don't let the UNSUB off the hook or enable him to cope with the crime. And don't piss him off at this stage by publicly referring to him as a madman or maniac. In fact, it might be a good idea to find a psychiatrist or psychologist who'd be willing to state publicly that the UNSUB is a victim of society, just as he perceives himself. This could provide a face-saving scenario and might encourage him to either call the doctor or visit (probably surreptitiously) his office. I didn't know that precisely as I was formulating that advice, Illinois attorney general Tyrone Fahner was on television calling the Tylenol poisoner a dangerous madman.

The media always have a role in these cases, because the UNSUB always reacts to the press coverage. What I really wanted to encourage the press to do here was simply to print the truth: the whole, complete truth about the victims. If they would do that, I would be very happy, both as a mindhunter and as someone very interested in victims' rights and the perception of victims as something more than horrible statistics. In other words, if the UNSUB could be made to relate to any of them as human beings, rather than just abstract targets of his rage, then, with this type of offender, we might have a chance of appealing to a sense of guilt or remorse. If I had my way, the newspapers would pull out all the stops—show pictures of the victims and where they were buried—and force the readers, and by extension the UNSUB, to see each of them as the complete and innocent human beings they were.

When I review the list of victims, it seems to me the most potentially productive victim to start with would be Mary Kellerman, who was just twelve years of age. If the media can't get through to people's emotions with that one, then my plan probably won't work anyway. But if the article describes the burial location, then I would advise the police to surveil the site, because there would be a good chance a remorseful UNSUB might show up to apologize to the dead girl.

Another possible avenue of press interest might be to concentrate on one of the stores that sold the poisoned Tylenol, and talk vaguely—giving away no real security tactics—about what measures it is currently taking to avoid a repeat and to protect its customers. This might be enough to pique the UNSUB's interest to come in and see for himself if the security measures really had changed. I reviewed the locations and settings of each of the affected stores and recommended one that was not close to a major highway; that would winnow out some of those who are just plain curiosity seekers. A variation on this would be to get the owner or manager of a drugstore that had not been affected to brag publicly about how his store was so secure and his management skills so sharp that the killer couldn't possibly slip any poisoned Tylenol onto his shelves. This would be perceived as a challenge. With round-the-clock surveillance of the store, this tactic might provide another opportunity for nabbing this type of offender.

Then I suggest a false-alarm scenario, in which police and the FBI are dispatched to a given store in an isolated area on a hot tip that turns out to be a false alarm. In this instance, the local police chief or investigator would boast publicly that his department's efficiency in responding "scared off" the offender. This might prove another irresistible challenge.

If we announce a nighttime vigil for each of the victims, I think there is a good chance the UNSUB might show up at one. I recommend placing a small cross or other marker at each of the graves during the vigil, hoping the killer will go back afterward to take one of the markers as a souvenir. I further suggest that the task force solicit volunteers to help answer phone calls and handle tips from the public, with the expectation that the UNSUB would volunteer.

When I finally finish the profile and case analysis, it's well into the evening. I give it in to be typed up and wait for Ed Hegarty and his colleagues to get back to the office.

I think it must have been close to midnight when they finally show up again. The SAC takes the six or seven single-spaced pages I've written and scans them while I stand there silently. When he finishes reading, he looks up and says, simply, "Very impressive." From Hegarty, that is high praise, indeed.

Meanwhile, Johnson & Johnson has taken bold steps, telling the media and the public exactly what's been going on and organizing a nationwide recall of more than 260,000 bottles of Extra-Strength Tylenol.

The next day, Tom DuHadway and I go over to see the state police folk working the case and give them my profile. But before I can get very far, their chief guy on the case starts in, giving me his concept of the Tylenol poisoner's personality. He'd been involved in prosecuting Richard Speck, and basically his criminal profile is just like Speck's—a mean, angry son of a bitch who'd kill anything he looked at. Aside from the fact that so simplified a profile fits so many people in Chicago or any other large city that it's virtually meaningless, I think it's wrong.

I listen stone-faced, getting increasingly aggravated. When he's finished, I simply stand up to leave. "Where are you going?" he says to me.

"I'm leaving," I reply. "What do you need me here for?" Many times in my career I've been accused of arrogance. But it seems to me that if you're going to stick your neck out with the kinds of opinions and suggestions I have to make, you'd better have a pretty high level of leadership and self-confidence, because you're potentially sending a lot of police resources down one particular alley, and if you're wrong, there's going to be a lot of hell to pay.

"No, let's talk about it," he says. So I stay.

As I recall, Tom was the diplomat and smoothed all the feathers. On the surface, he came across as very calm, but from the way he was always chewing on a toothpick, I figured there must be a fair amount of underlying tension here, particularly with the kind of job he had to do. Years later, interestingly enough, the state guy came through Quantico for an executive-level course. He was really nice to me and we got along famously.

We got a report that the tainted Tylenol bottles were traced to two different manufacturing plants, one in Pennsylvania and the other in Texas, making it extremely unlikely that the adulteration could have occurred anywhere other than at the store shelf level. And it probably happened shortly before the products were purchased, since the Cook County medical examiner's chief toxicologist told us that cyanide is corrosive—it wouldn't take long for it to destroy the capsules' gelatin shells. The number of poisoned capsules varied from bottle to bottle, and as far as we could tell, no more than a single bottle was tampered with in any one store.

I tell Hegarty and DuHadway exactly what I have in mind for the journalistic angle. Ed suggests approaching two well-known area columnists, Mike Royko and Bob Greene. I tell them I'd prefer an investigative reporter to a columnist, since he or she would be used to dealing with the police and other official agencies as sources and background information and would know how to make the kinds of agreements and arrangements that would give each of them what they needed without compromising the professional integrity of law enforcement or the press. But the local agents insist that it should be a columnist, a talented writer who has a following with the public. I'm the outsider, so I go along.

Hegarty contacts a number of local journalistic outlets to see if any of them might want to run the kind of story we've talked about. Let me make it absolutely clear here that I'm not talking about managing the news or printing anything that isn't true, because there's been some controversy about this. I'd already had to explain my ideas on proactive techniques to the legal counsel for the Bureau's Criminal Investigative Division in Washington, and I assured them that I was not in the business of lying to the press. What I can be, I explained, is a news source, and like any source, I have a stake in getting a certain perspective and point of view before the public. If the reporter I approach wants to take advantage of my knowledge and information, he or she can do so; and beyond that, I have no control over what is printed in the newspaper or broadcast on television or radio. I hope the press will be sensitive to the fact that it is our job to catch criminals, but really, all I can do is tell my story and hope for the best.

Bob Greene, a columnist for the *Chicago Tribune,* agrees to meet with me. He's already discussed it with his editor, Jim Squires, and the two of them had met in Squires's office at the *Tribune* with Hegarty and Richard Brzeczek, the Chicago police superintendent. Though I still would have favored a full-time investigative reporter, I respect and admire Greene a lot, having read his column for some time in my own local newspaper in Virginia.

He comes to my room at a Holiday Inn, accompanied by Tony De Lorenzo, a local FBI special agent who'd driven him there.

I give him some background about what my unit at Quantico does and tell him that our specialty is studying the personalities and trying to figure out the motives of serial murderers. I explain how they tend to depersonalize their victims, and that some types simply don't give a shit about other people. But there are other types who are capable of feeling guilt and remorse under the right circumstances; I say that I'm betting the Tylenol UNSUB is one of those.

As we talk, Greene and I agree that the Mary Kellerman story is a good and important one by any journalistic standards. She was the youngest victim, she'd taken Tylenol to relieve the symptoms of her cold, she'd collapsed and died on her bathroom floor in her pajamas, and that's where her parents found her. So far they hadn't talked to any reporters.

Greene says to me, "That's a story I would want to write even if I had never heard of you. If you can get me into the house, I'd like to talk to her parents."

De Lorenzo and I say we think we might be able to arrange it. Without suggesting what he ought to write, Tony and I take him into our confidence and describe what our strategy would be. If he runs a column, we would then place both the Kellerman house and Mary's grave under twenty-four-hour surveillance.

Dennis and Jeanna Kellerman agree to talk to Greene, and Tony drives him to their house the next morning. He's introduced to the grieving parents by LeRoy Himebauch, another FBI special agent who's been dealing directly with the family and has their trust. Jeanna tearfully relates to Greene how she was going to buy a smaller bottle of Tylenol but figured they'd still use it after Mary's cold was better, so she reached for the larger bottle. That bottle was one of the ones that had been poisoned. Mary was their only child; they'd been unable to have any more. Dennis tells Greene how intensely he wants this monster to be caught.

The column Bob Greene writes is eloquent, hard-hitting, and, I believe, from the heart. It begins:

If you are the Tylenol killer, some of this may matter to you. Or it may make no difference at all.

If you are the Tylenol killer, your whole murderous exercise may have seemed beautiful in the flawlessness of its execution. You doctored the capsules, and the people died, and you put fear in hearts all over the nation. If you are the killer, the success of your mission may be sustaining you.

If you are the Tylenol killer, though, you may be harboring just the vaguest curiosity about the people on the other end of your plan: the people who were unfortunate enough to purchase the bottles you had touched.

Then he describes the Kellermans' street and gives their address. Greene later reported that the copy editors who handled the column questioned his decision to include that specific and sensitive piece of information. Rather than explaining what had gone into his decision, he simply asked them to leave it in.

Greene went through a lot of soul-searching about the journalistic ethics of this column, so much so that he later wrote a column about the experience for *Esquire* magazine, where he was a contributing editor. As he stated in that column, "It is one thing to say that a reporter should never cooperate with a law enforcement agency; it is quite another, when seven people have been poisoned to death in the area where you live, to say that no, you will not help."

He concluded by saying, "You get up every morning and you go to work and you try to do your job. Sometimes you wonder if you're doing it right. In the end, as always, here we are. You put words on paper and you hope they reach somebody."

As should be obvious, I have total admiration for Bob Greene, not only from my perspective as an FBI agent but also as a concerned reader and citizen. To me he showed that you don't have to surrender your membership card in the human race to be a journalist, any more than you have to to be a police officer or FBI agent.

The Tylenol poisonings soon became a national story. No one felt safe taking the most ordinary medication. One of the outlets where the capsules were found was in a shopping mall near O'Hare Airport. What if travelers carried tainted bottles across the country? What if other common consumer products such as instant coffee were next to be hit?

"What kind of human being could conceive such a scheme, carefully open the capsules and pour in powder, then see to it that the product was placed among rows of similar medicine on the shelves of drugstores?" the *Washington Post* asked in an editorial on October 6, 1982. Random illnesses and deaths that actually had nothing to do with this became suspect. Copycat extortion threats started turning up. Psychics began offering their insights.

There was one dramatic and ironic incident associated with my stay in Chicago that I thought proved not only the viability of my theories but also the law of unintended consequences. Upon my recommendation, the Chicago police agreed to stake out Mary Kellerman's grave after Greene's column was published. They hung out there for several nights, and let me tell you, a stakeout of a cemetery at night is a pretty unpleasant experience, so no one was chafing for this duty. I could picture the guys who got the assignment rolling their eyes just as their superiors had, thinking, Yeah, Douglas, great idea; why don't you sit your own ass out in the boneyard all night? I think they were about to give up on my idea when they finally hit pay dirt.

A man comes up to the grave site and starts talking. There's no one else around, so he must be talking directly to Mary!

He drops to his hands and knees, sobbing. "I'm sorry. I didn't mean it. It was an accident!" This is great; they often try to make their murderous actions seem unintentional. The cops are all excited ("Maybe Douglas does have his act together"), imagining what kind of heroes they're going to be tomorrow when news gets out that they caught the Tylenol killer.

"I'm so sorry . . . Susan," the UNSUB cries.

They're about to pounce. But wait a second—Susan? Who the hell is Susan?!

It turns out he's standing in front of the grave next to Mary's! Buried there was the victim of an unsolved automobile hit-and-run, and the perpetrator just happened to come back while the police were there. So the good news is that we solved a hit-and-run that night and we confirmed what I'd found in my research about criminals: no matter who they are or what type of crime they commit, many return to the scene of their crime and/or their victim's grave for a variety of reasons. And I made at least partial believers out of some of the detectives. The bad news, of course, is that we hadn't ferreted out the Tylenol killer. We'd later learn that our prime suspect had already left town by the time the surveillance started.

I remained in Chicago for about a week, then followed the Tylenol case from Quantico. Task force investigators were working intensively. They interviewed disgruntled workers from each of the affected stores, went door-to-door with police sketches of suspicious-looking individuals seen in or near the stores, and tried to lift fingerprints from a tainted bottle they'd found still on a drugstore shelf. They pored over security camera footage taken at various affected stores. The FBI asked for news film taken at Paula Prince's funeral. One of the best leads was from an elderly lady who recalled seeing a man in a drugstore take something from his jacket pocket and put it back on the shelf. At the time she thought maybe he was having second thoughts about shoplifting.

Illinois attorney general Tyrone Fahner, who'd been coordinating the state, local, and national investigation teams, had been making public statements about how they thought there was more than one offender, in part because some of the poisoned capsules were put together more artfully than others. I believed we were dealing with only one depraved individual, and continued making my recommendations on that basis. Various psychiatrists and academics started weighing in with their own profiles, some stressing the disgruntled employee likelihood, which I'd abandoned. A psychiatrist at Northwestern University who'd testified for the defense in the John Wayne Gacy murder trial thought the poisoner would be a lot like Gacy.

As the weeks dragged on with no new poisonings but no arrests either, fear still remained high. Many jurisdictions around the country canceled trick-or-treating and other Halloween festivities. Practically every community had its own real or imagined scare. The U.S. Food and Drug Administration reported 270 cases of possible product tampering since the Chicago incidents, thirty-six of which it considered "hard-core."

"This is getting completely out of control," said the deputy commissioner of one state's Department of Consumer Protection.

Investigators looked into cyanide deaths in other states for possible linkages, including that of a graduate student in Philadelphia (which was ultimately ruled a suicide), another poisoning in California, and one in Kansas. Vernon Williams Jr., an unemployed father of two boys in his mid-thirties, was sentenced to two years in prison for mail fraud after trying to extort $100,000 from Johnson & Johnson, threatening to taint more Tylenol. The New Jersey man claimed he got the idea after seeing the news stories about the people who died around Chicago. This instance was only one of many.

With all of the investigative efforts, only a few solid suspects had been developed. One was a loading-dock worker at a food store warehouse who was known to dabble with chemicals and refused a lie-detector test. There was a suburban-Chicago man with a history of mental instability who made threats against some of the store chains where the tainted Tylenol was found.

And there was a thirty-six-year-old former Chicago accountant named James William Lewis, who attempted to extort a million bucks from Johnson & Johnson, mailing them a letter threatening further poisonings if this ransom wasn't paid into a Chicago bank account. In the letter he used the name Robert Richardson, an alias he had used before, and wrote, "So far I have spent less than $50, and it takes me less than 10 minutes per bottle." The pharmaceutical company was prepared to pay the money to avoid further incidents, but was advised not to by the FBI. The task force and Bureau were avidly looking for Lewis (who seemed to have left town right around the time the deaths began) both for the extortion threat itself and to see if his whereabouts at critical times matched up with the poisoner's. While on the run, Lewis sent several handwritten letters, signed Robert Richardson, to the *Chicago Tribune*, denying any connection to the poisonings and calling himself "a victim."

One contained these strangely paranoid and obsessive words: "We are not armed, unless one means in the anatomical, paraplegic sense. We shall never carry weapons, no matter how bizarre the police and FBI reports. Domestically, weapons are for two quite similar types of mentality: (1) criminals and (2) police. We are neither."

As soon as I read this, I sat up and took note. I had profiled the Tylenol poisoner as a cowardly type who would not feel comfortable with direct, one-on-one confrontation; and so, despite his strong inner rage, he would not be the type to carry a weapon.

The next day, the *Kansas City Star* received a letter from "Richardson" in the form of an essay titled "A Moral Dilemma." In it he attacked the Kansas City PD's handling of an investigation into the death of Raymond West, who had been a former client of Lewis's accounting business. After death, West's body had been dismembered and stuffed into a plastic bag and left in the attic of his home, where it was found on August 14, 1978.

"I have been wanting this case reopened for years," wrote Richardson/Lewis. "I know that I did not have anything to do with Mr. West's death. I hope this time the investigators will take the time to conduct more than a superficial inquiry."

The letters were postmarked New York City. From my research with killers, I knew it was common for those who had left the cities of their crimes to visit public libraries in their new locations to look at newspapers from their old hometowns to see if and how they were covering the criminal investigation. I suggested having New York FBI agents and NYPD comb the libraries, looking for anyone matching the descriptions or sketches who was studying Chicago papers.

Lewis was arrested in Manhattan on December 12 in the main branch of the New York Public Library. The next day, Lewis's thirty-three-year-old wife, LeAnn, surrendered at O'Hare Airport after a flight from Philadelphia. Her husband also appeared to have written a threatening letter to President Reagan in mid-October, which was one of the things I said in my profile that I expected to see. The letter was stamped by a postage meter from Mrs. Lewis's former office and complained about certain tax policies. If the president did not back off them, the letter warned, he would be assassinated. At Lewis's bail hearing, U.S. magistrate James T. Balog was also told that Kansas City, Missouri, authorities had come up with new evidence in the murder of Raymond West. Because of the state of the corpse, cause of death could not be definitively determined, but poisoning was suggested. Lewis was indicted for capital murder, but the charges were dropped after a judge ruled that Lewis's arrest and the search of his home had been improper.

Lewis was six feet one and weighed 167 pounds. An enhanced security camera photo of a man thought to be the UNSUB showed someone six-one to six-two, 170 to 185 pounds. Since Lewis left town right around the time of the deaths, he would not have been able to respond to Bob Greene's column in the way I had hoped the UNSUB would.

In the months after his arrest for the Tylenol letter, Lewis was also convicted of mail fraud in Kansas City, Missouri—this was unrelated to the Tylenol case—and sentenced to ten years.

At his trial for extortion in Chicago the following October, Lewis's attorney, Michael D. Monico, conceded that his client wrote the letter to Johnson & Johnson, but claimed that in spite of the $1 million demand, he never sought to profit. Instead, Monico suggested, Lewis was trying to get back at Frederick Miller McCahey, a member of the Miller Brewing Company family, who had owned the travel agency where LeAnn once worked and with whom she had lost a pay dispute after she was let go when the agency went out of business. It was to McCahey's bank that Lewis had directed the ransom money be sent.

"Intent is the issue in this case," Monico told the jury in his closing argument, and the intent was to expose supposed wrongdoing by LeAnn's former employer.

As we've noted, there is an all-too-common tendency to confuse intent with motive. All intent refers to is the willfulness of the action. Exposing this supposed wrong may have been his intent, but his motive was revenge.

James Lewis was convicted of extortion and sentenced to twenty years. LeAnn was not charged with anything. No one was ever charged with the murders, which stopped as suddenly as they had begun.

Lewis was released from the federal prison in El Reno, Oklahoma, on mandatory parole on Friday, October 13, 1995. It was reported that he would move to the Boston area, where LeAnn had been living. Despite the fact that he was convicted only of a related extortion, and that he vehemently denied involvement in the poisonings themselves, many law enforcement officials considered him the prime suspect. Former Chicago police superintendent Richard Brzeczek, however, did not. At the time of Lewis's release, he told the *Chicago Sun-Times* that he was convinced that one of the victims was singled out for murder and the others were killed to make it look like a random act.

Of course, in our system no one is guilty until proven so in a court of law, so none of us can say that Lewis was the Tylenol UNSUB. But I do feel confident in saying that the poisoner would be someone like this convicted extortionist, whose motive was anger and a desire to get back at specific individuals and the world at large for perceived wrongs done to him. And while Lewis never admitted any role in the poisonings, he did relate to police interviewers how a killer might have adulterated the medicine, by spreading the cyanide powder onto a cutting board and then carefully brushing it into the capsules.

"They asked me to show how it might have been done and I tried, as a good citizen, to help," Lewis told the *Chicago Tribune* in a 1992 prison interview.

Now, this is very interesting. During my own prison interviews, I found repeatedly that when I couldn't get a subject to admit to a crime or series of crimes, particularly murder, I could sometimes get him to "speculate," in the third person, about how a hypothetical offender might carry out a particular violent or predatory act. I found this when I interviewed Gary Trapnell, a notorious armed robber and airplane hijacker at the federal prison in Marion, Illinois. This was also the case with Ted Bundy, who through years on death row would not acknowledge his string of killings of young women across the country but would speak about how such a killer might go about the crimes in question.

Lewis also had the kind of background I would expect to see in a deadly extortionist type of offender. As reported in the *Sun-Times,* while growing up in Missouri, he'd quarreled so violently with his adoptive parents that he was sent to a mental hospital. Later he was arrested after fighting with his stepfather.

The Tylenol scare ended up costing Johnson & Johnson more

than $100 million and cost many millions more to the local, state, and national law enforcement agencies that investigated it. In 1991, Johnson & Johnson reached a settlement with the families of the seven victims. As a result, the drug company began triple-sealing the packages to thwart tampering. Other companies followed suit, knowing that Tylenol's fate could just as easily have been their products'. Congress made product tampering a federal offense with passage of the Consumer Tampering Act. And our innocence and trust as citizens were forever altered because some inadequate and ineffectual individual was pissed off at everybody.

As I learned after the Tylenol case, product tampering and other forms of extortion have become significant issues for law enforcement to deal with. It is crucial to try to understand the motive, because that, along with victimology and the means by which the act is carried out, is the key to who done it.

But because there are so many threat claims in our society today—as witness the aftermaths of *Doomsday Flight* and the Tylenol scare, to name just two—before we even deal with the issue of motive, the first thing we need to establish is the legitimacy of the threat itself. Is the threat for real, or is it a hoax just meant to mess things up and give the caller a sense of power? In some cases, the offender will demonstrate his ability by directing authorities to a sample of his work. But in most other cases, a threat involves police in a delicate process of evaluation to determine whether the UNSUB is capable of carrying it out.

From our perspective in behavioral science, some of this is done through what we call psycholinguistic analysis, which means actually using the subject's own words and phrases to determine his personality, level of sophistication, motivation, and therefore his capability. In other words: Do the offender's attributes as we understand them match up with the requirements of the threat scenario? If it's an extortion for money, we then look at the instructions for delivering the ransom, since the pickup is the most difficult part of this kind of crime to pull off: Has the UNSUB come up with a workable plan, or is he merely fantasizing?

One scenario that would tend to indicate the sophistication of the extortionist would be a directive to leave the money in a given telephone booth. So you, as the police, are surveilling this drop site. You see a guy go in and you arrest him. That's a mistake. He can claim he just went in to make a phone call.

Okay, so you watch while he pretends to make a call, then picks up the briefcase with the money and walks away. Then you arrest him. Hold on, though. He's still going to claim that he found this case in the phone booth, and good Samaritan that he is, he was taking it to the police station to turn it in. The point is, if this guy is sophisticated enough to have worked out this fail-safe ploy ahead of time, then you've got to be just as sophisticated in surreptitiously tailing him until he somehow proves his intentions are less than honorable.

Sometimes, I've found, threat letters are evaluated too closely, word for word or even letter stroke by letter stroke. I always told my people you have to hold it away and look at the big picture—the real message the writer is trying to get across. Because even if it is a hoax, you still have to try to catch that individual, if for no other reason than to cut down his harassment potential.

For example, if the threat is against a particular individual and the communication asks for $1 million, the first thing we ask ourselves as investigators is whether the targeted victim is reasonably capable of coming up with that kind of dough. If not, we're not going to take the threat so seriously. If the threat comes in on a Friday afternoon with a demand for immediate payment even though the banks are now closed for the weekend, that suggests an UNSUB with a fairly low degree of sophistication. Even if the threat is made by people against themselves in an attempt to garner sympathy or set up some kind of fraud, we have good ways of seeing through it.

But eventually, it all comes down to motive. In every case we come across, the first question we ask is *Why?* Why is this happening? Why does someone want to do something to this particular person or this particular company? What does the threatener actually want? Does the motive appear to be financial gain? love? sex? vengeance? punishment? recognition? excitement? guilt? satisfaction? hate? attention? What is the threatener telling us with the threat to our or someone else's well-being?

If he has a need for revenge, say, then we can start looking at the people who might have reason to feel that way. If he displays generalized anger, as in the Tylenol poisonings, then the case is going to be more difficult to crack. The general rule is that organized offenders extort for money and disorganized offenders for all the other reasons; though of course, there are many exceptions.

There's an old saying in law enforcement: "Killers don't call, and callers don't kill." What this means is that you can tell a lot about motive by the UNSUB's approach. If he calls first, or otherwise declares his intentions, then we start looking for a profit motive. If there isn't a call but people start dying, then we look to revenge and rage as motivation forces. Of course, this is a generality, and we have to look carefully at each of the details of the particular case.

If the threat is against an individual, the first thing I'm going to tell that person is to become very aware of anyone he comes in contact with, even casually. The reason for this, other than keeping up his guard, is that the UNSUB is going to have to inject himself, to observe what effect he's having; otherwise he's not going to get the satisfaction he's looking for.

Like arson, product tampering can be used to cover other crimes, and that's where our next case comes in.

In 1986, the Tylenol case was still fresh in the collective consciousness, but people had begun to relax a little and take safe consumer products more for granted again.

Then on June 11, Susan Katherine Snow, an attractive and well-respected forty-year-old assistant vice president of Puget Sound National Bank in Auburn, a suburb south of Seattle, dies in a hospital emergency room after being discovered by her fourteen-year-old daughter, Hayley, on her bathroom floor. She had been divorced twice and was newly married to Paul Webking, a forty-five-year-old truck driver with whom she was very much in love. In addition to Hayley, Snow had an adult daughter.

The quickness and drama of her death suggests a brain aneurysm or some kind of drug overdose, but there was no evidence of internal bleeding and Snow was not known as a drug abuser. Then, during the autopsy, the assistant medical examiner, Janet Miller, smells the subtle scent of bitter almonds. Though not always noticed and not detectable by everyone, when it is, it's practically a giveaway for cyanide poisoning.

Toxicology tests confirm the cyanide in Sue Snow's system. Family members insist that she would never poison or otherwise harm herself intentionally, and when investigators exhaustively try to reconstruct what she might have ingested, the only thing they come up with is two Extra-Strength Excedrin capsules. An examination of the bottle reveals three more adulterated pills. Paul Webking had taken some of the capsules from the same bottle, but nothing happened to him.

The agonizing drill has begun again. Within days, the FDA publishes the lot numbers Snow's bottle had come from and the manufacturer, Bristol-Myers, recalls its product nationwide. Seattle police comb store shelves looking for more tainted bottles and find two—one in Auburn and another in the neighboring community of Kent. And because of the new legislation following the Tylenol poisonings, the FBI gets involved. My unit at Quantico is called in to profile the UNSUB and come up with some possible proactive strategies.

Paul Webking agrees to take a polygraph test and passes easily. All of the investigation shows nothing but a grief-stricken husband who had truly adored his new wife.

We wait for some demand or other communication that might indicate the unknown poisoner's motive, but nothing comes. Authorities hold their collective breath waiting to see if anyone else falls prey. And unfortunately, one does.

On June 17, forty-two-year-old Stella Maudine Nickell calls Seattle police to report that her husband, Bruce, a part-time mechanic and heavy-equipment operator for the Washington Department of Transportation, fifty-two years of age and a recovered alcoholic, had died less than two weeks before at Harborview Medical Center in Seattle. The hospital listed the cause of death as emphysema, but she distinctly recalls that he had taken Extra-Strength Excedrin shortly before he was stricken. When she heard the publicity, she became suspicious. She checked the lot number of her bottle and it was the same as the one in Sue Snow's medicine cabinet. Investigators are very interested.

Bruce Nickell has already been buried, but since he had agreed to be an organ donor, the hospital has a sample of his blood. Sure enough, toxicology tests reveal the presence of sodium cyanide. No more deaths have been detected, and no threat or demand has been received. Paul Webking and Stella Nickell both file wrongful death suits against Bristol-Myers.

But then the investigators find something odd—the kind of little detail that stands out and, if it's followed up properly, can break a case wide open. Of all the thousands upon thousands of bottles of Extra-Strength Excedrin the authorities have gone through, they've been able to locate only five that were adulterated. Two of those five were found in Stella Nickell's trailer home, and she had previously said that she bought them at different stores on different days. What were the chances one person would happen to buy two of those five bottles at different times? Statistically, almost nonexistent.

Detectives start focusing on Nickell. She has two beautiful daughters and a grandchild—not exactly your most common killer profile. She's well liked by her coworkers at the private security firm where she's a dispatcher. She was visibly grief-stricken when Bruce suddenly passed away. We advised the investigators to look closely at the victimology and try to attach a motive.

Once Nickell falls under scrutiny, FBI agents start putting together other incidental findings. Roger Martz and Debbie Wang of the FBI Lab's Chem Unit discover that the tainted capsules contained not only cyanide but also traces of four other chemicals, two of which were in algicides commonly used in home fish tanks. In his spare time, Martz visits pet stores, reading the labels on all the fish tank cleaners. Finally he comes upon one that has all four of the suspect chemicals. It's a premium algicide called Algae Destroyer. Evidently, the UNSUB had mixed the cyanide powder in the same container he or she had previously used to mix the algicide.

Meanwhile, Seattle agents learn that in addition to Bruce Nickell's $31,000 life insurance policy as a state worker, in the past year Stella has taken out additional policies. In all, she would collect about $175,000—if Bruce died accidentally. Death by poisoning is considered accidental.

When one of the Seattle agents reads Martz's report, he remembers seeing a fish tank in the Nickells' trailer. Agents then go around to local pet stores with a packet of photographs, one of which was of Stella Nickell, and ask the clerks if they have seen any of these people. At one store in Kent, someone picks out the picture of Nickell and recalls special-ordering Algae Destroyer for her. He also recalls selling her a mortar and pestle to grind the tablets into powder.

The evidence is coming together now. Nickell fails a polygraph. The FBI's Document Section determines that Bruce's signature had been forged on two of the insurance policies. But the evidence needs to be stronger. Then, in January 1987, Stella's daughter Cindy Hamilton contacts the investigators and says she feels she has to come forward with what she knows. She tells them her mother had often spoken of killing Bruce, one time even mentioning cyanide as a means. She tried to kill him once before with toxic seeds, but nothing happened. Then she started thinking about the Tylenol poisonings and realized she had her scenario. Cindy says her mother consulted several books in the library on various types of poisons. Agents then find Nickell's fingerprints in several books that library records show she had repeatedly borrowed, including the titles *Deadly Harvest* and *Human Poisoning*.

When Bruce dies suddenly, Cindy reports, before she can even ask a question, her mother says, "I know what you're thinking, and the answer is no."

And that was the official word, too—the coroner had erroneously attributed Bruce's death to acute emphysema, rather than to a random act of poisoning. Stella had to have someone else poisoned so she could become part of a pattern of crime, respond, and get authorities to reconsider her case. Otherwise she'd miss out on the big accidental-death benefit.

The other appalling thing to consider is that even if she was committed to this course of action, she could have made a call or written a note to authorities to establish credibility rather than sacrificing another innocent life, but she was willing for some stranger to die just to make her point more emphatically. And if Janet Miller had not detected the bitter almond odor at Sue Snow's autopsy, Nickell would have had to keep killing until someone figured it out so she could come forward.

Her background revealed a stark counterpoint to the image she'd projected to her friends and associates. Between 1968 and 1971, while living in California, she'd been convicted of forgery, check fraud, and child abuse of her daughter Cindy. At the time of Bruce's death, the Nickells were deeply in debt and threatened with both foreclosure on their home and the prospect of bankruptcy.

On May 9, 1988, Stella Nickell was found guilty of murder and was sentenced to two ninety-year terms in prison for the murders and ten years for each of three counts of product tampering, to be served concurrently. She was the first person in American history to be convicted of murder through product tampering.

U.S. District Court judge William Dwyer characterized Nickell's acts as "crimes of exceptional callousness and cruelty" and recommended she be ineligible for parole for at least thirty years and that her assets all be used to compensate the families of her victims.

Joan Maida, the assistant U.S. attorney prosecuting the case, noted, "It is unnerving to think just how many people stood to die because of this woman's greed." According to the prosecution, Nickell planned to use the insurance money to buy the piece of land her trailer was sitting on and open a tropical fish store. She loved fish.

Cindy Hamilton received a $250,000 reward from an industry group for her part in her mother's arrest and conviction.

Ironically, Nickell had committed the perfect crime and then blew it. This is one of those instances in which we say that the postoffense behavior gave the offender away. Had she not been so greedy, she would have gotten away with killing her husband and collecting his more modest insurance policy. But since her motive was, in fact, greed, the oldest motive in the book next to jealousy (the Cain and Abel case), it's easy to see how motive prevented her from literally getting away with murder.

Unfortunately but not unpredictably, this was not the end of it. In the February 1991 issue of *Reader's Digest,* an article appeared about how the FBI had cracked the Stella Nickell case. Shortly thereafter, Joseph Meling of Olympia, Washington, got the idea to poison his wife, Jennifer, with Sudafed decongestant tablets laced with potassium cyanide to collect on her life insurance. As in the Nickell case, a relative came forward to testify to the defendant's murderous intentions. In this case it was Keith Meling, Joseph's uncle. Jennifer survived, but in the process Joseph killed two other innocent people, Kathleen Daneker and Stanley McWhorter. Like Nickell, Meling was found guilty on six counts of product tampering and related charges.

Are we encouraging others to try the same thing simply by relating this story? No, and I hope no one will be stupid enough to think we've given them a plan. Because I know that anyone who reads the story carefully will realize that this is one kind of crime that is not worth the effort, because you are not going to get away with it. Everything is stacked against the offender, including the inevitability of his or her own behavior.

Is poisoning a female crime? Not particularly. The great majority of poisoners are going to be males, just as other types of murderers are. But because of the nonconfrontational aspect of it, if a woman is going to attempt murder, poison is one of the means that would likely be near the top of her list. And if a man is the perpetrator, then we'd expect him to be a shy or cowardly, emotionally submissive male who would be equally uncomfortable with confrontation. If we were called in on a new poisoning or product tampering case, we'd begin by suspecting a white male, but if the scenario and victimology suggested a particular, rather than a random, target, this is one type of crime in which we might easily shift our focus to a woman UNSUB.

An extremely bizarre poisoning case involved Audrey Marie Hilley of Anniston, Alabama, who also poisoned her husband, but with a very different motive in mind. The case was so weird in all of its twisted details that it sounds much more like a fictional mystery story than a real-life case.

On May 19, 1975, Frank Hilley goes to see his doctor, complaining of nausea. He keeps getting worse, and on the twenty-third, he's put in the hospital. Two days later he's dead. Doctors attribute the death to infectious hepatitis. Hilley leaves behind his wife, Audrey Marie, and their fifteen-year-old daughter, Carol Marie. Two years later, Audrey's mother, Lucille Frazier, dies of the same thing. Then in August 1979, nineteen-year-old Carol is hospitalized with nausea, bouts of vomiting, loss of feeling in her hands and feet—the same symptoms her father had four years earlier. In the hospital, Carol is partially paralyzed and near death for several weeks, but finally starts recovering. She tells doctors that her mother gave her several injections while she lay in her hospital room.

The previous July, her mother had purchased a $50,000 insurance policy on Carol's life.

But this isn't the only incriminating evidence against Audrey. Lab tests revealed abnormally high levels of arsenic in Carol's blood. Frank's body is exhumed, and a careful lab examination now certifies the cause of death as acute arsenic poisoning. Arsenic is also found in the exhumed remains of Lucille Frazier, but the levels are ambiguous. At any rate, Audrey Hilley is indicted on October 25, 1979, and charged with the attempted murder of her daughter.

Free on $14,000 bond, on November 16 the five-foot-one, green-eyed, brown-haired forty-seven-year-old woman disappears from the suburban Birmingham motel where she's been living. Around this same time, Audrey's mother-in-law, Carrie Hilley, dies after being sick for several weeks. And she's not the only one who's become ill after some contact with Audrey. In the late 1970s, Audrey had complained repeatedly to police about hearing prowlers around her house and receiving threatening phone calls. Two police officers came to her house, where she told them of her complaints and served them coffee. Shortly after leaving, both officers developed nausea and severe stomach cramps. Neighbor children were sick all the time without doctors being able to figure out why. When they moved away, the children quickly got well.

I'm called in to do a fugitive assessment. I suggest looking for Audrey in areas where she might feel comfortable. Looking into her background, I think she might show up very close to where she came from.

Audrey's car is found in Marietta, Georgia, but with no sign of her. The FBI looks for her from coast to coast. Meanwhile, on January 11, a Calhoun County, Alabama, grand jury indicts her on charges of murdering Frank.

She manages to drop out of sight until January of 1983, when she's found by FBI agents in the printing shop in Brattleboro, Vermont, where she worked. It was not far from Marlow, New Hampshire, where she'd been living under an assumed identity. Calling herself Lindsay but going by the nickname Robbie, Audrey married a tool-and-die maker and boatbuilder in his thirties named John Homan. She then went to Texas, where she staged and fabricated her own death. Then she came back to Marlow and to John Homan—as Robbie's twin sister, Terri Martin, twenty pounds lighter and hair dyed blond!

Yep, you heard right.

"If I were taken into court today, I would swear they were two different people," a shocked Homan tells the Associated Press. "She's been nothing but a warm and wonderful woman." He says he thought that perhaps she'd staged her own death to spare him the anguish of eventually learning her true identity. She had told him she'd had a husband who died of a heart attack and two children who were killed in an automobile accident in Tyler, Texas.

John's younger brother, Peter, says Audrey "was the happiest thing that ever happened to him" and that "he really loved her."

I certainly concede that this all comes as a surprise to me. I expected she'd be found somewhere near her home in Alabama, and a whole lot sooner than now. As I evaluate the facts of the case, I conclude that Audrey Hilley is really a classic psychopath. Generally we don't see this in women. She's self-sufficient, she's got no regard for the truth, she can con people at will and sniff out vulnerability and gullibility in people. If she'd been a man, I wouldn't have been surprised if she'd been a serial rapist or predatory sexual killer.

As seductive as she was, there was something about her that made people vaguely uncomfortable. Acquaintances and co-workers of Robbie's were alarmed by the uncanny similarity of the "twins" and notified authorities. Even the details here are bizarre. Hilley, posing now as Terri Martin, placed a newspaper obituary for Mrs. Robbie Homan. But Ronald Oja, who's been Robbie's supervisor in the sales department of Central Screw Company in Keene, New Hampshire, before she supposedly left for Texas, thought it odd that the obit listed her as Robbie Homan, rather than using her "real" name, Lindsay R. Homan. So he checked out some of the details, such as that she'd donated her body to the Medical Research Institute in Texas and that she was a member of the Sacred Heart Church in Tyler. This all turned out to be untrue, so Oja contacted the New Hampshire state police and put them on to Terri Martin.

Okay? With me so far? The police are looking for a fugitive known to them as Terri Clifton, who has used the name Terri Martin, so they think maybe this Terri Martin could be her. The state police contact the FBI, which sends an agent to interview Terri Martin. In an effort to convince the agent she's not Terri Clifton, Audrey Hilley admits she's not really Terri Martin and reveals her true identity.

She waives extradition and is brought back to Anniston and thrown into the county jail, this time with considerably higher bail. She pleads not guilty to the murder and attempted murder and two additional counts of writing bad checks.

The folks who knew her in the old days are just as shocked as Homan. Olga Kennedy, the headmistress of the school Carol Hilley once went to, tells an A.P. reporter that Audrey was "an outstanding, attractive, cooperative parent. When there was something to be done, she seemed always to be willing to offer anything she could."

The case is so strange that Circuit Court judge Sam Monk grants a prosecution request by Assistant D.A. Joe Hubbard for psychiatric evaluation. It goes to trial at the end of May 1981 with Hilley's daughter, Carol, as the opening prosecution witness, telling about the mysterious injections her mother had given her, even before she went to the hospital.

Hilley's former sister-in-law Freda Adcock then testifies that she had found three jars of baby food and a container of rat poison in a box in Audrey's house. A state toxicologist testifies that a bottle found in Hilley's purse contained traces of arsenic. And Audrey's son, Mike, a thirty-year-old minister in Conyers, Georgia, tells the jury that his father had turned yellow days before his death and he wondered if he was losing his mind. Assistant D.A. Hubbard also produces a letter written by Mike in the fall of 1979 to Calhoun County coroner Ralph Phillips, saying, "It is my belief that my mother injected my father with arsenic as she apparently has done to my sister."

Priscilla Lang, a woman who had shared the same jail cell with Hilley, testifies that Hilley told her she had tried to kill her husband and daughter because Carol was a lesbian and Frank was "taking up for her." Her method of poisoning, according to Lang, was to put a little arsenic in her husband's food every day.

The prosecution puts forth anger over Carol as one possible motive. Another was the insurance money Audrey collected after Frank's death—$31,140—and the additional money she would have collected had her daughter died.

After a nine-day trial, the jury takes about two and a half hours to find Hilley guilty of murder and attempted murder. Facing Judge Monk for sentencing, Hilley states, "I still maintain my innocence," and, "I did not administer poison to anyone."

Monk sentences her to life plus twenty years.

In September, Alabama state lab scientists find no arsenic in the exhumed body of an eleven-year-old girl, a former playmate of Carol's, thought to be another possible victim of Hilley's. And in December 1985, the Alabama Supreme Court turns down Hilley's bid for a new trial on the claim that evidence used against her resulted from an improper search.

But the strange story doesn't end there. On February 19, 1987, Hilley is granted a three-day furlough from Julia Tutwiler Prison for Women in Wetumpka, Alabama, under the sponsorship of her husband, John Homan. Despite Hilley's previous record, it's the prison's policy to grant temporary leave to inmates who've been in prison at least six months and followed all the rules. Warden Hare says she's been let out on eight-hour passes before and always came back when she was supposed to.

Two and a half days into her leave, Homan contacts police and tells them she's (guess what?) disappeared. She left him a note saying she would not return to prison and was being helped to flee to Canada by a friend named Walter. She hoped he would understand and try to forgive her.

A possible sighting outside Alabama brings the FBI into the search. But the next time she's seen is on February 26, when she's found in a driving rainstorm on the back porch of a house less than a mile from her place of birth, shivering, soaked, muddy, and speaking incoherently. A nearby resident sees her and calls the police. On the way to the hospital, she dies. Cause of death: hypothermia and exposure. She was fifty-three years of age. Eight years after I wrote it, my fugitive assessment proves accurate.

"It's the end to a truly long and fascinating story," Joe Hubbard commented when told the news.

What was Audrey Hilley's motive? Was it greed, anger, a combination of the two, or something else altogether? Looking back on the case, I think you have to factor in her psychopathic personality as well as some probable mental illness. Certainly she was motivated by money in the successful attempt on her husband's life and the unsuccessful one on her daughter's, and certainly she had a fair amount of anger and rage, which also drove her to these seemingly unimaginable acts.

But I think that may be too simple an explanation in Hilley's case. Looking at her background and personality, and contrasting them with her life situation—married young and resentful of being saddled with a husband and family she really didn't want—I think she was motivated by a yearning for emancipation and a kind of free lifestyle that she could never have with Frank. I base this at least partially on the fact that even though she seemed to love John Homan, she left him, too, before long, and even went so far as to fake her own death to maintain her freewheeling style—to deceive both him and the authorities who were still on her trail. She needed to remain in control. As I say, we see this a fair amount in men, not too often in women.

As she got older, as her world grew farther and farther from what she wanted it to be, she may have grown weary of the effort it took to maintain this control and one-upmanship over the authorities and everyone else in her life. Even if she could evade all the people looking for her this time, she was now in her fifties, her hard life was catching up with her, and it wouldn't have been as easy to charm, seduce, and fool a new set of people as she'd done before in New Hampshire and Vermont. But still, she wasn't going back to prison; she wouldn't give the law that satisfaction. She would keep controlling things until the end—an end, I have to think, she chose for herself.

In October of 1988, Peggy Carr, a forty-one-year-old waitress in the central Florida town of Alturas, starts feeling sick. She goes to the hospital, but then recovers and they send her home. But then she gets sick and is hospitalized again. She has chest pains, severe nausea, tingling in her extremities. The symptoms keep getting worse; her hair falls out in clumps and she says she feels like she's on fire. Then her seventeen-year-old son, Duane Dubberly, and sixteen-year-old stepson, Travis Carr, also get sick, with the same complaints. Duane drops from 175 to 92 pounds. The doctors are baffled. Peggy's husband, Parearlyn, a miner known as Pye, looks on helplessly as his wife and the children suffer. Within a few weeks, Peggy lapses into a coma. Peggy's daughter, Cissy, herself the mother of a two-year-old daughter, is suspicious that maybe Pye poisoned Peggy. The two boys eventually recover, but Peggy lingers in the coma.

Doctors do every kind of examination and toxicological screen they can think of. Possibly this is lead, mercury, or arsenic poisoning. But when he factors in the hair falling out in clumps, one doctor considers the possibility of thallium, and a tox screen shows Peggy's urine to have a level twenty thousand times above normal! The two boys are also tested and come up positive. So do Pye and the other kids. Thallium was widely used as an insect and rat poison, but had been banned by the EPA since 1972.

A full-scale criminal and epidemiological investigation is launched. More than 450 items in the Carr home are tested. Finally, investigators come up with the answer: tainted bottles of Coca-Cola. But who? And why?

There is no life insurance in the family or any other source of financial gain to be had from Peggy's or the children's deaths, so the profit motive seems remote. Pye arouses initial suspicion, as the spouse always does. He was out hunting the day Peggy first took ill; they'd been arguing; and in fact, Peggy had moved out of the house for a while before all this began. And he'd been slow to take her to the hospital, at first thinking she wasn't too sick. On the other hand, everyone says what a terrific guy he is, he's known to love all his children, and he had elevated thallium levels in his own system. And there are no other reports of tampering with Coke in this region. The only people affected are in this one household. It seems to be a motiveless crime. And a particularly cruel and heartless one, because if it is not a random product tampering like the Tylenol case, then the UNSUB is consciously targeting not only adults and teens, but very young children as well.

But there is one possible clue. Several months before Peggy started getting sick, the family received a threatening note, typed on a yellow Post-it. It said, "You and your so-called family have two weeks to move out of Florida forever or else you all die. This is no joke."

Whoever sent the threat to Pye Carr had addressed it to the town of Bartow, rather than Alturas, which was actually the proper way to do it if the recipient had a mailbox at home, which the Carrs did. But only someone familiar with the area's mail system would know about this. When police question him, Pye mentions clashes between his family and the next-door neighbors, forty-two-year-old George James Trepal and his forty-one-year-old wife, Diana Carr (no relation to Pye and Peggy). None of the incidents had been very serious in Pye's judgment: arguments about loud music and the like—normal neighbor conflicts. But then he recalls that after Trepal complained about Carr's two Rhodesian ridgebacks chasing his cats, both dogs suddenly got sick and died. And just two days before Peggy began feeling ill, she and Diana had another argument over her sons' music blaring from the speakers of their truck while they were washing it. That one was heated enough that Diana threatened to call the police and Peggy finally ordered the other woman to get off her property.

The Trepals' house is surrounded by orange groves; they like their privacy. Polk County homicide investigator Ernie Mincey goes over to interview George Trepal, and he's not reassured. Trepal, who is short, bearded, and rather round, soft, and unkempt, tells him that someone in the community of six hundred wanted the Carrs to move away, and he sounds a lot like the threatening note, which was never made public. Mincey checks Trepal out further and discovers that a number of things he told him are not true, such as that he knew nothing about thallium. In fact, Trepal was arrested in 1975 and served two and a half years in Danbury Prison in Connecticut for working as a chemist for a large and illegal methamphetamine manufacturer—and thallium is used in the production of speed. While in prison, Trepal continually complained to corrections officials about the noise of other inmates' radios.

There's more. George Trepal and Diana Carr are proud of

their membership in Mensa, the elite society for brilliant people. To qualify, you have to score in the upper second percentile on IQ tests. Most of their socializing is with others in the Polk County chapter. They consider themselves intellectually diametrically opposite of the Carrs. There's no question that they're extremely bright. Not only is George trained as a chemist and now works on his own as a computer programmer, Diana is an orthopedic surgeon who also has a master of science degree and another master's in clinical pathology. In fact, they met at a Mensa meeting in Augusta, Georgia, where Diana was doing her residency. Since then, they've participated in Mensa "murder weekends," where they planned and acted out the perfect crime. At one such event, George prepared a handout that included these lines: "When a death threat appears on the doorstep prudent people throw out all their food and watch what they eat. . . . Most items on the doorstep are just a neighbor's way of saying, 'I don't like you. Move or else!'"

Ironically, George's father was a New York City police officer who switched careers and opened a TV and radio repair shop in North Carolina when the family moved there shortly after George's birth in 1949. George was essentially raised by his mother, Mabel, who wouldn't let anyone, including her husband, take care of him. She wouldn't let him get into fights, and when anything went wrong for him, she would always take care of it.

But tantalizing as all this may be, it doesn't add up to murder. Where's the motive? You don't kill your neighbors because they play their music too loud, particularly if you have a genius IQ. So Trepal is a suspect, but he's not a good suspect. The cops have got to find someone with a real reason to kill Peggy Carr and her family.

Meanwhile, the FBI has been called in to consult. The Lakeland, Florida, Resident Agency has referred it to the Tampa Field Office, where it's being coordinated by Special Agent Jana Monroe. (Jana, a former police officer and homicide detective in California, before long would come to Quantico to be a profiler in my unit, where she would stay until she went back to California as a squad supervisor in the San Diego Field Office.) Jana has researched the case extensively, including all aspects of thallium poisoning, and is planning a proactive investigative strategy with Ernie Mincey.

She refers the case to us at Quantico. Bill Hagmaier (who would go on to become chief of the new Child Abduction and Serial Crimes Unit after I retired) is the special agent in my unit with territorial responsibility for Florida, so he works up a profile on what kind of personality and behavior we should expect from this kind of poisoner-murderer. Bill states that this type of individual is not going to confront conflict directly; he'll be too cowardly for that. He'll try to settle his scores more through cleverness than by force.

Bill also says that someone who uses this type of deadly but rare and slow-acting poison is going to be very intelligent, clever, and organized. The offender would have had reason to believe that by the time the crime was discovered, the evidence—the Coke bottles—would already be out of the house. Just by luck, one of the bottles was still there when the epidemiological search was conducted. The fact that the UNSUB poisoned an eight-pack rather than one of the large two-liter plastic bottles the Carrs also had in the kitchen is significant. This guy is showing us he's up to the challenge. Despite the motive problem, all of this is pointing to George Trepal. He would be the type to be arrogant and think he's smart enough that he can do whatever he wants and get away with it. Hence, the overt reference at the Mensa meeting to poisoning one's neighbors as a way of saying, Get the hell out.

You won't have any luck confronting him, Bill advises Mincey.

You've got to get at him in a way he won't find threatening. On the phone, the two men and Jana talk about sending someone in undercover. At first, they consider her. Jana's done undercover work before and she's quite good at it, but they conclude that Trepal would be too smart to believe that a very attractive, intelligent, and glamorous blond like her would be attracted to a slovenly schlepp like him.

Around this time, it becomes clear that there is no medical hope for Peggy. The Carr family decides to turn off the machines artificially keeping her alive. She passes away on March 3, 1989. Now Ernie Mincey is handling a murder case. He calls in Susan Goreck, a detective with the sheriff's department, in her mid-thirties, who also has extensive experience working undercover and is highly intelligent, so she'll fit in in the Mensa environment. She poses as Sherry Guin, a woman from Houston extricating herself from a marriage to an abusive husband. Bill Hagmaier coaches her by phone on what to expect from George Trepal.

She meets Trepal and his wife at a Mensa murder weekend in April 1989, and the three of them really hit it off. Since Diana works such long hours, George and "Sherry" start spending a lot of time together. She plays to his intellectual pride and vanity, encouraging him to brag about his exploits. Goreck tries to be very careful. If they're eating in a restaurant, for example, and she gets up to go to the bathroom, she doesn't touch anything else on her plate when she gets back to the table. After observing the couple for some time, Goreck becomes convinced that it is, in fact, George rather than Diana who planned and carried out the poisonings. Diana is too dominant and assertive; George is the recessive one. He's the one who conforms to Hagmaier's profile. In fact, they eventually learn how closely he does conform. He never went out with girls growing up and, though brilliant, was an underachiever in school. Diana, on the other hand, is much more direct and to the point. If Diana were going to try to harm someone, she wouldn't hide behind a poisoning scheme.

George gives Sherry tips on how to get back at her soon-to-be-ex-husband, which include blackmail, lodging false child molestation charges against him, and sending threatening letters to the president over his forged signature. During a visit to the Audubon Nature Center, George picks some berries he says are poisonous, gives them to her, and tells her that three can kill a person. But as for direct confrontation, he's predictably a coward. At one point, another undercover agent is sent in, pretending to be Sherry's abusive husband. He and Sherry get into a potentially violent argument in front of Trepal in an airport, and Trepal backs off in fear, getting the hell out of there as soon as he can.

In December, George Trepal and Diana Carr move to Sebring, Florida, where she is going to begin a new medical practice. They rent their home to Goreck. When she and other investigators look around the house, they find thallium nitrate in the garage.

It takes almost a year to get a search warrant, but when police and the FBI finally examine the Trepal home in Sebring, they find, among other items, a supply of thallium, books on poison, including a well-worn text labeled "General Poisoning Guide" in George's handwriting, and an Agatha Christie novel titled *The Pale Horse,* about a pharmacist who kills by poisoning food and medicine with thallium. In the basement of the Sebring home, they discover a secret chamber with handcuffs and other bondage equipment, such as whips and a platform with stirrups attached. In this room investigators find books with titles such as *Whipped Women* and *Studies in Sadomasochism,* a magazine called *Advanced Bondage,* and pornographic videos about torture and murder. In the VCR is that modern classic, *Ilsa, She Wolf of the SS.*

Equally interesting is a set of journals Susan Goreck finds in a box in the house. Written by George about himself in the second person, they describe a withdrawn child with a rich fantasy life but constant feelings of isolation and outsider status. They go on to describe his feelings about women, sadomasochism, relationships that didn't work out, and repeated drug use.

The cops come to arrest George Trepal. He is meek and cooperative, but Diana is defiant and belligerent, trying to block their entrance to the house. George is brought in and charged with Peggy Carr's first-degree murder, six counts of attempted first-degree murder, seven counts of poisoning with intent to kill, and one count of tampering with a consumer product. Diana is not charged. George maintains his innocence throughout the trial, but in the end, he's found guilty on all fifteen charges. On March 6, 1991, just over two years after Peggy Carr's death, Circuit Court judge Dennis Maloney sentences him to death in the Florida electric chair upon recommendation of the jury. The defense didn't present character witnesses at Trepal's sentencing hearing, possibly because they knew or suspected that prosecutor John Aguero was ready with evidence from the secret basement room in Sebring of the hidden side of the mild-mannered, bespectacled defendant's life.

Susan Goreck, who got to know George Trepal as well as anyone in law enforcement, said that he had a real disdain for people who weren't as intelligent as he was. She believed that the murder and attempted murders were carried out not so much out of rage or hatred of the Carrs as out of contempt for them, and arrogance, and for the sheer intellectual satisfaction of winning the game against them.

A fellow prison inmate reported that he'd accidentally folded the cover on a dictionary he'd borrowed from Trepal, who then told him that people like him "should be put to death." How's that for motive?

One final note: it has been reported by one of Trepal's friends that he finds his time on death row "boring" because "there aren't a lot of interesting people to talk to." Oh well, if the justice system takes its course in a timely manner, maybe he won't have to deal with that burden too much longer.

None of us is completely safe from the kinds of crimes we've been examining in this chapter. Jud Ray, who went on to distinguish himself as one of the outstanding members of the Investigative Support Unit and is now the chief of the International Training and Assistance Unit at Quantico, was a new special agent in his first assignment, in the Atlanta Field Office in 1981. But he was far from a novice in law enforcement. Before joining the Bureau, this Vietnam combat veteran had been a police officer and shift commander with the Columbus, Georgia, Police Department, where I first got to know him during the Forces of Evil murder case, recounted in *Mindhunter*. A few years later, we worked together briefly on ATKID—the Atlanta child murders. I say briefly because Jud had to leave the case. He almost left this world.

He was having severe marital problems, and he had given his wife an ultimatum: either stop verbally abusing him, drinking heavily, and acting erratically, or he was going to take their two young daughters and leave.

Things did improve for a while. She treated him better and even started making dinner regularly. Then she hired two guys to have him killed. Jud was severely wounded, near death. He spent weeks in the hospital and gradually, when he was well enough, solved his own case, sending his wife (who'd taken out a sizable insurance policy on him) and the shooters to prison.

But when he started reviewing things in his own mind, Jud realized in retrospect that the ambush in his bedroom was the second attempt on his life. Before taking such decisive action, she had tried gradually to poison his food.

It suddenly dawned on him that he had been telling her all the interesting details of a fascinating case he'd been briefed on by this guy John Douglas up in Quantico, whom he'd taken courses from and worked with on other cases—about a fugitive poison murderer by the name of Audrey Marie Hilley.

# CHAPTER FIVE

# GUYS WHO SNAP

A couple of years before I retired from the Bureau, I got a call from the assistant director at Quantico, who wanted to put me in touch with a former SAC who was now the head of security for a major industrial corporation. The guy had an internal problem he wanted us to consult on.

"What's the problem?" I asked.

"Someone's pissing in the window cleaner bottles—you know, like Windex bottles."

"What?" Was I hearing him right? "I don't have time for this," I say. "I've got a million cases down here. I'm busy."

"John, he's a very nice guy. Just give him a call."

So I called the guy and tried to be serious about this. He had nothing to send me, so I asked him to just give me the facts.

"Well, in our computer room the machines are very sensitive. We have workers—both men and women—they wear white coats and they're responsible for keeping the machines clean themselves. Someone has been urinating into these spray bottles. Everyone on the shift is really—".

"Pissed off? I can understand that. How long has it been going on?"

"About a month. And it's always on the same shift. We have three shifts a day. Not all the bottles—usually like one a shift."

I said, "I think I can come up with something here. Take it from the beginning. What's going on with the company? Is there anything going on with the unit? What about the particular shift? The fact that it's always the same shift has to tell you something right away. How many people are there?"

"At any given time, there's like forty people on the floor."

"Could any one of them have access to the bottles?"

"Yes. All the bottles are kept out on a tray." That meant that one bottle was not assigned to a given machine or worker, so whoever was contaminating a bottle would have no way of predicting who was going to end up using it.

I told him that this is a symbolic, indiscriminate act. He's not saying, "Piss on you, Joe or Jane." He's saying, "Piss on everybody." He's trying to cause chaos and disruption among the entire group. Then we went through the specifics. I questioned him about how the urine might have gotten into the bottles. There were restrooms right off the main floor, and it would be easy to carry a bottle in under a lab coat.

The first thing I did was eliminate the women as suspects. It wouldn't be impossible for them to target a Windex-type bottle, but it would be a lot harder physically than for a man. If a woman was going to do this, she'd come up with some means that was easier for her than a narrow-necked bottle.

"From here on it should be pretty easy," I said. In a situation like this, I didn't spend any time on the traditional profile elements (white male, thirties, dropped out of high school, no girlfriends, conflict with parents, that sort of thing), because it didn't matter. What mattered here was motive, and the behavior that would lead to this sort of offense and then give the perpetrator away.

"Is there anyone on the floor who's wanted off this shift, who's been angry with everyone and isolated himself? He's probably filed complaints or written letters and he feels that no one has paid any attention. You may have seen a personality change. He's living alone, his social life isn't going well, or he's got marital or financial problems. And most important, he'll be the one complaining most about the piss in the bottles; all the more reason he should be allowed off this shift."

And it was like a lightbulb went off. "Yeah, there is one guy. . . ."

I suggested that they bring him in for a "routine" interview, one-on-one, where the supervisor would be supportive, recognizing the strain he might be under, and tell him how they were trying to get him off the shift, which was true—there just hadn't been any other openings.

They brought this guy in and questioned him. He was in his thirties, and he had been writing letters. Unbeknownst to anyone at the company, he was having marital problems. He was no longer living with his wife and had gone home to live with his parents. He felt that everything in his life was crumbling. Eventually, after finally getting all this off his chest to a sympathetic listener, he admitted that he was the anonymous pisser.

Like the cases in the last chapter, this would qualify as a sabotage and product tampering. Fortunately, it was not nearly as serious—no one's life was ever in danger, and it was so basic that it was a very easy case to solve if you kept your eye on the motive. *Why* is this happening? *Who* is the victim? It's not for money. It's not extortion. It's a nuisance crime. Someone is angry enough to do something harassing and disgusting, but not violent. What is this telling us?

Was this one ever a real threat? I don't think so. But could something like this evolve or escalate into one? Well, maybe.

What if the company isn't supportive of his emotional problems? What if they don't even recognize them? And what are you going to do with him? Are you going to reward negative behavior by giving him the new job he wants?

Okay, so you don't give him a new position and you just tell the supervisor to keep monitoring him. Is he always sitting by himself at lunch? Is he reading *Soldier of Fortune* or gun magazines at his desk? Does someone overhear him saying, "One day I'm going to get those bastards"?

Or, the other alternative, you fire him right after you solve the pissing case. You escort him to his car and kick his ass right out. And maybe his parents are getting tired of him sitting around the house. His wife doesn't want him back, he's having trouble seeing his kids. Now we've entered the danger zone.

But how do you monitor the guy in this situation? The head of the company can't assign someone to tail him and see if he's abusing alcohol or drugs or if his life is falling apart around him. His motive remains the same. But at what point does he start feeling he's got nothing left to lose? The outburst could come months, or even years, later.

Violence in and around the workplace has become a major and frightening factor in society today. The only thing you can do here is have good, alert security and keep up a list of people who you feel might have reason to cause trouble. Make the security staff aware of them and have procedures in place to deal with it if a potentially dangerous former employee enters the premises.

And as we shall see, there are a lot more dangers resulting from guys who snap, many of them far more serious than peeing in a bottle: situations that suddenly become deadly if they're not recognized ahead of time and defused. But like that simple case, we use motivation and behavior to get to the bottom of them.

On Monday, December 7, 1987, at 4:16 in the afternoon, Pacific Southwest Airlines flight 1771 from Los Angeles to San Francisco slammed into a hillside along California's central coast near San Luis Obispo, killing all forty-three passengers and crew members aboard. Among the dead were James Sylla, president of Chevron USA, California's largest corporation, and Wolfgang Studemann, an astrophysicist at Germany's famed Max Planck Institute and one of the world's leading authorities on comets. Also on the plane was Kathleen Mika, assistant director of alumni programs at the University of Southern California, who was planning the upcoming Rose Bowl parade.

The crash impact was so intense that twenty-seven of the victims could not be individually identified, and so when time came for burial, they were placed in vaults buried in a single plot with a marker listing all their names.

But this airline crash was even more upsetting than most. Only a few minutes before the four-engine British Aerospace BAe-146 jetliner disappeared from the radar screen—just as it should have been descending from its 22,000-foot altitude for its scheduled 4:43 landing at SFO—air traffic controllers in Oakland heard pilot Gregg N. Lindamood report gunshots in the passenger cabin. The badly damaged flight recorder told National Transportation Safety Board investigators even more: an intruder had entered the cockpit, fired additional shots, and then the plane rapidly accelerated downward.

Who could have done this? And why?

The critical clue was found among the debris scattered over the hill and twenty acres of surrounding countryside—a scorched and crumpled air sickness bag with the following message scrawled across it: "Hi Ray, I think it's sort of ironical that we end up like this. I asked for some leniency for my family, remember. Well, I got none and you'll get none."

Without the note, the investigation would have had to begin at square one, with a systematic victimology of everyone on the flight's manifest. But with this piece of evidence, the FBI was quickly able to determine that "Ray" was Raymond F. Thomson, forty-eight years of age, the LAX manager of customer services for USAir, parent company for Pacific Southwest commuter airline. The author of the note, verified by handwriting exemplars, was David Augustus Burke, thirty-five, a passenger services rep with the airline, also at LAX. Thomson had been his supervisor. A bent and broken Smith & Wesson .44 magnum was found in the debris field and the fingerprints on a hand discovered in the cockpit wreckage matched Burke's. A friend and fellow USAir employee in San Francisco, Joseph Drabik, identified the weapon and confirmed that he had lent it to Burke along with a box of twelve shells.

The FBI believed that Burke first shot Thomson at point-blank range and then made his way into the cockpit.

The Bureau's affidavit, filed in U.S. District Court, stated, "There is evidence to believe that David Burke was involved in the destruction of PSA Flight 1771."

Richard Breitzing, SAC of the FBI's Los Angeles Field Office, who had put more than thirty agents on the case, was more direct when he told the *Chicago Tribune,* "If he were alive, we would charge him with air piracy and murder."

The psychological autopsy began.

David Burke was born in England in 1952, one of five children of Altamont and Iris Burke, both immigrants from Jamaica. When he was a young child, the family moved to Rochester, New York, where Altamont went into the construction business as a heavy-equipment operator. David grew up there, apparently a pretty average kid. In 1973, he went to work for USAir as a baggage handler at the Rochester airport, progressing steadily to customer service rep and then supervisor.

From most reports, he was just the kind of agent you'd want to deal with, always going out of his way to take care of customers and make sure they got where they wanted to go. On many occasions, he would take over for another agent and solve difficult ticketing and transfer problems. Not only that, he never forgot where he came from, and was always trying to help others, particularly blacks and other minorities like himself, to get jobs with the airline and at the airport.

Burke was stocky and handsome. He was a well-known and popular figure in Rochester's growing Jamaican community, where his expensive suits, flashy jewelry, and champagne-gold-colored Mercedes with the license plate REGGAE were in sharp contrast to what most of the underemployed immigrants could afford. No one resented him, however, because he was generous and always more than willing to do whatever he could for anyone else. And the neighbors in his predominantly white, upper-middle-class suburb southwest of the city described him as a real nice, quiet guy.

Yet there was apparently another side to Burke. He was not actually married to the woman he lived with in the Rochester area and called his wife, and he had at least seven children by at least four different women. The woman he lived with refused to marry him when he would not promise to be faithful. From all reports, the greatest trauma of his life was the heroin overdose of his brother Joey in 1980. David had been trying desperately to help him, and told others he felt responsible for his beloved brother's death. The only thing David was ever convicted of was a charge of shoplifting a package of meat in 1984. He pled guilty and got probation. But there were always rumors and questions about how he lived such a lavish lifestyle on his $32,000-a-year airline salary. A two-year investigation pointed to his being a key player in smuggling large quantities of Jamaican cocaine and marijuana into Rochester, by way of Miami. When undercover agents tried to nab him for cocaine dealing, he stopped the investigation cold when he figured out who they were and casually said, "How ya doing, Officer?"

And there were other allegations—that Burke was involved with a Mercedes-Benz auto theft ring and that he sold USAir tickets to friends at low prices. None of these charges was proven, though the Monroe County District Attorney's Office believed they were the reason he suddenly left Rochester after working there for fourteen years and went to Southern California, even though it meant taking a demotion and pay cut from the job he loved. After several months on the job out there he filed a complaint with the California Department of Fair Employment and Housing, claiming that Raymond Thomson had promoted over him two whites with less experience.

Despite his normally easygoing and helpful personality, he was also reported to have a disturbing temper. Jacqueline Camacho, a USAir ticket agent and Burke's girlfriend in Los Angeles, let him live with her and her daughter for a while in her place in Hawthorne, but after his promotion was denied, the relationship began rapidly deteriorating. During one argument, Camacho told police, he dragged her from her bed, choked her, and nearly strangled her. Camacho obtained a court order preventing him from coming near her. He brought his teenage daughter Sabrina out to live with him in California after she began having problems at home, but neighbors reported violent clashes in which Burke screamed at her for long periods of time, calling her a "little slut" and a "whore." The neighbors believed they could also hear him hitting the sobbing girl. But when he emerged from the condo, he was all smiles.

We always look for a precipitating stressor as motivation for any crime like this, and the FBI investigators found one in their interviews with airline officials. On November 19, eighteen days before the crash, Ray Thomson fired Burke after a surveillance camera recorded him taking $69 in cash that had been collected for cocktails on a flight that had recently landed. USAir security took Burke to LAPD's Pacific Division station, where he was booked and released on his own recognizance. On December 1, prosecutors decided to drop the charges, thinking it would be a difficult case to make based on the content of the surveillance tape. But Thomson, known as a straight arrow and tough manager, would not take him back, despite several visits and pleas from Burke. The last visit was only hours before the two men boarded the plane.

As an airline employee well known to the personnel at LAX, Burke had no trouble getting the large gun past security. All he had to do was go in back of the ticket desks and take the direct passage down to the plane. Thomson worked in Los Angeles, but his home was in Tiburon, just over the Golden Gate Bridge from San Francisco, so he returned there as often as he could. When Burke learned which flight Thomson would be on, he paid cash for a one-way ticket on the same plane.

That same day, Burke left a message on Camacho's answering machine saying that he loved her. In his condominium in Long Beach, agents found a recently revised will and new insurance policies.

"I don't know," said Burke's longtime friend Owen Phillips when he heard about what had happened. "Maybe he just snapped."

This is an extremely sad and tragic story on many levels. David Burke was not an inherently evil person in the way that many of the sadists and sexual predators I have hunted are evil. But the destruction of PSA flight 1771 is what can happen when you combine a volatile personality with some powerful stressors, easy access to a weapon and even easier access to a target, and the people in charge don't recognize a dangerous situation ahead of time and act to defuse it. As a result, a lot of innocent people died. This is not a question of blaming the victims. I never do that. But as I counsel individuals who have to place themselves in potentially dangerous situations, increased risk requires increased vigilance.

Where were there chances to prevent this tragedy? When David Burke first started displaying violent behavior. When he came back repeatedly to Thomson asking for his job. When he asked a friend to borrow a powerful handgun and shells. When he was allowed through airport security because he was recognized. And there were probably others.

But was it predictable that David Burke's motive for revenge would be so strong that he would take his own life and the lives of however many passengers were on the plane? In retrospect, maybe, but unless someone makes overt threats, this is very difficult to anticipate. That's why you have to have a *general* policy of being prepared to deal with these situations; you're probably not going to be aware or precise enough to pick out the one that might blow.

So, how do we attempt to implement this? We can't track or intensely monitor every seemingly frustrated, unhappy employee or coworker. In other words, how do we assess danger, determine who is merely pissed off, and who is so motivated by anger he doesn't even think about all the innocent people he's going to take out with him?

Simply put, we have to look at the behavior.

As a rule, people on the job are not going to want to sit down with you, their supervisor, and discuss intimate details of their personal lives, even if you were willing to take the time and make the effort to do so. So we all have to train ourselves to observe behavior.

What is this person's normal behavior? Is that what we're seeing? Have there been changes? Is he suddenly becoming obsessively religious after having been unobservant in the past? Was he a social drinker who is now either displaying signs of inebriation or, alternately, criticizing others who are drinking or not going to church? Is he complaining about others in a way he never did before? Is he obviously eating more or eating less?

Is there a change of pattern?

In the early 1980s, when I went into a coma and nearly died while working the Green River case in Washington, I came to realize that I had no balance in my life. I worked very hard, but I was neglecting my family, my health, my faith, just about everything else. I was essentially working by myself in those days, and the few other people who were doing some profiling, such as Roy Hazelwood, had their hands full with their own cases and teaching loads. So there was no one at work who could take me aside and say, "John, are you all right? You look like you're having some problems." My wife, Pam, and my parents knew what I was going through, but since they couldn't actually experience it the way a colleague could, I wouldn't listen to them in the same way.

Fortunately, I got the wake-up call, as severe and intense as it was, that told me I had to start putting things more in balance. But this is what you're looking for—someone whose life is no longer in balance.

Then someone has to take responsibility. If you are the boss and something seems radically wrong or different, you have to make meaningful contact with this individual. You can't go to the police unless there's some overt threat, but you can try to help, try to ameliorate his problem, and you can notify others in the organization to watch for potential trouble. This is not foolproof. All you can do is be alert and try to cut down the odds.

One former SAC was a well-respected and very tough figure in the FBI who served in several senior positions during his career. He was one of the few higher-ups who always believed in and supported the profiling and criminal investigative analysis programs, and I considered him a great Bureau resource. When he retired, he went to work as an executive at a major airline. We ran into each other about a year or so later at the retirement dinner for the head of the Secret Service and exchanged all the normal greetings.

"John, how are you doing?"

I said, "Fine, how are you doing?"

"Oh, it's great. You know, life after the Bureau . . ."

"What's it like?" I asked.

"You know, at the Bureau we had to deal with all this personnel bullshit," he said, "but here at the airline, you have someone who's not doing a good job, you call them into your office, you have security come and escort him out, scrape the sticker off his car, and say, 'Adios.'"

It sounded good to me.

A couple of years later, he calls me and he's singing a different tune. The airline is reorganizing to stay competitive and is in the process of laying off thousands of employees, which they haven't had to do before. He's been handling threats; specifically, people have been trying to sabotage the air-conditioning system that services the computers, and he's got all kinds of things to address. He tells me he wants to come to Quantico and discuss them with me and the unit.

We had a conference with him and basically told him the airline would have to handle the issue from both a security and a human resources point of view. We gave him some ideas about how to force the UNSUB or UNSUBs into the open if the threats escalated. But the main thrust had to be working with the people affected by the layoffs and letting them know the company cared about them and would try to do something for them.

Because of all his FBI management experience and his own sophistication, this individual could deal with problems like this about as well as anyone. He was able to get the airline to take his suggestions, and serious trouble was avoided. But what this underscores is that you've always got to be prepared, not just when the shit hits the fan—because the main problem my former colleague was facing was the sheer number of possible suspects. If, God forbid, something really serious or life-threatening had occurred, it would have been a far harder case to solve than, say, David Burke's.

I refer to this proactive approach as doing "psychological preventive maintenance."

In the past, there has been a tendency in many companies to deal with a potential employee behavioral problem by getting rid of it—if not through firing, then by trying to transfer the individual out or make it the task of some other department, like personnel. An encouraging trend I am seeing today, and I hope it continues, is to give all managers or supervisors in a company the kind of training and guidance they will need to recognize a potential behavioral issue and know how to deal with it. Unlike some of the crimes we've talked about earlier, workplace violence is not the kind of thing where you're going to be able to look at a young kid or teenager and say, One day he's going to come into work with an AK-47 and wipe out all the other employees.

This is often a fine line that managers have to walk. If you appear to invade someone's privacy, that person may sue you. If you don't do anything and then the individual goes bad, you or the company could be sued for not taking proper precautions. Sometimes it seems like a no-win situation. One of the best and most effective things a company can do, particularly a large company, is to have the resources available where people can go and seek help; they should know it's there for them and that it will not be held against them if they take advantage of the service.

We're all familiar with the horrifying incidents that have occurred involving "disgruntled" U.S. Postal Service workers and how some of them have had deadly consequences. In fact, in certain circles the phrase "going postal" has become the sick cliché for emotionally snapping and shooting up your workplace. In fact, the Postal Service has had a frightening recent history of on-the-job violence. Since 1986, thirty-five postal employees have been killed by their coworkers (who sometimes then killed themselves) in ten separate incidents. There's even a perverse video game out called *Postal*. (I don't have to tell you the object of play; you can easily guess.) But as troubling as these statistics are, the Postal Service isn't the only organization having to come to grips with this phenomenon of modern life. It just happens to be big and conspicuous, and deals with the kind of unrelenting volume and mechanization that highlight any problems brewing just beneath the surface.

About two years before I retired from the Bureau, some top Postal Service people came to meet with us in ISU and the Behavioral Science Unit at Quantico. We met in the office of John Henry Campbell, my opposite number on the training side.

They were genuinely frustrated, saying things like, "What can we possibly do? We're so big, we've got so much mail to handle, our people are responsible for processing X amount per hour, and it's so impersonal."

I said that at the very least they had to start giving the impression that they were doing something, that they cared and wanted to take care of their people; and that was the responsibility of their human resources unit. Additionally, I told them I thought they needed to have some kind of behavioral science unit of their own. On one basic level, it could be ass covering if something went wrong. But on a more positive level, the reality was that violence is always best dealt with before it reaches that intensity, if you can somehow nip it in the bud; and that meant training your people on how to do their own profiling and assessments.

One very encouraging and innovative program is being tried in southern Florida, where the Postal Service has brought in local law students to act as mediators between workers and management. Oftentimes they find that problems can be resolved simply by listening and caring. The point is, many issues can be resolved before they reach the critical level if the employee feels he has some recourse, if he feels he can get through to someone without having to make a dramatic public statement.

I always tried to be responsive in my own unit. If someone appeared to be having a problem, if he had isolated himself or otherwise broken his own behavioral pattern (as I discussed a little earlier), I would try to bring him into my office, sit him down one-on-one, and, without snooping, say, "Is everything okay? Can I do anything for you?"

I knew that all of my people, special agents and support staff alike, had highly stressful jobs. So I'd try to do whatever it took to make them as happy, comfortable, and effective as possible. Maybe that meant just lending an ear at the right time. Maybe it meant covering for them if they needed to take some time off. Maybe it meant letting them work at home for a while. Obviously, mail sorters can't do this. Neither can members of Quantico's Hostage Rescue Team, for that matter. But you try to do what you can. The point is, if any significant part of the employee's life is in chaos, at least there's someone letting him know he's getting some kind of support or understanding. I may not be able to solve the problem with his wife or child. I may not even be able to solve the problem he's having with his coworker or office mate. But I can't take the chance of ignoring him. That lesson has been driven home loud and clear.

Sometime around the mid-1980s I had a case out of Chicago. It was a big company, a bank. A threat had been made in the form of a note—and reported to the head of security—to the effect that "we're going to come into your goddamned lobby and blow up the whole goddamned place." There was something else in the note approximating, "You sons of bitches. Look how you're treating us!"

So, *Who?* and *Why?* I asked the bank's security guy what was going on in his company, and he told me about major layoffs. The note was typewritten and the style and word choice suggested someone with education. I concluded this was likely someone in middle management who was facing a layoff he never expected and who was really rocked by it. That basic profile represented most of the affected population, so it would be an incredibly large investigative task at this point to try to discover the UNSUB's identity. Sometimes a general proactive strategy is going to be more efficient.

I asked what the bank was doing about all the layoffs. He told me they weren't doing much; there wasn't a hell of a lot going on.

How were these people learning that they were losing their jobs? They found out when the interoffice mail was routed to them. Very frigging sensitive.

I said, "Is anyone talking to them afterward . . . following up?" No. Has the president or the chairman of the board spoken to them? Well, no; but as it happens, he's making a speech before all the employees today.

The president of this bank is not a people person. He gets up there in front of close to a thousand employees. But he's shy and taciturn. He doesn't even bring up the layoffs until people start raising their hands, and then he's not prepared to deal with it. He can't give these people the decent answer they're entitled to, and essentially he's booed off the stage.

So the security director calls me back after this, relates the incident, and says, "In light of this and the threatening note, what are the chances of this actually happening?"

I tell him the chances are very, very good. He asks what he should do. I say it's a two-prong approach that seems pretty clear to me. You'd better start showing these people you care and that you're trying to do something real and substantial to help them through the transition and secure other jobs. And in the meantime, while you're working on this, you'd better have security beefed up across the board, particularly in the lobby of your main branch.

As it turned out, they did implement these suggestions and nothing happened. But it easily could have. They got lucky. But it doesn't always work out that way, particularly when you've gotten behind the situation like this and you're trying to play catch-up.

This is terribly important because despite what some organizations are doing, the problem is getting worse, particularly if we define the workplace in broad terms. Probably the single most alarming trend we face today is the violence in our children's workplace—the school. And though there is no simple solution to what is an extremely complex problem, among the things we've got to do is just what I suggested for the Postal Service and the airline and the bank: we've got to educate the "managers" and "supervisors"—the teachers and principals and administrative staffs—to recognize the danger signals. When some kid makes a statement about shooting someone, don't just think he's playing games. We can't afford to ignore this.

And keep in mind that kids are even more impressionable than adults. If, as we discussed in Chapter Three, well-publicized crimes can give other criminally oriented individuals ideas on how to commit their own, what about children who watch the news and see other children shooting up their schoolyard or classroom? A badly adjusted child, motivated by anger and resentment, may see this act as the logical and dramatic solution to his own problems. He won't think about the horrible aftermath, the fact that his family will be devastated and he will spend years in confinement, destroying his own life. In fact, depending on his age and psychological makeup, he may not even think beyond the act itself. Just as the skyjackings of the 1960s and 1970s fed on one another, so do acts of school gun violence; and we're all left wringing our hands about how this could happen. We're not going to prevent all of them, but let's at least be sensitive to the warning signs, just as we must be in industry.

Those of us who study crime and criminals for a living know that crime evolves as time goes on, just as other trends and social phenomena do. Unfortunately, one of the ways violence in the schools is evolving is from kids beating up other kids on the playground to vent their anger to, instead, bringing guns to school, which, essentially, they use like toys. The horrific child-on-child killing in Jonesboro, Arkansas, in the early spring of 1998 was the fourth such shooting spree on school grounds in the United States in just a little over a year!

When the assistant principal of Pearl High School in Pearl, Mississippi, subdued the sixteen-year-old who had just killed two of his fellow students and wounded seven more, after having just stabbed his mother to death, he asked him, "Why, why, why?"

The student replied, "The world has wronged me, and I couldn't take it any longer."

Remember, the same triggers apply for poorly adjusted kids

as apply for poorly adjusted adults, including the precipitating stressors, such as relationship problems, problems at home
or the work environment (in their case, school). And those in
authority—parents, teachers, administrators, school psychologists,
and social workers—should be looking for many of the same red
flags, such as obsession with firearms, isolation in social situations, seemingly idle threats, or casual talk of murder. We can't assume that just because they're kids they won't commit adult-level
violence. Remember, we're dealing here with all the things we're
dealing with in violent adults, plus even poorer impulse control,
an even less sophisticated worldview, and the invincibility of youth.
As we've seen all too frequently recently, that's a dangerous combination.

In fact, there are many dangerous combinations, and even if
we understand the motive, we can't always anticipate them all, as
our next case demonstrates.

Around 9 A.M. on March 6, 1998, Matthew E. Beck, a
thirty-five-year-old accountant at the Newington, Connecticut,
headquarters of the state lottery, shot and/or stabbed a number of
his fellow employees, killing four. Beck, who had worked at the
lottery for eight years, then took his own life, shooting himself in
the head with the Glock nine-millimeter semiautomatic pistol he
had used in the rampage.

The first victim was Michael T. Logan, thirty-three years of
age, the director of information systems and Beck's former data
processing supervisor; he was shot twice and stabbed seven times
with a hunting knife in the abdomen and chest. Beck sustained a
leg wound during this assault and left a trail of blood from Logan's
office to where he found Linda A. Blogoslawski Mlynarczyk, the
lottery's thirty-eight-year-old chief financial officer. He reportedly
walked into the conference room where she was in a meeting and
said, "Say good-bye, Linda." She was shot multiple times and also

had defense wounds on her hands from the knife. It was her job to meet with Beck after his return from a recent stress-related leave of absence to discuss his responsibilities in the new job he was to hold. The night before the attack, she had confided her concerns to her husband.

Frederick "Rick" W. Rubelmann III, forty, vice president of operations and administration, was the next to die. He was shot four times—twice in the back as Beck chased him through the building, the last wound in his head. Rubelmann was hit as he tried to direct other employees out of the building to safety.

The fifty-four-year-old lottery president, Otho R. Brown, was shot in the buttocks as he fled across the parking lot. After this first wound took him down, Beck fired twice more as Brown lay bleeding on the ground, begging for his life. It was clear to several employees that Brown was attempting to divert Beck away from the building, and by doing this he probably saved at least several other lives.

Officers arrived on the scene within two minutes of numerous frantic 911 calls. As police confronted him, Beck put the gun up to his own head and pulled the trigger. He was medevaced by air to Hartford Hospital, where he died shortly after arrival.

The day before the shooting, Beck left a vague message for a reporter at the *Hartford Courant* newspaper, saying he wanted to talk that day, if possible, about "lottery issues."

Matthew Beck was unmarried and had moved in with his parents the previous September. He was described by friends as "an avid gun enthusiast." On an application for a state auditor's position, he said he'd been a security guard, had experience with firearms and "tactical response training and situational analysis." Beck had returned to work less than two weeks before the rampage, following a four-month leave of absence for stress. He was authorized to stay out an additional two months, but came back on his own.

Someone who had worked with Beck noted that he had recently lost weight and seemed more withdrawn than usual. Afterward, one colleague remembered him commenting in the days before the shootings how easy it would be to build a bomb just from what you could learn on the Internet. Other coworkers described him as disturbed when he got to the building that final morning, refusing to talk to anyone until the moment he stood up and walked toward the administrative offices, where he began his assault. He showed no emotion as he stalked and killed the supervisors who were involved in the seven-month process of addressing grievances he'd filed against the lottery.

These included complaints about other people being promoted over him, wanting a special orthopedic chair, and an environment that he felt thwarted his career growth and opportunities. The letters he wrote were described as calm and businesslike. He'd applied for jobs at Central Connecticut State University and the University of Connecticut Health Center, and also requested a transfer to the state Department of Special Revenue or the Department of Social Services. Karen Mehigen, the human resources director, informed him that they were trying to take care of all of his concerns, including finding him a chair that met his needs.

As far as I can tell from my study of the case, these people were already doing everything I would recommend (and have) that organizations do to protect themselves and minimize the risk of trouble.

Beck was on at least two medications prescribed for anxiety, depression, and obsessive-compulsive disorders, and was under psychiatric care. He had a history of mental illness and twice had been committed to an institution, once voluntarily following threats of suicide and an attempted drug overdose.

Donald Beck, Matthew's distraught father, sadly told the

*Hartford Courant* that saving his son then "might have been a mistake."

In a poignant and, I believe, very moving statement, Donald and his wife, Pricilla, shared with the public how they felt:

> What our son, Matt, did was wrong, terribly wrong. Nothing anyone can say can justify or condone his actions. In spite of the comfort of coworkers, the love and help from friends and family and the treatment, counseling and medications from his doctors, he chose the wrong path. A path of hopelessness when other avenues were open to him.
>
> Unfortunately and tragically, he decided to take others with him. His murderous act was monstrous, but he was not a monster, as his friends and family can attest. At this time of grief for many, we offer our sincerest sympathy to all the families and apologize for Matt. I cannot ask you to forgive him for we have not yet forgiven him for what he did.
>
> He failed his coworkers, his friends, his family and most of all, himself.
>
> We love you Matt—but why?

We'll never know all the whys of a tragedy like this. Some of them are forever locked in the mental illness with which Matthew Beck seemed to have struggled for much of his adult life. But by analyzing the crime itself, we can still begin to reach certain conclusions about his motive.

Unlike stalker Richard Wade Farley, who shot the object of his obsession, Laura Black, killed seven people indiscriminately, and wounded another four at her workplace; unlike Thomas Watt Hamilton, the butcher of the Dunblane schoolchildren; unlike the junior high and high school student shooters; unlike anyone who enters a place of work and just opens fire, Beck was highly selective in his targets. He killed four people who actually had been trying to help him. But by his logic, he targeted the people he thought were responsible for his difficulties at work. His motive was anger and the need for revenge against these specific people based on his own paranoia. A lot of these guys will depersonalize their targets. Matthew Beck evidently deeply personalized his grievances, and this was his way of dealing with them.

I wish I could end this case on a hopeful note, or at least with an enumeration of the concrete lessons to be learned from it. Unfortunately, I can't. I've often said that our struggle against crime has to be dealt with as a war, and just as in war, there are going to be civilian casualties. In this instance, it seems that the company was doing everything right but was dealing with someone too angry and, by most evaluations, too mentally ill to be receptive.

To minimize the number of lives lost, though, we have to try to learn more and figure out where and how we can make a difference, before the die is irretrievably cast, because ultimately, we're all vulnerable, and not just when we're on the job.

The workplace isn't the only one where guys snap.

On December 7, 1971, officers went to a large but poorly maintained old Victorian mansion on Hillside Avenue in Westfield, New Jersey, a suburb eleven miles southwest of Newark, after neighbors reported lights burning in the house both day and night for weeks on end. Through the window they could see a scene of horror. Several bodies lay on sleeping bags on the floor of the house's impressive ballroom. Patrolman George Zhelesnik got in through an open side window. As he moved toward the bodies, he heard what sounded like an organ playing a funeral dirge. It turned out to be a record set on automatic and sent through the house's loudspeaker system. The dead were all identified as members of the List family: Helen, forty-five years of age; her sixteen-year-old daughter, Patricia; and two sons, John Frederick, fifteen, and Frederick, thirteen. In addition to the neighbors' general concerns about the lights, what had motivated the police visit was the concern of Patricia's drama teacher when she just stopped showing up.

Mrs. List lay against one wall; her face was covered with a cloth. Her three children were lined up in a row, perpendicular to the body of their mother. And that wasn't all. When they searched the house, officers found the body of Helen List's eighty-four-year-old mother-in-law in a storage room on the third floor. Each was dead of gunshot wounds, apparently administered from behind.

Before the officers left, they already knew who their prime suspect was: the one missing member of the family, forty-six-year-old John Emil List.

The evidence consisted mainly of a series of letters that John List had meticulously written out, but never sent, to various people of significance to the List family's life, apologizing for and explaining what he had done. In addition, he had canceled the paper, stopped the milk delivery, informed the children's schools and part-time jobs that the family would have to be away for an extended emergency, and, it was soon discovered, withdrawn the remaining $2,289 from the family bank account.

His car was found abandoned at Kennedy Airport in Queens. The title and owner's identification cards were left inside. John List had disappeared . . . vanished, as they say, without a trace.

Had there not been the documentary evidence to support John List's involvement, the presentation of the crime scene still would have led us to conclude that the killer was a family member. The fact that the bodies were all laid out uniformly and placed in *sleeping bags* was a form of undoing, of placing the victims in a position of repose because the killer felt bad or uncomfortable about what he'd done. When we see a baby murdered, for example, if the body is just tossed into a Dumpster or left by the side of the road, the killer was probably a stranger. If, however, the child is wrapped up or otherwise "protected" and left in some orderly or dignified manner, then the killer was probably a parent or close relative.

If there was ever a case where one is absolutely compelled to ask, How, in the name of God, could a father and husband do such a thing? it is this one. And as it happened, one of the letters the investigating officers found detailed how, in the name of God, he did what he did. It was written by John List to his pastor at the Lutheran church he attended, Eugene Rehwinkel, and it spoke clearly and directly to motive.

> *Dear Pastor Rehwinkel:*
>
> *I am sorry to add this additional burden to your work. I know that what has been done is wrong from all that I have been taught and that any reasons that I might give will not make it right. But you are the one person that I know that while not condoning this will at least possibly understand why I felt that I had to do this.*
>
> *1. I wasn't earning anywhere near enough to support us. Everything I tried seemed to fall to pieces. True, we could have gone bankrupt and maybe gone on welfare.*
>
> *2. But that brings me to my next point. Knowing the type of location that one would have to live in, plus the environment for the children, plus the effect on them knowing they were on welfare was just more than I thought they could and should endure. I know they were willing to cut back, but this involved a lot more than that.*
>
> *3. With Pat being so determined to get into acting I was also fearful as to what that might do to her continuing to be Christian. I'm sure it wouldn't have helped.*

*4. Also, with Helen not going to church I knew that this would harm the children eventually in their attendance. I had continued to hope that she would begin to come to church soon. But when I mentioned to her that Mr. Jutze wanted to pay her an elder's call, she just blew up and said she wanted her name taken off the church rolls. Again this could only have an adverse result for the children's continued attendance.*

*So that is the sum of it. If any one of these had been the condition, we might have pulled through but this was just too much. At least I'm certain that all have gone to heaven now. If things had gone on who knows if this would be the case.*

*Of course, Mother got involved because doing what I did to my family would have been a tremendous shock to her at this age. Therefore, knowing that she is also a Christian I felt it best that she be relieved of the troubles of this world that would have hit her.*

*After it was all over I said some prayers for them all— from the hymn book. That was the least that I could do.*

*Now for the final arrangements:*

*Helen and the children have all agreed that they would prefer to be cremated. Please see to it that the costs are kept low.*

He goes on to give various practical instructions, such as where to bury his mother and whom to contact in the family, what to do with the remaining property. Then he gets back to what is always for these guys the most important subject—himself:

*As for me please let me be dropped from the congregation rolls. I leave myself in the hands of God's Justice and Mercy. I don't doubt that He is able to help us, but apparently He saw fit not to answer my prayers the way that I hoped they would be answered. This makes me think that perhaps it was for the best as far as the children's souls are concerned. I know that many will only look at the additional years that they could have lived, but if finally they were no longer Christians what would be gained.*

*Also I'm sure many will say, "How could anyone do such a horrible thing?"—My only answer is it isn't easy and was only done after much thought. . . .*

John got hurt more because he seemed to struggle longer. The rest were immediately out of pain. John didn't consciously feel anything either.

*Please remember me in your prayers. I will need them whether or not the government does its duty as it sees it. I'm only concerned with making my peace with God and of this I am assured because of Christ dying even for me.*

*P.S. Mother is in the hallway in the attic—3d floor. She was too heavy to move.*

*John*

Well, there you have it. Amazing, isn't it? A couple of notes may help clarify the situation.

List was an accountant, a CPA, seemingly a perfect profession for this timid, mild-mannered milquetoast of a man. He was apparently a very good one—he always knew where he stood with numbers; everything was either right or wrong, black or white. But he kept losing jobs. I could see a guy like this getting promoted to higher managerial positions, where he just couldn't hack it because of his peculiar personality. Reportedly, after List lost one job at a bank, he would spend the workday reading in the commuter train station rather than confess to his family that he'd been fired from another position. He had so little insight into his own professional weaknesses that he once took a job selling life insurance, even though people who knew him said he couldn't look another person in the eye. So that became another failure in his life.

He grew up an only child under the domination of a strict religious mother who, while not physically abusive, would not let him get dirty or do the things other boys did, and always made sure to keep him on the straight and narrow. His father was in his sixties when John was born and apparently didn't exert much of an influence. When John got to be a teenager, he was not allowed to dance. Even his mother Alma's own church pastor said she was being excessive. And that was the way John grew up. He was able to marry Helen Morris Taylor, a beautiful woman whose first husband, a dynamic man, the diametrical opposite of John, had been killed in the Korean War. They had one daughter. Helen also had syphilis—which John didn't know—apparently contracted from her first husband. The disease would grow progressively worse during the marriage, Helen would suffer from atrophy of the brain, which made her more and more mentally dysfunctional and alcoholic. List was afraid she had already had too much of a negative effect on the children. Patty wanted to become an actress. In John's religiously rigid, carefully ordered mind, that was the road to hell, or more likely, only one of many. He was also concerned that she had expressed interest in witchcraft and might have tried marijuana.

Even though Helen and Alma did not get along well with each other and John resented the strictness of his upbringing, Alma was living with them because she had supported them to the tune of about $200,000, which John had gone through in an attempt to make ends meet and support the large eighteen-room house that was so important for his self-image and public image.

Many, if not most, of the killers I've studied and interviewed have, while admitting their actions, found someone else to blame—a mother, a wife, a boss, a political conspiracy, society in general—whoever or whatever fits into their own emotional context. List's context—the way he saw himself and the world around him—was that of a proper, religious, God-fearing churchgoer, so when he decided to put the blame on someone else, that someone was God. According to the note, had God come across for him and answered his prayers, then none of this mess would have been necessary. John was trying to make us believe that he was only playing the cards he was dealt.

The real motive, I suggest, is that things got too messy and complicated and uncomfortable for him, and so he snapped. Here's a rigid, obsessive-compulsive type who needs all the numbers in his life to add up. The pressure cooker built up too much steam, and this was his way of removing the lid. He essentially admits that he didn't want to go bankrupt and live like a pauper, though he transfers this feeling onto his children, and the only way out is to start fresh. If that means shedding his family, well, okay then, best to send them off to heaven. It is as if he purged himself, then rationalized the act so that he could have another life.

I don't want to sound as if I'm making light of this, or that I minimize List's mental and emotional problems, because clearly, anyone who would wipe out his own family and even try to suggest that it was for their own good has a serious mental disturbance in addition to whatever character disorder psychiatrists might define in him. The important issue to people in my business, though, is whether this mental disturbance was such that it *compelled* this man who obviously knew the difference between right and wrong to kill his own family. And that's probably a question for which psychiatry wouldn't have a definitive answer.

But it is interesting and significant to note that John List was completely organized throughout this entire episode, including

his effectiveness at disappearing. A mentally unstable or delusional offender would be disorganized and leave a trail of evidence
that would lead to his being found. Not so John List. And as we
shall see shortly, this was not a mass execution. Each member of
his family was killed separately, at a different time and under a
different circumstance than the others.

If List really killed his family to send them to heaven but
did not kill himself because suicide would have prevented his
entering—though only God knows how he thought he could
wipe out his entire family and still earn a ticket of admission—
why didn't he just turn himself in to the police right afterward and
face the consequences? Why didn't he go to his pastor and speak
to him personally? Sometimes you will find these guys claiming
that they have sent their loved ones to heaven and that they have
remained on earth to suffer. But there certainly is no evidence
that List suffered after the murders, or that he intended to suffer
as he went forward in his new life, hiding from the authorities
hunting for him.

Even if he had decided to commit suicide, someone like this
probably still would have killed the rest of his family first. He was
so rigid and control-oriented that it would have been unthinkable
to him that these people remain on earth without him being able
to control them.

John List made a choice. He proved himself to be little more
than a narcissistic coward, a coward who made it easier on himself by shooting each of his family members in the back. Remember, this was a guy who couldn't even look business associates in
the eye.

The List disappearance became an obsession for the cops who
worked the case, particularly James Moran, one of the first detectives on the scene, who went on to become chief of the Westfield Police Department. I provided a fugitive assessment, with

periodic updates, to help the authorities aim their search. As with other fugitives, I noted List would likely flee to an area where he would feel comfortable, maybe someplace he had lived or traveled to before that he liked. And with his nature, he wouldn't stray far from the types of things he had done all along. If he had a job, it would either be working with numbers or something menial, where he would not have to interact much with others.

In 1989, the case got the attention of *America's Most Wanted,* which at that time had been on the air just a little more than a year. The television show was hosted by my friend John Walsh, an attorney, who along with his wife, Revé, had lost their six-year-old son, Adam, to a vicious child killer in Florida. The experience transformed John's life, a life he dedicated to bringing criminals to justice and to the victims' rights movement.

In trying to decide how to present a fugitive whom no one had seen for eighteen years, the show's producers turned to Frank Bender, a Philadelphia artist and sculptor who had an uncanny talent for re-creating human heads and faces in three dimensions from whatever evidence he was given to work with—a skull, a decomposing body, an old photograph. His re-creations showed more than physical accuracy; the true artist that he was, he was also able to render personality. Bender had done a lot of volunteer work for the National Center for Missing and Exploited Children in Arlington, Virginia, and I had seen him lecture and conduct demonstrations at Quantico. His work was very impressive.

Bender was given some photographs of List taken shortly before the murders, as well as whatever profile information the producers had to work with, which was pretty basic. Within about a month, he had come up with a life-size bust of John List as Bender imagined he would look if still alive, including the kind of glasses he would have, even what his typical facial expression might be.

The program aired on May 23, 1989, and featured both a re-creation with actors typical of the program and Frank Bender's bust of what John List might look like at the moment. The hotline was flooded with hundreds of tips. The FBI went through the tips and put in enormous manpower.

One of them paid off.

It was from a woman named Wanda Flanery in Colorado, who thought the bust looked amazingly like her old neighbor Bob Clark, an accountant and tax preparer. Bob's wife, Delores, had given her their forwarding address when they moved to Midlothian, Virginia, near Richmond, so that Bob could take an accounting job there. This location was interesting, I felt, since John List had met his wife, Helen, outside Richmond. If Bob Clark turned out to be John List, the fugitive had indeed returned to a place that was familiar and comfortable to him.

On June 1, 1989, FBI special agent Terry O'Connor went to the Clarks' house and showed a photograph of the bust to Delores. She admitted that it certainly looked like her husband, whom she had known since meeting him at a Lutheran church social function in Denver in 1977 and had married in 1985. But he was such a kind, quiet, and mild-mannered man, he couldn't possibly have done anything like what this John List did.

That same morning, agents went to the firm where Clark worked. He denied any knowledge of the crimes or who John List was. He was arrested, taken away, and fingerprinted. Bob Clark and John List were the same person.

John Walsh credits the List case with giving *America's Most Wanted* the momentum it needed to establish itself and stay on the air. And a quiet, methodical killer who had managed to evade justice for almost two decades would finally stand trial.

Police and the FBI now were able to fill in the remaining details. List shot his wife, Helen, in the kitchen as she had her morning toast and coffee. Then he went upstairs and shot his mother, Alma. Later in the day, he picked up Patty, drove her home, and shot her. Next he went back out for Frederick, got him home, and shot him. John Jr. came home earlier from soccer practice than expected, surprising his father, who had to shoot him with two guns a total of ten times before he was sure his son was dead.

After the murders, he ate dinner and slept in the house, then ate breakfast the next day before beginning his life as a fugitive. He had thoughtfully turned down the thermostat because he didn't want the oil tank to run out before the bodies were discovered, causing the pipes to freeze and burst. That would have created unnecessary expense for the bank holding the mortgage on the house, and since the bank hadn't done anything wrong, List reasoned, it shouldn't suffer from his actions. He flew to Denver and began his new life, applying for a new Social Security card. He even chose his assumed name with care. It was a common name, but there had been a Robert Clark in List's graduating class at the University of Michigan. So if any potential employer wanted to check his background, they would find school records to support it.

He admitted that he had planned the crime, that he had bought and tested the weapons ahead of time: a nine-millimeter semiautomatic and a .22 caliber revolver. Investigators found the murder weapons carefully stored in a desk drawer labeled "Guns and Ammunition." He had never bothered to pick up the gun permit he had applied for less than a month before. On the application, under his reason for wanting a firearm, he had written, "Home protection."

(Parenthetically, my New Zealand colleague Trevor Morley reports that in his country, the firearms application process includes contacting and visiting the applicant's spouse, neighbors, and anyone else close to him, to ascertain whether anyone who knows him has a problem with him having a gun or whether this represents anything strange or out of character. If this very sensible procedure were followed in the United States, I wonder how many murdered people, including the List family, might still be alive today.)

During the months after his arrest, List was always described as a quiet, courteous, and cooperative prisoner who never gave anyone any trouble.

Defense attorney Elijah J. Miller Jr. told the jury in his opening statement of the nine-day trial that List killed his family "with love in his heart for his mother, wife, and children." Several defense psychiatrists stated that while John List did know the difference between right and wrong, he'd essentially had a mental breakdown, which caused him to do these things in the name of religion. List told the prosecution's psychiatrist that, after a while, he'd been able to put the murders behind him and thought of them only on the anniversary date, and had begun enjoying life again. His brother-in-law said that List had a collection of books on crime and murder, especially unsolved mysteries. He also liked war games.

The defense argued against admitting into evidence the letter List wrote but did not send to his pastor. New Jersey Superior Court judge William Wertheimer ruled that the letter, like the rest of the house and its contents, was abandoned property, and therefore not covered by the "priest-penitent" privilege.

On April 12, 1990, after nine hours of jury deliberations, John List was convicted of five counts of first-degree murder. Despite a plea for leniency, in which List expressed sorrow, asked forgiveness, and explained that the crimes were "due to my mental state at the time," Judge Wertheimer sentenced him to five consecutive life terms, the maximum allowable under the law. The sixty-four-year-old defendant would not be eligible for parole for seventy-five years.

"Defendant's name and his deeds in November 1971 have proven to be a specter that will not as easily be obliterated from the community's mind as they were from his own conscience," the judge declared in an extremely articulate and moving sentencing speech. He went on to say, "After eighteen years, five months, and twenty-two days, it is now time for the voices of Helen, Alma, Patricia, Frederick, and John F. List to rise from the grave."

Sadly, a John List–type domestic murder situation would have been very hard to predict and, therefore, prevent. Maybe even harder than Matthew Beck's. List's family and—if he was working—people at work probably would have noticed him becoming stranger, more and more rigid as he tried to keep control of his life and situation. Ultimately, it just becomes too exhausting to maintain this level of control, and that's when someone like this is liable to snap. But the problem is, this type will not let people close to him emotionally, so all they can observe is outward behavior. And he's not the kind you'd figure to do something like this, anyway. That's why it's so important to study these cases and see what we can learn from them, so that maybe in the future we will be in a better position to spot the trouble before it escalates into a crisis.

How much of a threat was John List in his new life as Bob Clark? We teach at the Academy that the only truly reliable predictor of future violence is past violence. But this guy had only one violent episode in his life. Is it likely he could have had another and possibly killed his second wife? The answer is, it all depends on circumstances. If things went along okay, if he had the financial security and self-respect he needed, everything would probably be fine. But if similar circumstances occurred again, if he were faced with the potential of personal ruin and public embarrassment, he'd already have in his mind the scenario that would get him out of it, and like any successful repeat offender, he'd know how to carry it out.

Or, since we've acknowledged that crime patterns evolve, was there much of a threat he would shoot up his workplace instead of his own family? I don't think so. List was too cowardly and nonconfrontational to ever contemplate something this direct.

Having said that, I do feel that in the current climate of acting out one's rage in scenarios of indiscriminate violence, a lot of people who previously would have killed themselves or staged a murder-suicide at home might today just as easily vent their frustrations on their coworkers.

But in this particular case, unlike a Matthew Beck or a David Burke, John List was trying to extricate himself from his situation, not end it. He got away after doing in his family. There wouldn't have been any such escape for a more public violent statement. This wasn't a curtain call for List as it was for those other two. This was a possible solution.

And as we'll see even more in the next chapter, the fugitive has his own set of agendas and motives.

# CHAPTER SIX

# ON THE RUN

There are three possible outcomes for a fugitive: He's caught. He's not caught. Or he goes out in a blaze—a blaze he might perceive as one of glory but that my colleagues and I would more characterize as a pathetically characteristic brand of cowardice.

With John List, we've looked at a fugitive who was eventually caught, even if it took close to twenty years. Let's begin here with a crime that looks similar on its surface, with similar motivations. But as we'll see, the behavioral evidence shows us a very different type of offender. And after that, we'll contrast chilling examples of those other two outcomes.

When we teach FBI agents or National Academy fellows at Quantico, we want them to see beneath surface similarities—so many of the offenders are underachieving, underemployed loners, for example—and understand the components that in any particular case make up that most crucial of all equations for us: *Why? + How? = Who.* And of course, those components are going to break out differently, get weighted by the profiler differently, in each case, and there's no formula to tell him or her exactly how to do it. It's a matter of experience, instinct, and skill, which is why it takes us about two years to train a smart and seasoned agent who's already shown an aptitude in the local field office to work effectively in my old unit. In short form, the types of distinctions and considerations we teach our agents are what we're dealing with in this book.

On the second of March 1976, a forest ranger found five bodies burning in a shallow grave in the swampland of rural Tyrrell County, North Carolina, about two hundred miles south of Washington, D.C. She had seen the smoke from what she assumed to be a forest fire and went to put it out. The medical examiner determined that the victims—a woman in her thirties, an older woman, and three boys ranging in age from about five to about fifteen—had been bludgeoned to death, but there was no identification on any of them, so no one knew who they were.

The only clue was a pitchfork found near the graves. North Carolina Bureau of Identification investigators were able to trace it to the Poch hardware store in Potomac, Maryland, in the affluent Montgomery County suburb of Washington, D.C.

More than two weeks later, on March 18, a maroon Chevrolet Malibu station wagon was found in Great Smoky Mountains National Park on the North Carolina–Tennessee border. The car's luggage area was covered with drying blood, and bloodstained blankets were found inside, along with a shotgun, an ax, and a box of dog biscuits. In the glove compartment were maps of the Southern states and a container of Sereax, a prescription tranquilizer.

The Chevy Malibu was registered to William Bradford Bishop Jr. of Bethesda, Maryland, thirty-nine years of age, a Foreign Service officer with the State Department.

The bodies found on March 2 were identified by neighbors from photographs as those of Bishop's thirty-seven-year-old wife, Annette; their three sons, William Bradford III, fourteen,

Brenton, ten, and Geoffrey, five; and Bishop's sixty-eight-year-old mother, Lobelia, who lived with them in their split-level California contemporary house in Bethesda's Carderock Springs subdivision. The three boys were all wearing pajamas. The neighbors had thought nothing of the house being empty at first because the Bishops were known as a fun-loving family who took spur-of-the-moment trips. It was assumed that this time they were away skiing. When police searched the house, they found bloodstains in the bedrooms and the front hall, where it seemed from the evidence that a violent struggle had taken place.

William Bradford Bishop Jr., known as Brad, and the family's golden retriever, Leo, were still missing. A huge manhunt was organized, involving the FBI, the National Park Service, and state police from both North Carolina and Tennessee. Tracker dogs detected Bishop's scent near the tourist center at the park where the car was found. Some of the authorities who went looking for him speculated that he had hiked off into the mountains and either killed himself or died of exposure. They couldn't find Leo, either.

So who was this Brad Bishop, and what the hell happened?

Actually, he seemed like the all-American boy: a handsome, charming Foreign Service officer with the State Department; a Yale graduate; fluent in Spanish, Italian, French, and Serbo-Croatian, which he learned for work in Yugoslavia with the Army. He won commendations for this work in counterintelligence. One of his assignments involved infiltrating the Yugoslav Army ski team while it was training in Italy. After the Army he earned a master's degree in Italian, joined the State Department, and served in the U.S. embassies in Ethiopia, Italy, and Botswana. Before this last posting, he earned a second master's in African studies, and in Botswana he also received pilot's training. He was an enthusiast of competitive sports and an experienced camper who took private whitewater canoeing lessons, which later led to speculation he might even have used a canoe to leave the park unseen. The blond Brad and his equally good-looking auburn-haired wife were high school sweethearts back in California, where he was quarterback of the football team and she was a cheerleader. The only time they were apart was when he went east to go to Yale while she went to Berkeley. They married when they graduated, in 1959.

As Montgomery County sheriff's officers and detectives tried to piece together what had happened, they learned that Brad uncharacteristically left work early on March 1, complaining that he was coming down with the flu. He was upset over losing out on a promotion. Earlier in the day, he'd withdrawn $400 from his bank and on the way home stopped at the Sears Roebuck store at Montgomery Mall and bought a heavy ball-peen hammer and a five-gallon gasoline can, then drove to a Texaco station, where he filled the gas can.

Though neighbors didn't hear anything suspicious, investigators speculated that sometime that same night, Bishop used the hammer to kill his wife, mother, and all three of his children. Then he placed their bodies in the back of the Chevy and drove south to the Outer Banks of North Carolina.

From the bodies and crime scene clues, it probably happened something like this:

Bishop first attacked Annette in the den. Just after he killed her, Lobelia returned home from walking Leo and surprised him. He tried to hide the body with one of his jackets, then attacked and killed his mother. Bishop then went upstairs to the bedrooms where the three boys were sleeping and bludgeoned each of them to death. He wrapped all five bodies in blankets and loaded them into the family station wagon, then drove all night to North Carolina, accompanied by his dog, Leo—the only "family member" he deigned to let live—successfully making it through several toll stations with his grisly cargo unnoticed.

Credit receipts indicated that his BankAmericard had been used on March 2 to buy sneakers in a sporting goods store in Jacksonville, North Carolina, about a hundred miles south of where the bodies of his family members were discovered. Police were able to get witnesses to confirm that it was Bishop himself. An unidentified dark-skinned Caribbean-looking woman was seen holding Bishop's dog's leash while he paid. The owner of the store recalled Bishop as polite and well-spoken and said that he and the woman seemed like a couple.

In subsequent weeks, there were sightings by hikers along the Appalachian Trail, and other possible appearances at various points along the Southeastern coast, down as far as Daytona Beach, Florida.

William Bradford Bishop Jr. remains missing to this day. There have been possible sightings all around the world, all of them unconfirmed, and authorities have been unwilling to have him declared dead since murder is a crime without a statute of limitations.

More than two years after the murders, in July 1978, a former acquaintance claimed to have spotted him on the street in Stockholm, Sweden. A Swedish woman who knew him when he was stationed in Ethiopia in the 1960s said she saw him twice on the streets of Stockholm but didn't approach him or contact the police right away because she'd forgotten he was wanted for murder in the United States. She described him as bearded and well dressed. Swedish police didn't find any evidence he was there, but it's not customary in that country to launch a publicity blitz about fugitives. Some publications there even refuse to print the names or photographs of criminal suspects.

Then in January 1979, a State Department employee on vacation in Sorrento, Italy, claimed to have seen him at a public restroom. At this sighting, Bishop was said still to be bearded, but poorly dressed and bedraggled-looking. Bishop had lived in Italy before—in Verona when he was in the Army, in Florence as a grad student, and Milan as a diplomatic envoy—and knew the country well.

We did a fugitive assessment on him at Quantico and updated it from year to year. Unlike a John List or even an Audrey Hilley, whom you'd expect ultimately to find in situations similar to the ones they left (when List was caught, he was doing pretty much what he had in his previous life; Hilley was found close to where she was born), because of his Foreign Service background and language and social skills, Bishop would be able to operate practically anywhere in the world. And because the authorities wouldn't be looking for him as aggressively overseas as they would be in the United States, a foreign country, particularly in Europe, would constitute his greatest comfort zone. We went back over his life to find out where he seemed to have been the happiest, and those were the places we suggested he would most likely be hanging out. But despite a lot of effort on the part of a lot of people and his appearance for a time on the FBI's Ten Most-Wanted List, Bishop has managed to stay on the run. If he is still alive, he still might be caught, but it would take a lot of luck at this point. John List wasn't equipped to go someplace where programs like *America's Most Wanted* are not shown. William Bradford Bishop Jr. was very well equipped.

Bradford Bishop has, of course, never been convicted and, as such, is legally entitled to a presumption of innocence. Consider the case for a moment, however, as if he were found guilty. The similarities to the List case five years earlier are striking. Both were professional, educated suburban family men, and each lived with his wife, a dominant mother, and three children. And at a certain point, apparently disappointed by the way things were going in their lives, it seems that both men cracked, killed their families in their own homes, and took off.

But the differences are equally striking. You'd be hard-pressed to find two individuals seemingly more opposite each other than John List and William Bradford Bishop Jr. List was a timid, obsessive-compulsive tight-ass in his late forties with virtually no social skills, who used religion as a crutch. Bishop was a career diplomat in his late thirties with a diplomat's social graces and skills at getting along, an ability to function on his own in the wilderness, and an equal proficiency at being able to live overseas, if and when necessary. List was kind of a pathetic figure. Bishop was a man most people would envy.

The differences in postoffense behavior are also significant. List remained in the house after the murders and ate breakfast there the next morning before setting out, which was the one noticeably disorganized offender trait he displayed. But he laid out the bodies, as we've noted, in a "caring" manner consistent with what we would expect of a killer with a close relationship to his victims.

Bishop, on the other hand, got the hell out of Dodge right after the killings and took the evidence with him. The maps in the car show a degree of sophistication and planning. What is unusual (relatively speaking, of course; this is all highly unusual, thank God) and perplexing is the way his family was killed: up close and personal, and very brutally. It wasn't "clean," like a surprise gunshot to the back of the head. The Bishops were literally beaten to death—including a peaceful, sleeping five-year-old. As a parent, I remember how—even during some of the most trying times in my life—watching my children as they slept always grounded me in what was really important. After a child's worst day, he or she still looks completely beautiful and innocent in sleep. In that state, they have that magic ability to calm and soothe, as though reaching right into a parent's soul, evoking utter love and devotion. So, knowing what I do as a parent, while it goes against all tenets of nature to imagine hurting your child, it's inconceivable to plan to brutally bludgeon him as he sleeps! And if Bishop killed them as police believed, it had to be a completely willful act on his part. He had to be able to visualize what the end result of his actions would be. And that's a damn chilling thought. And then there is the disposal of the bodies, which shows more concern with destroying evidence than seeing to the dignity of the bodies and the eternal rest of the deceased.

But I keep coming back to the behavior—the way the crime was committed. To bludgeon one's family to death, there has to be some very deep and volatile anger, which just wasn't present with List. Even if you are a manic-depressive, and there is some evidence Bishop was, you don't just suddenly, on the spur of the moment, decide things are really out of hand, go out and buy a hammer and some gasoline, and beat your family to death. There has to be some emotional buildup to it. So in some form or other, the idea of what he was going to do had to have been brewing in Bishop's mind for some period before the actual crime on March 1, 1976. This man would have been covered in the blood of his wife, his mother, his children.

Assuming Bishop was the killer, what could have accounted for his rage and desperation? Disappointment at being passed over for promotion for the first time in his golden career? Depression? (He was being treated by a psychiatrist.) Tension with his mother? A secret girlfriend? None of these seems a very likely or logical motive—and they certainly don't explain the manner in which he committed the crimes. They aren't even internally consistent, as List's motive appears when you look at things from the offender's own perspective. Basically, nothing seemed that wrong in Bishop's life. Couldn't he have just gotten a divorce or changed jobs, after all?

Despite what we know, so much of Bishop's life remains a mystery. I have a high degree of confidence that I've accurately explained why John List did what he did. I'm not as sure about Brad Bishop. We've seen cases in which some people are so consumed with their own image of themselves that their personal view of success and achievement has little to do with what other people think—just as an anorexic might have a completely different sense than those around her of whether or not she's fat. Someone like Bishop, for example, would have a real problem with admitting marital difficulties. It would show he was less than perfect. So would being passed over for a promotion. There is a phenomenon with some of these guys we refer to as the "dangerous forties." When they get to that age and take stock, if it doesn't look as though life is going quite the way they planned it, they can pop.

In addition to the fact that Bishop had been seeing a psychiatrist, the investigators found some financial problems, but nothing terribly unusual for people in their thirties living in that kind of neighborhood. There was some tension over Brad's mother living with them, and Annette, apparently, wasn't keen on picking up stakes again for another overseas tour. But still, there were none of the kind of stressors we'd expect to see. And even with the report of the woman holding Leo's leash in the sporting goods store, there was no conclusive evidence Bishop was carrying on an extramarital affair. It just didn't add up.

It's also doubtful Bishop could have effected his escape completely on his own as List did. Not only was he seen in the company of another woman the day after the murders, but he abandoned his car in the middle of a national park. How did he get out? Maybe he hitchhiked. Maybe it was the canoe. But then what? It's more likely he had a planned ride.

And as with List, we have to ask whether someone like Bishop might be motivated to kill again. And here, the answer is the same. As long as things are going well for him, then he won't be dangerous. But if anything comes up that he perceives to be a serious stumbling block, then the same emotional forces could come into play. Even though they both wiped out their families, this guy (again, if indeed he did it) shows a far more violent streak than List. He is more resourceful, and if he's threatened with capture, I'm not sure he'd be quite as docile, either. Nor would he be quite as much of a physical coward. Rather than face capture, I could see a guy like this committing suicide.

So, like D. B. Cooper, the notorious air pirate who bailed out of a commandeered Northwest Orient airliner somewhere between Portland and Seattle with $200,000 in ransom money in November of 1971 and was never heard from again (nor was his body found), William Bradford Bishop Jr. has become the stuff of legend, immortalized in novels, TV movies, and ballads played on the radio. The FBI is still looking for him, and the Montgomery County, Maryland, sheriff's office, which has never given up the hunt, would dearly like to find him and bring him to justice.

So would I, because more than almost any of the others, this is one case where I feel a tremendous need to know *Why?*

Like the infamous Charles Starkweather and Caril Ann Fugate, who terrorized the Midwestern United States with a vicious crime spree for weeks in the winter of 1957, Alton Coleman and Debra Denise Brown led their own reign of terror throughout the Midwest in the summer of 1984. Seldom in my career have I come across a more depraved individual than Alton Coleman, willing to rape or kill practically anyone or anything that moved and totally unconcerned with the consequences.

He was born into bad circumstances in Waukegan, Illinois, in 1955, to a prostitute who already had two other children. Mainly, he was raised by her mother. He was often teased by his peers, who called him "Pissy" because he wet his pants. Early on, he got involved with a black street gang and started building his rap sheet. He dropped out of school in the ninth grade. When he was eighteen, he was arrested for raping and robbing an elderly woman in Waukegan, but was able to bargain it down to simple robbery, which earned him a stint in the tough Joliet penitentiary, where I've interviewed many dangerous and violent offenders. He wasn't exactly a model prisoner: he sexually accosted several other inmates until he was paroled. It didn't take him long to rack up another string of sexual assault charges in the late 1970s, two of which he beat when his lawyers were able to convince juries that the acts were consensual. One victim during this period was his own niece. With his dysfunctional background and psychological makeup, Coleman seemed to have no conscience, no concern for the rights, feelings, or pain of others. Somebody like this would perceive that nothing was given to him and nobody cared, and also he was entitled to take whatever he wanted and didn't have to care what anyone else thought.

The rape charges kept piling up, and he was suspected in the rape-murder of a fifteen-year-old girl in 1982. He was out on bail, awaiting another rape trial, when his 1984 rampage began. By this time Coleman had been briefly married to a teenage girl, who left him and went to the police for protection. Now twenty-eight, he was involved with twenty-one-year-old Debra Brown, a woman from a solid, stable background, who broke off her engagement to another man when she met Coleman and moved in with him. Throughout his life, Coleman never held more than an occasional odd job.

On May 29, 1984, using aliases, Coleman and Brown convinced a nine-year-old girl in Kenosha, Wisconsin, named Vernita Wheat to go with them to Waukegan. They never returned, and Vernita's mother was quickly able to pick out a police photo of the man who took her daughter. A federal grand jury indicted both suspects on kidnapping charges, which brought the FBI into the case.

On June 18, Coleman and Brown were driving through Gary, Indiana. They stopped when they saw two young girls—seven-year-old Tamika Turks and a nine-year-old relative—walking down the street. They asked for directions and said they would give the girls money if they got into the car and helped them find their way. They drove the girls into a wooded area some distance away, and while Brown held Tamika down on the ground, Coleman raped and strangled her. The other girl was also raped and beaten, but managed to escape. She identified the attackers from police photos.

The next day, Donna Williams, a twenty-five-year-old beautician in Gary, was reported missing after agreeing to pick up a "couple from Boston" she met at the salon who wanted to see her church. Other people in the salon identified Coleman and Brown as the couple from police photos. The same day, Vernita Wheat's body was discovered, strangled, in a derelict building in Waukegan.

On June 24, Coleman and Brown, now in Detroit, kidnapped a woman at knifepoint in front of her home and ordered her to drive them to Ohio. She intentionally crashed the car into a parked truck, jumped out, and ran away. The two outlaws escaped in her car. Four days later, they broke into the Jones house in Dearborn Heights while the middle-aged owners were having breakfast; they beat them both, robbed them of a small amount of cash, and stole their car. By now the FBI and every law enforcement organization in this part of the country were after them.

On July 2, they broke into the home of another middle-aged couple in the Detroit area, beat them, and stole their car. They drove it to Toledo, Ohio, where they broke into another house, assaulted the owners, and stole their car. They later went into a bar and tried to kidnap someone inside, but were foiled when the bartender came after them with a gun. They still managed to escape, and on July 7, they raped and strangled Virginia Temple, thirty years of age, and her ten-year-old daughter, Rochelle, left their bodies in a crawl space, and robbed the home. And on July 11, with the discovery of beautician Donna Williams's strangled body back in Detroit, Alton Coleman was placed on the FBI's Most-Wanted List, even though it was filled. They made him a rare Number Eleven.

In Cincinnati, fifteen-year-old Tonnie Storey disappeared. Witnesses once again picked out Coleman and Brown as the people she was last seen with. Her body was discovered four days later, repeatedly stabbed and shot in the head.

So far, all of the victims had been black, though clearly there was no particular victim of preference, since they ranged in age from prepubescent up to senior citizen. On July 13, Coleman went to the home of a white couple in their mid-forties, Harry and Marlene Walters, in the Cincinnati suburb of Norwood, gaining entry on the pretext of wanting to buy their camper, which was parked in the driveway with a For Sale sign on it. Both were bludgeoned viciously, even after Harry pleaded with the attacker not to hurt his wife. Marlene died of her wounds. According to police descriptions, the entire back of her head was missing from the attack with a crowbar and pliers. The victims were found by their teenage daughter, Sheri, when she returned home. Harry, who was hospitalized for more than three months, managed to give police a description of the young black couple, who had arrived on bicycles and left in Harry's car.

Three days later, they kidnapped a college professor named Oline Carmichal and stole his car, driving with him in the trunk to Dayton, Ohio, where they abandoned the vehicle and uncharacteristically left him inside alive. He was rescued the next day and described being abducted by *two* men and a woman—a discrepancy that would soon be explained. The same day, an elderly Dayton minister and his wife were bludgeoned in their home, but survived the attack. They told police that they had welcomed a young couple into their home for several days and that the minister had driven them to Cincinnati for a prayer meeting. But then the couple returned, attacked them, and stole their car.

That car was found the next day in Indianapolis, abandoned next to a car wash. The car wash owner, seventy-seven-year-old Eugene Scott, was abducted and his car stolen. Scott was found several hours later in a ditch, like teenage Tonnie Storey before him, stabbed and shot in the head. These two would go after anyone.

Meanwhile, Dayton police arrested a man named Thomas Harris, who admitted to being an accomplice in the kidnapping of Professor Carmichal and claimed he had talked Coleman out of killing this victim, which would explain why he was left alive.

My unit in Quantico was asked for a fugitive assessment on Coleman and Brown. Despite the fact that they were extremely vicious, it became clear to me that unlike someone such as Bradford Bishop, they weren't terribly sophisticated or smart. They were sufficiently organized to repeat the same crime over and over again, and seemed to have it down pretty well. Yet they left fingerprints and clues wherever they went and made no real attempt to disguise themselves, even though they knew Coleman was already wanted on a fugitive warrant. I didn't go so far as to think of Brown as a compliant victim, since she went off with Coleman more than willingly, but definitely he was calling the shots. And though she was enamored of him, I suspected there was some fear and domination in there, too.

This tied in with Coleman's motive, in my estimation. And

despite the horrible destruction he caused, that motive was actually pretty mundane. As I studied his background and rap sheet, it was clear to me that from an early age, Coleman had this fantasy of sexually dominating and controlling other people, because, like so many other serial rapists, this is what made him feel good and gave him the most satisfaction in life. Certainly he didn't get it from personal accomplishment or relationships. And the fact that all of his early violence was directed against other blacks speaks to me of the essentially sexual nature of the crimes, rather than primarily a general rage against society, which was also there and showed up in some of the later crimes. In fact, while he was beating a middle-aged black couple in their own home in Detroit, he went into a practically incoherent tirade about how blacks were forcing him to murder other blacks, as if that could somehow explain and justify his actions. Since what he knew was a life of lawlessness from a very early age, Coleman was able to assimilate his sexual crimes into a way of providing for himself. In other words, not only would he rape and beat and sometimes kill, but while he was there he would also rob and carjack. Essentially, these guys view their criminal activities as their job. Why do you go to work? Because that's what you think you're supposed to do. There's no reason to believe Coleman would think any differently.

What we found by tracing the spree on a map and assigning dates to each appearance was that Coleman couldn't go out too far or stay away too long from someplace he found familiar or secure. Once he was out of Waukegan or the Chicago area, he was really out of his element. The nature of this criminal, I thought, would be to go back to his roots, where he felt comfortable. In fact, he was so predictable we later learned that we actually predicted the highway he'd be taking back home. We told the authorities that before too long, Coleman would return to Waukegan or possibly

Chicago; they should start looking for him there and putting out his description.

On July 20, police in Evanston, which is about halfway between Waukegan and Chicago, responded to an anonymous tip from an acquaintance who thought he'd spotted them, and found Coleman and Brown sitting in a park, on a row of bleachers facing the basketball courts. The police surrounded the couple with guns drawn, and faced with this overwhelming force, they surrendered. Coleman gave them a false name; Brown identified herself accurately. Coleman had two bloodstained knives on his person, and Brown had a .38 revolver in her purse. She also had sunglasses belonging to Sheri Walters, daughter of one of their murder victims. That afternoon, the police located Eugene Scott's car blocks from the park. The crime scene techs were able to lift Brown's fingerprints from the interior.

Alton Coleman and Debra Denise Brown were tried separately on multiple murder counts in various jurisdictions. Both were found guilty and sentenced to death. Altogether, from May 1985 through January 1987, Coleman received four separate death sentences in different states, and Brown two. In January 1991, outgoing Ohio governor Richard Celeste, a known death penalty opponent, commuted Brown's sentence in that state (along with those of six other convicted killers) to life imprisonment, citing a report from his staff stating that Brown was mentally retarded. Her Indiana death sentence for the murder of Tamika Turks, however, still stands. On April 26, 2002, Alton Coleman was executed by lethal injection at the Southern Ohio Correctional Facility in Lucasville, Ohio.

Of the various trials, perhaps the most interesting and bizarre aspect was Coleman's repeated attempts to act as his own attorney. He did this in the trial for the murder of Marlene Walters, in Hamilton County, Ohio, Common Pleas Court, and in the final trial, in Wisconsin, for the murder of nine-year-old Vernita Wheat. He thought he could do a better job of defending himself than any court-appointed attorney.

Brown was almost equally uncooperative with her own lawyers. During her trial for the murder of Marlene Walters and the vicious attack on Harry Walters, she would not let her attorneys bring her to the stand or call witnesses who might have attempted to mitigate her guilt as a compliant victim.

Dayton attorney Dennis Lieberman, who defended the couple in connection with the abduction of Professor Carmichal, told the *Chicago Tribune,* "I can accurately say that representing [them] was one of the worst experiences in my legal career." He went on to say, in a very telling and insightful remark, that Brown "has decided to tie her future in with [Coleman], for whatever result. It's something that's always troubled me from the very beginning, as if she's under some sort of mystical, hypnotic trance. There is no doubt in my mind that Alton Coleman has a certain effect on Debra Brown."

Just after Debra Brown's case went to the sequestered jury and nothing else she said or did would affect their judgment, she got a subpoena from—you guessed it!—Alton Coleman to testify as a witness in the trial in which he was both defendant and defense counsel.

Coleman got her to state on the stand that she was the one who attacked Marlene Walters.

"I'd say yes," Brown said.

"Could you make that a little clearer? Did I or did I not have anything to do with this?"

"No," Brown replied.

"Did you get her downstairs in the basement?"

There was a long hesitation, then Brown said, "Yes, I did."

"Did you hit her in the head?"

"I hit her, but I can't recall hitting her in the head."

"Where was I when you was in the basement?"

"You was upstairs."

It was Coleman's contention that he was only trying to "control" the victims when he struck them in the head with a four-foot wooden candlestick holder, but that Brown had gone crazy in a fit of vengeance and killed Mrs. Walters.

Amazingly, a little later in this examination, Coleman had the balls to say, "Debra, you're a little afraid, aren't you?"

"Yes," she replied.

"Bear with me, Debra. You know this is rough."

During cross-examination, prosecution attorney Carl Vollman got Debra to contradict what she said and admit that she had been using cocaine and marijuana at the time of the crime. Coleman had been drinking vodka. When Vollman asked her how much blood there was in the basement, she responded, "I don't know. I wasn't down there."

In his own summation to the jury, Coleman told them how much he loved Debra and how much courage it took on her part to say that he was not responsible for Mrs. Walters's death.

Coleman had also requested that he and Brown, who had proclaimed themselves common-law husband and wife, be allowed to have sex in jail. Judge Richard Niehaus turned down the request. He told reporters he had found Coleman's performance in court "incredible" and said, "I've never seen anything like this before. I hope I never get another one of these."

In an effort to spare her lover from the electric chair during the penalty phase, Brown said under oath, "I killed the bitch, and I don't give a damn. I had fun out of it."

Coleman got the death penalty in his trial. Brown received a life sentence in hers. When told of her testimony in Coleman's trial while they were sequestered, one of her jurors expressed regret at not sending her to the chair, too.

Again, in the Wheat murder trial in Illinois, not being satis-fied with the prior performance of his various court-appointed attorneys, Coleman asked Lake County circuit court judge Fred Geiger to let him represent himself, a request the judge reluc-tantly granted. After the jury reached another guilty verdict and was about to enter the sentencing phase, Coleman asked the judge to reinstate his two lawyers. Although prosecutor Matthew Chancey objected that the defendant had had the opportunity to be represented and decided the lawyers weren't good enough for him, Judge Geiger approved the reappointment, saying, "I think Mr. Coleman has shown good sense right now."

It made little difference, though. The jury, which had taken only a little more than four hours to find him guilty, examined the evidence and decided, as other juries had before them, that Alton Coleman should die for his crimes.

After the trials were over, I interviewed Debra Brown in prison. I wouldn't say I thought she was retarded—that isn't my field—but I did find her to be a very passive, compliant person who would be defined by whoever was influencing her—whether Alton Coleman or Mother Teresa. This confirmed my theory about them when we were still looking for them. Her relationship with Coleman was almost one of slave to master. On her own, I didn't think there was much chance someone like her would stand up to someone like Coleman, or leave him when things got too violent and scary. It would be scarier to risk his wrath.

When they were still on the loose, I suggested we ask the media to publicize the fact that we considered her submissive to him and in increasing danger of being harmed by him. The im-plication of this was that we considered her far less culpable than him and that she should turn herself in for her own protection. Had they not been caught when they were, I think we would have pursued this strategy aggressively.

Let me hasten to add, though, that so-called compliant victims may be defined along a continuum, with someone such as Debra Brown much more compliant and much less victim. We are, after all, talking about a woman who could hold down a terrified child to help her boyfriend rape the girl. With someone like Patty Hearst, on the other hand, who robbed banks with the Symbionese Liberation Army after being kidnapped and virtually brainwashed by them, to say nothing of being locked in a closet and, by her own account, raped, I would stress the victimization over the compliancy. A woman like Karla Homulka, wife of the predatory Canadian monster and sexual sadist Paul Bernardo—who helped her husband with the crimes we described in our previous book *Journey into Darkness,* including the rape and fatal drug overdose of her own younger sister—would fall somewhere in the middle: both victim and perpetrator.

This does not mean that every woman who comes in contact with an Alton Coleman or a Paul Bernardo is in danger of becoming a compliant victim. It has more to do with her personality than his, and we all make our choices. While I was on the West Coast doing a radio program as part of a book promotion tour, a very sensitive and concerned woman called in and said that her daughter had been acquainted with convicted killer and accused serial killer Glen Rogers, who was captured after a high-speed chase in Kentucky in 1995 and, because of his wide swath and boastful swagger, soon became a universal suspect for practically every unsolved sexual murder throughout the South and Southwest.

Rogers was under lock and key by this point, but just thinking about her daughter with this man sent shivers down this mother's spine. "What were the chances of my daughter being murdered by this guy?" she asked me.

I said, "Well, the reason your daughter wasn't murdered and

that nothing bad happened to her is because, I'm guessing, she's not a very passive person, is she?"

"No, you're right," she replied.

"In fact, I'd bet she's very assertive, very aggressive, a real self-starter."

"Yes, exactly," the woman said, as if I were a psychic.

"What does she do?" I asked.

"She manages a bar."

I said, "Well, see. She knows how to take care of herself. She has contact with a lot of people. She doesn't take any B.S. off anyone. So someone like this, a guy like Rogers—even if he could date her—he couldn't control her in the way he'd like, he couldn't dominate her. For his victims, Rogers would choose people he could control, who were vulnerable, who lacked self-esteem, who were in the throes of a separation or divorce or some other life trauma. And these predators are good at spotting those women, at sensing who they are."

Just as we tell parents that their greatest weapon against child molesters is being able to instill self-esteem in their kids, I could tell this radio audience that sexual predators home in on victims in whom they sense a lack of self-esteem and self-worth—the ones they feel they can entice, mold to their own purposes, and separate from family, friends, and values.

Alton Coleman found what he wanted and needed in Debra Brown.

And Brown is not the same kind of offender as Audrey Hilley or Stella Nickell. I don't think she would go out on a killing spree on her own. But does that mean she isn't dangerous? Not necessarily. People like Alton Coleman will always find people like Debra Brown. One of the points I make over and over again is that violence is situational. For example, the mere fact that a child molester is a model prisoner in no way suggests that he will not go back to being a child molester as soon as he is released from prison and once again given the chance. By the same token, while I think Debra Brown would be "safe" on her own, she has displayed no evidence of a conscience, and I have little confidence that, once again put under the influence of someone like Alton Coleman, she couldn't resume pretty much where she left off. Because whatever rage and sexual obsession went into Coleman's motive, hers had to do with acceptance and being given a direction in life, however perverse that direction may seem from the outside.

Each in his or her own way, Alton Coleman and Debra Denise Brown represent to me what the philosopher Hannah Arendt referred to as the banality of evil. They each made a choice, and from my analysis of Coleman and examination of Brown, it doesn't appear that either one of them had to invest much moral depth or struggle in that choice. And that's as good a reason as any other why I don't want them ever getting the opportunity to make another choice as long as either one of them is alive.

As decent, sensitive human beings, anytime we see someone capable of multiple murders, we are instantly repulsed. The circumstances hardly matter. For those of us in the business of criminal investigative analysis, the repulsion remains the same but the circumstances are very, very important. In the FBI, we divide multiple murderers into three basic categories: serial, mass, and spree killers. And there is a very different and distinct set of motivations we've learned to attach to each one.

First, the definitions.

A *serial killer* is someone who has murdered on at least three occasions, with what we call an emotional cooling-off period between each incident. This cooling-off period can be days, weeks, months, even years. Occasionally, it is only hours. But the important consideration is that each event is emotionally distinct and separate.

A *mass murderer* kills four or more victims in one location in one incident. That location may be a building with numerous rooms, and the incident may stretch over a period of minutes or hours, but the killings are all part of the same emotional experience.

A *spree killer* is defined as someone who murders at two or more separate locations with no emotional cooling-off period between the homicides. Therefore, the killings tend to take place in a shorter period of time, though, of course, if the serial killer's cooling-off period is short enough, he might even work faster than the spree killer.

I've spent much of my career hunting and studying serial killers, because, frankly, they're the ones who require the most hunting and studying if we're going to put them out of business. We all know their names: Ted Bundy, John Wayne Gacy, the Son of Sam. Also Clifford Olson and Michael Ross. So terrifying are serial killers that they've taken on a significance out of all proportion to their numbers, occupying a permanent dark corner of our collective psyche. But it's just as important to understand the other two types of killers. In the cases we've covered so far in this book, Thomas Watt Hamilton (the Dunblane killer), John List, and William Bradford Bishop Jr. would be considered mass murderers. Coleman and Brown would be spree killers; so, in my opinion, is the next one we're going to look at.

Why are the circumstances so significant? Because they speak directly to motivation, to what the offender "wants" out of the act, to where his head is at when he's contemplating the crime.

These are generalizations, but speaking in terms of motivation, a serial killer expects to get away with it, a mass murderer doesn't, and a spree killer probably hasn't even gotten that far in his thinking. Along with manipulation, domination, and control, a significant motivator for almost all serial killers is sexual, even if, as with Son of Sam David Berkowitz, the crimes themselves are not overtly so. They commit them because it makes them feel fulfilled, and they will keep doing them as long as they can. The very fact that they can be labeled as serial killers means that they have been successful in what they set out to do, and the longer they succeed at it, the more confident they become. They tend to develop a sense of superiority over the police and investigative authorities who can't catch them, and this empowers them even further.

For our purposes here, there are two kinds of mass murderers. There are the kind who go to a public or semipublic place (like a business or school) and open fire, for example. These types are making a statement, a statement that is so important to them, has taken on such significance in their lives, that they are basically willing to sacrifice their own lives to get that point across. When someone like Hamilton walks into a schoolyard with his high-powered weapons, he doesn't expect to come out alive. These types are mission oriented. It's as if each of them is writing a novel about himself in which the final chapter is violent death.

If the crime is committed in private, or away from witnesses, on the other hand, there is more chance the killer is thinking about getting away. John List told investigators he didn't expect to remain free as long as he did, but it is clear from his behavior he certainly hoped to get away with his crime. Likewise Brad Bishop.

Spree killers are moving pretty rapidly from one experience to another and, after a while, almost consider themselves on a roll. Of the three types, these are the ones, I've found, who think least about the future—that is, either having one or not. I don't think Alton Coleman was deep enough to worry about how long that could all go on. And someone like Charles Starkweather probably harbored the thought that he would eventually be caught or killed, but the idea was at best hazy in his mind—not really a consideration one way or another.

With a serial killer, we generally don't know the UNSUB's identity until or unless he's captured. With a mass murderer, we learn the identity of the killer after the fact, when we sort through the mess. With a spree killer, we usually know the identity and we're after him as a fugitive. And this is an important point, because the stress and strain of knowing we know who they are—and everyone's looking for them—helps us even as it takes its toll on them: they begin drinking or using drugs to cope with the daily pressure, and they start making mistakes.

Just as we can have crime scene presentations that are mixed between organized and disorganized elements, so we sometimes see these designations of killers combined. The most common of these would be the serial killer who degenerates into a spree killer, as Ted Bundy did at the end. As he worked himself up into more and more of a frenzy, his cooling-off period grew shorter and shorter until it essentially went away. At that point, the stresses grew; he became more intense, sloppier; he exercised poorer judgment in terms of being able to get away. And we're always looking for that phase with a guy who's on the loose and active.

Often, when a particular crime or series of crimes becomes the focus of the national media, several of my former colleagues and I are approached by reporters and television and radio producers to comment and give our perspective. This happened over and over again in the Simpson-Goldman case; it happened with Glen Rogers; it happened with the Oklahoma City bombing and the capture of the Unabomber, to name only a few. But I never before experienced anything near the media frenzy that occurred when designer Gianni Versace was murdered outside his home in Miami's South Beach, on July 15, 1997. The killer was thought to be Andrew Phillip Cunanan, who, it was believed, had already left a trail of death halfway across the country. Such was the intensity of the interest, fear, and horror that there was hardly a news organization or television show throughout the United States that didn't call me.

It was as if this young man and this senseless, execution-style murder somehow crystallized everything we felt about this kind of killer and our own vulnerability.

Andrew Phillip Cunanan was born on August 31, 1969, the youngest of four children, and grew up in the nice middle-class San Diego suburb of Rancho Bernardo, California. His father, Modesto, known as Pete, was from the Philippines, had been a U.S. naval officer, then made his career as a stockbroker after he retired from the Navy in 1972. Andrew was a bright, inquisitive boy, an early reader, who, according to available reports, including those of his mother, MaryAnn, never got into any serious trouble. She was a staunch Catholic and took pains to instill religious values in her children. By the age of twelve, Andrew was tall, dark-haired, and very handsome. He was known for his charm and wit at the private Bishop prep school in San Diego, where his parents sent him at considerable financial sacrifice.

When we look for shaping influences on Andrew's development, a couple of possibilities emerge. According to Andrew Cunanan's account, Modesto was a strict disciplinarian, sometimes physically punishing his son in ways that would leave bruises. For a smart, highly sensitive boy like Andrew, this would have created anger and resentment, as well as a sense of guilt that he had driven his father to resort to such severe measures. Andrew seemed to think his self-destructive behavior began as a result of, and reaction to, this harsh discipline. But when two of his siblings were later interviewed, neither remembered any severe corporal punishment. In fact, they claimed Andrew was the revered, pampered "white sheep" of the family. Modesto himself asserted in an interview with ABS-CBN Philippines TV that "Andrew never saw violence in our household. That was never part of his growing up years."

MaryAnn could be domineering on her own. Relatives noticed she and Andrew seemed especially attached to each other and she seemed to want to screen all of his friends to make sure they were appropriate for him.

Then, of course, there was the fact that, as early as his teen years, Cunanan was reportedly openly gay—at least, away from home. He had his first sexual encounter with another boy when he was thirteen, and rather than hiding it, he bragged about it. As with just about everything else in his life, there seem to be two opposing interpretations supplied by observers. One is that this was a healthy manifestation of his pride and secureness in his own sexuality. The other is that he was self-absorbed and always eager to be the center of attention, able to manipulate others to get what he wanted, with little capacity for appreciating or caring when he hurt others. This is one of the key traits we find in the development of individuals who grow up to be violently antisocial.

For his senior high yearbook, Cunanan is voted "Most Likely to Be Remembered."

Not only is he handsome, he appears older than his years. By fifteen years of age, but looking eighteen, he's frequenting the gay bars in the Hillcrest section of San Diego. He thinks "Cunanan" sounds too Filipino, so he constructs himself some more romantic-sounding Latin names, complete with personas and personal histories, including "Andrew DeSilva" and "David Morales." He begins a relationship with an older married man, who buys him expensive gifts, sets him up in an apartment in Hillcrest, and shows him the good life that Andrew would crave from then on. The relationship reportedly ends when the man finds clothing belonging to another of Andrew's lovers in the apartment. Andrew has to move back home, which he finds a strain. It's also difficult to conceal his sexual activity from his mother, who at this point apparently does not suspect his homosexuality, though his father does. For his sixteenth birthday, his parents buy him a used red Nissan 300ZX as an enticement to keep him living at home. According to a friend, Andrew sees through the ploy and considers them "pathetic" for thinking they "can just buy back my love."

By the time he's actually eighteen, he's regularly dating significantly older men, who open up the wealthier social circles of San Diego to him. He's been living by his wits for years, and knows how to get what he wants out of a situation. This seductive, manipulative power is another of the traits we see in the early development of sexual predators.

In October 1988, while Andrew is a nineteen-year-old freshman at the University of California at San Diego, Modesto is fired and, according to a lawsuit later filed by his wife, he is accused of misappropriating more than $100,000 of clients' money. He sells the house and instructs his wife to live on the proceeds while he goes back to the Philippines to find a new job. The meager proceeds from the house sale and Modesto's Navy pension add up to barely enough for MaryAnn and Andrew to scrape by on. The situation is full of tension, and, by at least one account, in a violent falling-out with his mother over his homosexuality, Andrew throws her against a wall. From a developmental perspective, you would not expect to see in Andrew the homicidal triad of bed-wetting, fire setting, and cruelty to animals that you would in a future serial killer or sexual predator; his impulsive, explosive outburst is, however, more in keeping with the emotional makeup of a spree killer.

After the falling-out with his mother, Andrew drops out of college and joins his father in a small town near Manila. But he's shocked, when he arrives, to find his father living in a squalid little shack without running water, selling cheap merchandise on the street, and expecting his son to help him. For a young man as concerned with self-image as Andrew, this is another critical blow. He earns money for his fare back to the States as a (sometimes cross-dressing) prostitute, with a clientele composed largely of diplomats.

When he returns to America in the spring of 1989, he moves into a boardinghouse in San Francisco's Castro district and gets a menial job to support himself. Meanwhile, he begins refining his cast of alternate identities to serve his purposes: the naval officer graduate of Choate and Yale, the aspiring actor, the construction contractor; one of them even has an ex-wife and a child. Each character has his own wardrobe and personality and peculiar traits, and Cunanan is such a good actor that most people who know him as one don't recognize him as any of the others. Cunanan's goal, as always, is the wealthy, sophisticated older man who can maintain him in the lifestyle to which he desperately aspires to become accustomed. He has fancy clothes, drinks the best champagne, smokes the finest cigars, is showered with expensive gifts and given a generous monthly allowance. By the fall, he's selling marijuana on the side and hustling the older, wealthy gay men he meets. He also dresses and looks straight enough when he wants to, so that prominent men trying to hide their sexual identities don't feel uncomfortable being seen with him. Despite all his charm, sophistication, and pretense, at this point he has never had what one would consider a real job and he is completely dependent for his status on being a kept man.

On Halloween night of 1989, Cunanan meets another older man, this one an actor, who soon moves him into his house and tells people Andrew is his secretary. Cunanan keeps dating younger men on the side, but is supported by the actor and accompanies him to the theater, the opera, and parties attended by the wealthy and beautiful. There is some suggestion that he may have met Gianni Versace at a restaurant reception the following

October. Andrew's actor partner is said to have introduced him to the heavy sadomasochistic whips-and-chains scene.

By 1992, he's traded up again, landing another older man, who gives him a credit card, which Andrew uses to entertain younger lovers and friends. When that relationship ends, he returns to San Diego and quickly finds a new lover, who allows him to live well and throw around cash the way he likes to do to impress people. That summer, though, he finds himself short of funds and forced to move in again with his mother so they can both afford to pay the rent. Though she no longer hassles him about his lifestyle, she keeps urging him to go to church. The arrangement is pretty trying for both of them.

According to writer Wensley Clarkson in his book *Death at Every Stop,* in 1994, as a favor to a friend and for a $1,000 fee, Cunanan marries a Spanish woman so she can get her green card. They part company immediately following the wedding ceremony, but run into each other a couple of months later and kind of hit it off. Cunanan admits he really likes the woman and is intrigued by his own bisexuality. The woman becomes pregnant by him, and they even consider the idea of a real marriage. But that would mean getting a real job rather than depending on rich sugar daddies, and that doesn't fit in with Cunanan's lifestyle. So by the time the baby is born, Clarkson reports, the one significant heterosexual relationship of his life is over.

He profiles the people he wants to meet just as certain types of serial killers, rapists, and child molesters do. In his case, it's wealthy gay men not tied down by families, and he finesses himself into their circles.

The following year he takes up with Norman Blachford, a semiretired businessman in his sixties, who gives him a monthly allowance and a new green Infiniti to drive. This arrangement allows him to move out on his mother, who, no longer having his contribution, is herself forced to move—into a public housing complex in Eureka, Illinois, near Andrew's brother Christopher.

The Blachford connection gives Cunanan an even better lifestyle, a wallet full of credit cards, and trips to Europe. But history repeats itself, and that relationship reportedly ends when Blachford grows tired of having his money spent by his boyfriend on other men. But the ever-resourceful Andrew quickly hooks up with a wealthy interior decorator in his fifties whom he met while involved with Blachford, and this guy becomes his entree to another circle of exclusive parties. Still, I have to believe that seeing his mother go into public housing reminds him of how tenuous and flimsy his whole affluent lifestyle is.

One of the younger men Cunanan becomes involved with is a ruggedly handsome Naval Academy graduate named Jeffrey Trail, assigned to the Navy in San Diego. Cunanan falls for him hard, even though the secretly gay officer wants only a platonic relationship with him. When Trail leaves the service in 1996 and moves away from California with a new lover, Andrew is devastated. But the next trauma is, perhaps, even greater and represents one of the tantalizing mysteries of Andrew Cunanan's life.

In January 1997, he gets sick, and even though the symptoms aren't acute, he can't manage to shake them off. He becomes worried that he might have HIV and goes in for a test and counseling. But he never specifically tells the counselor what he knows—if anything—of his HIV status, and we still have no definitive evidence one way or the other on this.

At this point, Jeff Trail is in Minnesota, manager for the local gas company in Bloomington. After learning that Jeff and his companion have split up, Cunanan goes to visit him in Minneapolis for a several-week stay, and while there becomes friendly with Trail's friend David Madson, a talented, blond, good-looking thirty-three-year-old architect whom he knew briefly in the San

Francisco gay scene. This time, the three of them hit it off well. Cunanan pays for expensive dinners and throws around money as if he were actually a man of means. He apparently becomes quite smitten with Madson, whom he later refers to as the love of his life. But Madson soon begins distancing himself because he is uncomfortable with how much Cunanan seems to be hiding (reportedly even his address and phone number) and how little Madson really knows about him. And if, as suspected, Andrew is dealing and personally using drugs, the guy could be dangerous.

Back in Southern California, Cunanan continues to mix with the beautiful people, but is painfully not one of them. He meets Madonna at a party but perceives that she treats him as if he is nothing, which, in many ways, he is. I mean, think about this: he is so egocentric and narcissistic he is pissed off when a big star doesn't treat him as an equal. This boy is living in a fantasy world. At another party he gets introduced to actress-model Elizabeth Hurley, who also ignores him. This is particularly irritating to him since he had unsuccessfully auditioned as an extra for her boyfriend Hugh Grant's film *Nine Months.*

He can't seem to latch on to another wealthy benefactor. Without one, he's powerless, and his emotional deterioration continues. He worries he's losing the looks and charm that have been his fancy meal ticket. In his business, by your late twenties you may not be quite over the hill, but you're certainly looking at the downslope. He puts on weight and stops exercising. For about a week in the spring of 1997, he works the streets of Los Angeles as a transvestite prostitute.

Returning again to Hillcrest, Cunanan sells his car and takes a small apartment with a roommate. He transforms his bedroom into a virtual shrine to actor Tom Cruise, covering the walls with posters and telling his roommate he wants to tie Cruise up and make him "beg for more." He confesses that he'd like to kill

Cruise's wife, Nicole Kidman, so he can have the actor all to himself. This is classic stalking behavior—both the obsession and the magical thinking that if one fact is changed, the stalker and the object of his "affection" can enjoy a life together. What's interesting and significant in this case is that we frequently see stalking behavior in assassins—both of political leaders and of show business figures—prior to the actual assassination or attempt. We'll go into that more in the next chapter, but by this point in his life it is clear Andrew Cunanan is developing an assassin type of personality.

In April 1997, he announces that he's moving back to San Francisco permanently. After a lavish going-away party, friends discuss his deteriorating appearance among themselves—he looks bloated and isn't being as careful as usual about his hair and dress—and rumors circulate that he may have HIV or AIDS. Around this time he has a screaming argument over the phone with Jeff Trail, whom he suspects of carrying on an affair with Dave Madson behind his back. They get over the tension, but Cunanan reportedly threatened to kill Trail, and Trail is worried.

Instead of going to San Francisco, Cunanan flies to Minneapolis, where, despite his reservations, Dave Madson picks him up at the Minneapolis airport, on April 26, and takes him back to his loft apartment. It is significant to note that despite being way over his credit card limit, Cunanan bought a one-way plane ticket to go there—forget what he told his friends about his plans to move to San Francisco. He and Madson go out to dinner with some of Dave's friends. The next night, Cunanan invites Jeff Trail, who's got his own live-in lover, to the loft.

When Trail arrives, they argue. We don't know exactly what happened, but neighbors hear shouting and screaming, and investigators believe that Cunanan goes into the kitchen, seizes a claw hammer from a drawer, walks back into the living room, and attacks Trail, bludgeoning him until he collapses. The floor and walls are spattered with Trail's blood. When police examine his body days later, his watch is stopped at 9:55 P.M. You don't need a series of murders to infer quite a bit about motive from this particular crime scene: nearly thirty blows from a hammer indicate a kind of overkill we see when the killer knows his victim very well. And the type of jealousy and impulsive rage Cunanan was apparently capable of would certainly support the theory that this was a personal-cause homicide.

Cunanan and Madson wrap the body in an Oriental rug from the bedroom and stow it in the apartment. Later, there is some speculation that Madson is held against his will by Cunanan, but there's no solid evidence one way or the other. The two men are even seen walking Madson's dog after the murder would have occurred. Madson's coworkers grow concerned that he hasn't shown up for work and hasn't called. They contact the building superintendent, who goes into the apartment with a neighbor, sees the blood, and finds the body. It's possible Cunanan and Madson are still in the apartment at the time. The super calls the police. When they arrive, they find Cunanan's gym bag and Trail's empty gun holster and an empty box of bullets. What they don't know is that Dave Madson has made the mistake of his life.

One point I always make is, if you are unfortunate enough to be the victim of a crime and the offender orders you to get into a car with him—don't do it! Your chances of survival are greatly reduced if you follow his instructions and go anywhere with him.

But Andrew and Dave have taken off in Madson's red Jeep Cherokee. On May 2, they show up at the Full Moon restaurant and bar in Stark, Minnesota, just off Interstate 35 north of Minneapolis. According to observers, Madson looks nervous, but there is no evidence of tension between him and Cunanan. In fact, from time to time they hold hands as they sit across the table from each other.

After lunch, they continue heading north, until Cunanan pulls the Jeep off the road and onto a trail that leads to an abandoned farmhouse. From the crime scene, it seems that he tells Madson to get out of the vehicle, then pumps several rounds from Trail's gun into his companion's head and back, including one through Madson's eye. This method of killing provides an important clue: even if Cunanan and Madson had not been seen together, anytime we see an attack to the face delivered from close range like this, we immediately think personal-cause homicide. Hours later, some fishermen find Dave Madson's corpse. When Chicago County, Minnesota, sheriff Randall Schwegman examines the body, he notices defense wounds on the fingers, indicating the victim knew he was about to be killed.

Madson's family is not only grief-stricken but shocked. They insist that he could not possibly have had anything to do with Trail's murder. His parents believe Dave might have walked in on the killing and been taken hostage by Cunanan, who then killed him when he threatened to escape and talk. And there is some good evidence that Madson did come in on the scene after the fact. As a rule, he takes his Dalmatian for a run about ten o'clock in the evening. And though there is a lot of blood on the floor and a lot of footprints, the neighbors hear no barking and there are no paw prints in the blood. If the dog wasn't in the apartment at the time of the killing, it's likely Madson wasn't, either. When authorities go to Madson's apartment, they find the dog there.

The motive to kill Dave Madson is a tough one, but there are probably several factors involved. One, there is the practical problem of keeping a witness from going to the police. But probably even more significant, Cunanan has now begun to settle scores.

THE ANATOMY OF MOTIVE

If he killed Jeff Trail for spurning him, now it is Dave Madson's turn. And if Cunanan had his way, he'd get back at everyone who ever spurned him in his whole sorry life.

Sheriff Schwegman travels to San Diego and, with police there, goes through Cunanan's apartment looking for clues. He's struck by the Tom Cruise shrine and alerts police to take extra security measures with the actor. He finds sadomasochistic sex pornography, including videos featuring animals.

By now, Andrew Cunanan is a known and wanted man. Police watch his apartment in case he returns. Be-on-the-Lookouts are issued throughout the country, and the public starts to be aware that a new serial killer is on the loose.

Cunanan's next stop is Chicago, where he frequents some gay bars and sleeps in Madson's Jeep because he's just about out of cash. In the evening, he drives to the city's celebrated Gold Coast area and ends up in front of the two brownstones that have been put together to form the home of Lee Miglin and his wife of thirty-eight years, Marilyn. Miglin, seventy-two, is a prominent real estate developer and father of the business park concept, which he developed from old warehouse sites. The self-made son of a Lithuanian immigrant father, he is a rags-to-riches story, modest and quiet but extremely smart, with an excellent reputation in the building and philanthropic communities. Marilyn, fifty-nine, is a success in her own right with a multimillion-dollar cosmetics business. They have two grown children. On this night, Marilyn is in Toronto on business.

Somehow—and this is another of the many details we still don't have about this case—Cunanan is able to gain access to the house. Earlier in the day Miglin was working in the garage with the door open, so that point of entry is the most likely. It's possible Cunanan wanted to rob Miglin of the cash he assumed a wealthy homeowner in this neighborhood would have on hand.

But once he's inside, it gets crazy. In the garage, he binds Miglin with orange electrical cord and wraps his entire head in duct tape, leaving only a breathing hole at the nose. He then subjects Miglin to hideous torture, stabbing him repeatedly with a screwdriver and pruning shears and then sawing through his throat with a bow saw while he watches the blood spurt. He gets into Miglin's green 1994 Lexus and runs over the body several times on the garage floor. Then he stashes his victim under another car, goes into the house, fixes himself some food from the refrigerator, makes himself at home, and goes to sleep in the Miglins' bed. The next morning, he takes several thousand dollars in cash, a leather jacket, and an expensive wristwatch, and heads off in the Lexus.

Why he practices this degree of overkill on someone he's never met before and has nothing personal against is an open question. But I wouldn't be surprised if Miglin did or said something that provoked his rage. My guess would be something like telling this young punk he wasn't going to give him his car or money and he should go out and get a damn job. Miglin is a tough businessman. Despite his age, I don't think he would have been easily intimidated by this young intruder. But this kind of resistance would point up for Cunanan all the inherent problems in his life and he would want to exact revenge on a successful person who recognized that about him and humiliated him with it. So he not only had to kill Miglin for strategic reasons, he had to dominate and destroy him for emotional ones. Miglin had become symbolic to him. He may even have been a symbol in Cunanan's mind of a judgmental, punitive father.

It's this kind of murderous rage and frenzy that leads me to believe that even if Cunanan started off as a serial killer, by the time of the Miglin murder he is definitely on a spree. The crime-scene indicators are mixed. In some cases we will see him killing for the thrill, for the manipulation, domination, and control that are absent from the rest of his life. In other cases, he will kill in a burst of anger, or because he needs something. The fact that he doesn't attempt to cover up his crimes speaks against a pure serial sexual offender.

In my mind, unlike most spree killers, Cunanan is a sexual predator, which we see demonstrated by many aspects of his personal life. That he had not killed up until Trail's murder is due to the fact that until then, everything was reasonably under control in his life. Violence, as I've noted many times, is situational. And I don't believe he went into the meeting with Trail expecting to kill him. The weapon was one of opportunity that he found at the scene. But once he gets started, it's as if each killing merely raises the ante and stokes his lust for more. Also, while he may not yet consciously be playing an endgame strategy at this point, he is not thinking long term. He's not taking care to avoid leaving clues as a successful serial killer does. He's no longer an UNSUB; he's in known fugitive status. He's going from day to day, incident to incident, and if he's considering the future at all, I don't believe he expects to come out of this spree alive.

Cunanan conforms to the spree killer profile on many levels: a white male killing within his own race. A drifter. Intelligent but an underachiever who's never really made anything of himself. Unlike a serial killer, who will fantasize the crime before committing it, there is no evidence this was the case after the murders of Trail and Madson. The spree killer's rage is unplanned and unpredictable. That's why, as Cunanan does here and later in his spree, he is much more likely to leave clues and use his own name. The trick with the spree killer is not so much figuring out *who* he is, as in the case of a serial killer, but *where* he is—and where he's going next. And let me add, this group is much more difficult to study directly (as I have studied serial offenders) because they don't often end up in prison, where we can talk to them. More often they'll end up on a medical examiner's slab.

Back in Chicago, Marilyn Miglin is worried as soon as her husband is not at the airport to pick her up on Sunday, May 4. When she arrives home, she finds the place a mess and calls the police. They are the ones who find Lee's brutalized body in the garage. There are no signs of forced entry, so police theorize that Miglin might have known his killer. In retrospect, however, other than the extremely tenuous possibility that Cunanan may have met the Miglins' actor son in Los Angeles—which the younger Miglin denied—there are no known links between them.

But this is the kind of crime that can easily throw investigators off. Consider that had Cunanan not taken Madson's Jeep to the crime scene, had he not stolen and later pawned an easily trace-able item like Miglin's collectable gold coin, and had he gener-ally behaved in a more criminally sophisticated manner, instead of leaving clues to his identity everywhere he went, investigators would have no reason to look for Andrew Cunanan in connection with this murder, no reason to view it as part of a killing spree. This would likely be investigated as a personal-cause homicide, based on indicators like the lack of forced entry and the overkill, and the crime scene read totally differently. You could lose a lot of time going down blind alleys with that theory.

In fact, though, police find Dave Madson's red Jeep Cherokee less than a block from Miglin's home, collecting parking tickets. There are photos of Cunanan inside and other evidence of him. And an S&M video found in his San Diego apartment contains a scene that is a virtual script for what he did to Lee Miglin.

From Chicago, then, Cunanan heads east toward Philadel-phia, using Miglin's cell phone to call a friend in San Diego. But when he hears on the radio that the police are after him, tracing him from the phone's signal, he pitches it out the window over a bridge. On Friday, May 9, he shows up at the caretaker's lodge in Finn's Point Cemetery, a Civil War burial ground in rural Pennsville, New Jersey. The caretaker there is forty-five-year-old William Reese, an electrician by training who is also an amateur Civil War scholar and takes part in reenactments. He and his wife, Rebecca, an elementary school librarian, have a twelve-year-old son.

Cunanan probably approaches Reese with some pretext like asking for directions. He then pulls out Trail's gun, forces Reese to hand over the keys to his red 1995 Chevy pickup truck, then shoots him once, point-blank in the head, execution-style. He leaves the Lexus behind, full of clues—including shell casings, the screwdriver used to stab Miglin, and a passport—and drives off in the pickup. Later that day, Rebecca Reese comes looking for her husband. When she sees his truck is missing, another car there in its place, she calls the sheriff's office. They find Reese's body slumped over his desk.

This shows the desperation into which Cunanan has by now fallen—and his total lack of criminal sophistication. Had he not just swapped vehicles here and had he used a different weapon, for example, there would again be no reason for police to suspect him in this crime. Moreover, if all he needed was a vehicle, plenty of criminals obtain them every day without implicating themselves in a murder! Cunanan realizes he needs another means of transportation for his getaway, but is not criminally sophisticated enough to just steal a car or hot-wire it in a deserted parking lot. The only thing he can figure out is to kill the owner and take the keys.

How do we know Cunanan is motivated simply by the need for a new vehicle? This is the first murder that contains no element of emotional release for the killer: the up-close-and-personal delivery of multiple fatal blows/gunshots/torturous wounds present in the first three indicated rage and anger were big motivators in the killer's psyche, either because he knew his victim personally or because (in Miglin's case) of what the victim represented and how he reacted to his killer. But here there is no attempt to torture or torment the victim. Add to that some victimology: unlike conditions on the reenactment battlefield, in real life Bill Reese was described as a nice guy with no enemies. He is merely in the wrong place at the wrong time.

The spree is in full bloom; Cunanan will do whatever he can within his limited abilities to keep it going, but the more the inexperienced offender tries to control the situation, the more out of control he becomes, which is a common phenomenon with spree killers. Also characteristic of this type: inside the Lexus, Cunanan has left newspaper clippings about the three other murders. Many of the serial offenders I talked to told me why they do this—to document their "accomplishments" and revel in them, reliving them in fantasy over and over as they read details of their exploits during their cooling-off periods. A spree offender has no such luxury, however. There's just not a lot of time for someone on the run, always looking over his shoulder, to stop and relive the past. While he gets off on reading of his "accomplishments," he's also gathering intelligence information, looking to see how much we know about who he is and where he might be going, and this adds to the pressure on him.

Following Reese's murder, Cunanan sees he's placed on the FBI's Ten Most-Wanted List. He's featured repeatedly on *America's Most Wanted*. Now the general public is taking notice. This serial killing business isn't just a homosexual grudge match any longer. He's murdering all types.

Despite his mental degeneration and sloppiness, Cunanan has his wits enough about him that in a Kmart parking lot in Florence, South Carolina, he spots a truck similar to the one he's driving and steals a license plate to throw cops off his trail.

On May 10, he checks into an oceanfront room at the Normandy Plaza Hotel in Miami Beach on a weekly rate under one of his old aliases, Andrew DeSilva. The low-rent, pink stucco–fronted hotel is a far cry from the elegant establishments he's used to. A week later, he pays by the week for another room, higher up, and a week after that he pays for a third, higher-up room by the month. Early in his stay, an employee at Miami Subs Grill, a couple of blocks from the hotel, recognizes him from TV photos and calls 911, but by the time police arrive he's gone.

Cunanan spends his nights barhopping and frequenting trendy South Beach's gay clubs. During the day, he keeps mainly to his hotel room, watching TV and poring through S&M pornography, living mainly on subs and take-out pizza. Meanwhile, his mother has moved back to National City, San Diego, and after the Miglin murder tells authorities she's afraid her son will come back to harm her. She gets an armed guard.

On the afternoon of July 7, Cunanan goes to a pawnshop near the hotel called Cash on the Beach and pawns a gold coin he stole from Lee Miglin. He uses his own passport for ID and lists the Normandy Plaza as his address. He also provides a thumbprint. But the store owner doesn't recognize him. As required by law, she forwards a copy of the pawn transaction to Miami Beach PD, but since this is a routine thing, it goes to a processing clerk's desk. There's another sighting of Cunanan, this one by tennis pro David Todini, who recognizes the fugitive as he walks down Collins Avenue, the main drag of Miami Beach. Todini calls the police, but by the time they arrive, he's gone again.

Some interpret his risky public appearances—and the clues he leaves behind—as him taunting the police. But in fact, it's all carelessness, which shows not only that he's coming apart, but also that he is never very together as a criminal, despite his public image. Basically, unlike most sexual killers, he's gone into the big leagues without spending much time in the minors perfecting his technique on less-high-profile crimes. So what he's doing is ultimately suicidal. Despite the interval between the later murders, there really is no cooling-off period.

One of South Beach's most celebrated residents is Gianni Versace, who bought a pair of dilapidated buildings on Ocean Drive and spent millions converting them into a palatial mansion that he calls Casa Casuarina. Versace's presence in the area, beginning in 1991, mirrors the transformation of South Beach from a depressing and seedy vestige of Miami's past to a happening, ultra-with-it Art Deco playground for the young and beautiful. In South Beach, anything goes. And though the fifty-year-old Versace also owns magnificent homes in Manhattan and Milan, and a huge villa on Lake Como, he loves his time here, the social scene and the freedom he feels to walk about as he wishes. On this particular visit, he and his entourage arrive on July 12. Cunanan is immediately aware of his arrival and, according to police reconstruction, stakes out the front of Casa Casuarina, which happens to be two blocks from the garage where Cunanan has stashed the pickup.

At around 8:30 on the morning of Tuesday, July 15, Versace leaves the mansion and walks a couple of blocks to the News Cafe, where he buys coffee and some weekly magazines. When he returns home a few minutes later, he begins to unlock the wrought-iron gate of Casa Casuarina. As he does this, according to a woman described as the police's best witness, a young man wearing a white shirt, gray shorts, and a black baseball cap and carrying a black backpack walks up and shoots him from behind. Versace collapses on the stone steps, mortally wounded. The assassin leans over him and shoots him again in the head, then takes off. From inside the house, Versace's companion, Antonio D'Amico, hears the shots and rushes outside, running after the assassin, who then turns and points his gun at D'Amico before disappearing in the direction of a nearby parking garage.

When police search the garage, they find William Reese's red Chevy pickup with the stolen plate, its windshield bedecked with parking tickets. Inside the cab they find the bloody clothes D'Amico identifies as having been worn by the killer, along with a United States passport issued to Andrew Phillip Cunanan. Also in the truck are more newspaper clippings, one of Cunanan's checks from Bank of America, and a list of other celebrities he wants to target. Two of them—Madonna and singer Julio Iglesias—have homes near Versace's. All of them are warned.

The two spent cartridges found at the murder scene match those found with David Madson's body. A nightclub security camera places him at an establishment called the Twist, which Versace was known to frequent. Employees and witnesses in neighboring establishments can identify Cunanan as having been there in the preceding weeks, which indicates that he was stalking Versace and staking out his residence.

Investigators try to establish a link between Versace and his killer. It was unusual for the designer to go out by himself, so perhaps Cunanan called first and arranged to meet him, but nothing solid can be established. The FBI is called in and helps conduct what is described as one of the largest manhunts in U.S. history. Police stake out the memorial service for Versace in hopes of finding his killer there.

With the killing of such a flamboyant celebrity on the steps of his own home, the entire nation is terrified. Cunanan could strike anywhere, anytime. And after his trail of terror has been pieced together with previous accounts of his many costumes and disguises, Andrew Cunanan is suddenly transformed by the media into this super-killer master of disguise. He's a chameleon who can blend in anywhere, we are told, and the police won't even notice him. Not since the fictional Hannibal Lecter has there been such a criminal genius. The clues are perceived by some to be a cat-and-mouse game he's playing with the police to show how clever he is. In fact, a former friend receives a call on his answering machine from Cunanan saying, "Hi, it's Andy. The FBI will never catch me—I'm just too damn clever." What this says to me, though, is that he's starting—and desperately needs—to believe his own mythology. This is always a risky proposition, regardless of your line of work.

This image is bolstered when, on July 17, Metro Dade police, responding to a burglar alarm, find the naked body of Dr. Silvio Alfonso in his Miami Springs home, ten miles from Versace's mansion. Like Versace, Alfonso has been shot in the head, execution-style. A man fitting Cunanan's description was seen fleeing the home. But several days later, with Cunanan still at large, another man with a passing resemblance is arrested and charged. His motive related to an argument with Alfonso over money.

The number of possible Cunanan sightings becomes virtually unmanageable.

In real life, of course, Cunanan is nothing like the master criminal he's portrayed to be. He's not nearly as sophisticated as a Bradford Bishop, a John List, or an Audrey Hilley. He's really a desperate, disorganized loser who is now very much at the endgame. The telephone message he left is wishful thinking. He has to realize that once he's let his murderous rage take hold of him and he's killed Jeff Trail, he can't go back to his old ways and lifestyle. It's not that he's clever; it's that the system is very unwieldy for this type of crime. In fact, several opportunities to catch him are missed. Not only is there the pawnshop evidence, but when police finally go to his hotel following Versace's murder, they search the wrong rooms. And there are other missteps that, unfortunately, are not unusual in a criminal investigation—

which is not an exact science and, despite such breakthroughs as DNA analysis and laser imaging, probably never will be. He's also just plain lucky that every time the police arrive on a tip, he's left minutes before.

As I explained earlier, in my opinion the clues he leaves have nothing to do with a clever cat-and-mouse game; they're just evidence of a sloppy offender who's running out of time. The big problem, as Mark Olshaker and I write in an op-ed column in the *Wall Street Journal* on Wednesday, July 23, is that there are so many individual police agencies throughout the country that before they can coordinate with one another, serial killers can easily get away with murder. In spite of this, we predict that he will be caught soon. In our view he's too inefficient at this point to last on the run much longer, and we know that he's only going to grow more careless and desperate as time passes. As control-oriented as he's been, he's not the type to surrender to police and go to jail. More than likely he will either kill himself or set up a situation in which the police have to kill him to protect themselves. This will be all the more likely if, as it was rumored, one of the triggering events for the spree was that Cunanan found out he was HIV-positive and could otherwise look forward to a slow, wasting death from AIDS. Since his autopsy records have not been made public, however, the matter remains open to speculation.

On the afternoon of the same day that our *Journal* article appears, Fernando Carreira, a seventy-one-year-old caretaker of a two-story houseboat docked in a marina in Miami Beach's Indian Creek, notes an intruder inside, thinks he hears a single gunshot, and calls the police, who seal off the area while the SWAT team surrounds the houseboat, which is captured on national television. Various pundits and some of my former colleagues go on the talk shows speculating about whether this is Andrew Cunanan or not, and whether he'll come out peaceably. A good many of them think it can't be Andrew Cunanan; this doesn't fit their profile of him; he'd be too smart and resourceful to place himself in such a vulnerable position. In all likelihood, he's long gone from the Miami area, which accounts for all these sightings around the country, including just under the FBI's nose in Washington, D.C. As I'm watching, I wonder how long it's going to be before they have to eat those words.

Around 9 P.M., after several hours of watching and waiting, the assault crew fires in tear gas canisters, then bursts in with weapons at the ready. They find Andrew Cunanan faceup on the bed, clad only in boxer shorts, shot through the mouth with the same .40 caliber handgun he had killed with four times before. He was down to his last bullet. He had obliterated the face that no longer served his needs. Evidence suggests he was living there about a week. As I anticipated, there is no suicide note.

It is psychologically tempting to speculate that Gianni Versace represented to Cunanan the wealthy older gay men on whom he had depended and that he killed the designer to symbolically get back at all of them for using him, and there might be some truth to this. Many crimes have multiple precipitators and determinants. But from my study of this type of offender, I think the most important element in the murder is that Versace represented a person Cunanan could never be, with a celebrity he could never attain and a lifestyle he could never achieve on his own. Versace was creative and accomplished and his lifestyle came from his own effort and talent, and he could keep it as long as he wanted. Cunanan was a glib, charming, empty shell who was already losing his appeal and moving farther and farther away from the life he always lusted after. The bleak, sordid existence he could afford on his own was too dismal to contemplate. I think it's likely that, had Versace remained overseas for another week or so, a desperate Cunanan, out of cash and resources, would have found another target in celebrity-rich South Beach for his final sensational act, and another of the beautiful people would have been murdered in broad daylight in Versace's stead—and it *would* have been in broad daylight, since part of the appeal for this offender was the notoriety of his act.

I also think it likely that once he found himself in Lee Miglin's wealthy home, though there was no sexual relationship between the two men, Miglin was in some ways a tune-up for Versace, in that Cunanan saw in him a successful, hardworking man with all the trappings that Cunanan could never have on his own. In other words, at his age, Miglin represented a future Cunanan knew he could never grow into. If we think of the offender in his mid-forties who kills in frustration that he's worked all these years, has the wife and kids, but hasn't achieved more of what he'd hoped for, Cunanan is like the stalker-assassins who kill in their mid-to-late twenties when they realize they can't even get things going in their life in the first place. Every profession has its own cutoff point at which you realize you're either going to make it or you're not. For offenders such as Cunanan, like athletes, that cutoff comes in the late twenties.

Homosexuality happened to be Cunanan's orientation, and it happened to be Versace's, so Cunanan could identify with him as a successful role model. Aside from that, homosexuality is merely incidental to this case. The types of rage and behavior Cunanan demonstrated are far more often displayed by heterosexual offenders. What he became, regardless of his orientation, was a stalker and, ultimately, an assassin.

And so, like other stalkers, he set out to destroy the object he most admired, that he most coveted, and in doing so accomplish *something* of note. The stalker and the nonpolitical assassin are obsessed with the object of their attention and/or what they represent. In some cases, as with Mark David Chapman, killer of John Lennon, they out-and-out want to be that person. And when they can't, they decide that no one else can be, either. I think this is what happened to some extent between Andrew Cunanan and Gianni Versace, who knew him hardly, if at all. To the extent that he could, Andrew Cunanan would go out in a blaze of glory. And like Chapman with Lennon, John Hinckley with his actress idol Jodie Foster, and other stalkers, there was a part of Cunanan that wanted to be forever linked to his target, and so he shall be.

When we consider a killing spree like this one, a lot of our study of motivation and behavior comes into the analysis. As with every other type of crime, in this case the first crime is the most significant. While Cunanan's first murders are not within his physical zone of comfort, which we would have to assume is around the Hillcrest area of San Diego, his victims are people close to him, within his emotional zone of comfort. They are easy to get close to, and so they are easy to strike out against. The first crime, and probably the second, is a crime of passion. Once he realizes he can do it, he expands his circle of violence out into the spree it becomes. And here again we see how important it is that Cunanan gave us clues to link all the cases together. Had there been only enough evidence to indicate Reese's case as the first, for example, the investigation would have been completely thrown off track. That's why I advise, when crimes in a series look as disparate as these appeared, you often have to question whether the first one you see is truly the first done by that offender.

Let me also add here that while I believe Cunanan was a sloppy, rage-driven amateur rather than a master criminal, I take strong issue with the so-called experts who claimed, and continue to do so, that Cunanan subconsciously wanted to be caught. In my opinion, there is nothing in his behavior, profile, or final actions that support this. If he had had more opportunities, he would have killed again. There was no reason for him to stop.

You've got to deal with each offender on his own terms and using his own weaknesses. Alton Coleman was much better at crime and—in terms of time at it and number of offenses—much more "successful" than Andrew Cunanan. He'd had a lot more experience. And he kept it relatively simple for himself and committed the same offense over and over again. What he didn't have was the worldly sophistication to go far from his comfort zone and blend in. Cunanan had that, and so he was able to travel. The more we know about each offender, the more we can do. For example—though some of this was tried—I think the authorities, and I include the FBI, could have been more proactive with Cunanan. We could be pretty sure that wherever he was, he would be hanging around the gay nightlife scene. We also had strong evidence that he was, and stayed, in the Miami Beach area. And we knew that the gay community in general was worried about this person in their midst. It would therefore have been logical to spend a lot of time and effort circulating his picture and behavioral description to restaurants and clubs, and—just as important—to have had a mechanism in place to respond immediately when a sighting was reported. Waiting for a normal police response, as we learned, just wasn't going to do the trick.

As with most serial killers, it would have been very difficult here to prevent the first murder. But if there is any lesson from the Cunanan case, it is the point we made in the *Wall Street Journal*: we have to have an organized, nationwide system for law enforcement to share information on a real-time basis. It won't stop serial murders or spree killers from getting started, but it sure can help stop them in their tracks. And once a violent offender is on the run, that is exactly what we need to do.

# CHAPTER SEVEN

# SHADOW OF A GUNMAN

At about twenty-five minutes after eleven on the morning of August 1, 1966, in the cloudless, typically oppressive central Texas heat, a blond, six-foot-tall, 198-pound former Marine and current architectural engineering student, dressed in sneakers and blue nylon coveralls over jeans and a red plaid shirt, drove his black Chevrolet Impala up to the gray, 307-foot limestone-faced clock tower adjoining the administration building of the University of Texas at Austin. He parked and, lugging an olive-drab military footlocker out of the backseat, proceeded by service elevator to the twenty-seventh floor, and from there by stairs to the observation-deck level, which circled the entire tower about 230 feet above the ground, just under the four large clock faces. There is no indication he ever intended to come back down under his own power. In fact, there is strong indication he considered this to be the last day of his life.

This Florida native's name was Charles Joseph Whitman, and that morning it was unknown outside his family and his small circle of acquaintances. Within the next hour and a half, though, thirteen unwary strangers would be dead by his choice and action, and within an hour after that, he would be known around the world as "the sniper in the tower." His name would be forever synonymous with spontaneous horror.

Also in those first hours, his tally would rise by two, when police found the bodies of his wife, Kathleen, and his mother, Margaret, both dead of multiple bayonet stab wounds to the chest, lying in their respective homes. In addition, he had shot his mother in the back of the head. Notes Whitman left near each corpse professed his deep love for both women. He had taken the precaution of leaving a note for the building super-intendent, supposedly from his mother, on her apartment door, saying she was sleeping late and not to disturb her; he had then called his wife's boss at the telephone company where she worked to say she was sick and wouldn't be coming in that day.

The footlocker he hauled into the tower contained both an incredible arsenal and a survivalist's ration pack. Among his weapons were a sawed-off twelve-gauge shotgun, a bolt-action six-millimeter Remington rifle fitted with a four-power Leupold sight, a pump-action .35 caliber Remington rifle, a .30 caliber M-1 carbine, a nine-millimeter Luger pistol, a Smith & Wesson .357 magnum, and more than seven hundred rounds of am-munition, in addition to three hunting knives, a machete, and a hatchet. His survivalist pack included canned ravioli, sausage, Spam, fruits, water, matches, gasoline, high-power binoculars, coffee, Dexedrine, Excedrin, and a radio so he could monitor the reports he knew would be coming in on him.

Other than Whitman's wife and mother, the victimology was completely random. He took out his first three victims while he was still setting up in the tower. He encountered Edna Towns-ley, forty-seven years of age, the divorced mother of two sons who served as a receptionist-greeter, when she welcomed him to the observation deck. Whitman struck her with the stock of his shotgun with enough force to crack her skull, then turned the weapon around and shot her. He was stowing her body when a young couple, Don Walden and Cheryl Botts, came down from the observation deck in time to see the good-looking young blond man carrying two rifles. They thought it odd, but when he offered them a friendly greeting, they proceeded down the stairs to the elevator. By the following day, the local media were describing Walden and Botts as "the luckiest couple in Austin."

But the next people Whitman encountered were not so lucky. Martin Gabour, called Mark, a sixteen-year-old high school student from Texarkana, Texas, and his eighteen-year-old brother, Mike, who had just completed his freshman year at the Air Force Academy, were in Austin with their parents, M.J. and Mary, visiting M.J.'s sister Marguerite Lamport and her husband, William. All six of them had come to the University of Texas tower this morning. By the time they got off the elevator at the twenty-seventh floor and reached the stairs that would take them up to the observation deck, Whitman had moved Edna Townsley's desk to the top of the stairs to keep anyone else away. Mary assumed that a janitor was in the process of cleaning the area, but Mark and Mike decided to check out the situation for themselves. They pushed the desk aside so they could squeeze by and find out what was happening.

As soon as Whitman noticed them, he wheeled around with the shotgun and fired, hitting both. They tumbled back down the stairs at the impact, and Whitman continued firing down the staircase at the rest of the family. Before the shooting stopped, Mark Gabour and Marguerite Lamport lay dead, and Mike Gabour and his mother were severely injured.

They were the last interruptions to Whitman's plan to set himself up outside on the observation deck, where the four-foot-high stone parapets would provide him with protection and the thin rectangular rain spouts would serve as gun slits.

And then, quite simply, he began firing below, covering a four-block area with his carnage. People on the ground saw others next to them dropping in pools of blood and looked up helplessly, not understanding what was happening. In terror, they huddled behind whatever cover they could find—a car, a lamppost, even a mailbox or trash can. The already wounded held still against the blistering, sun-baked pavement so the shooter, wherever he was, wouldn't go for them again.

Even after the emergency calls started coming in and Austin police raced to the campus that had suddenly become a killing field, there was no immediate solution. Having studied military tactics and understanding well the strategic value of a fortress and high ground, Whitman had bought himself a lot of time to continue his massacre.

Quickly determining that the most effective approach might be from the air, the police got access to a small plane and, with flying instructor and part-time Williamson County deputy sheriff Jim Boutwell as the brave volunteer pilot, sent up a sniper, Austin police lieutenant Marion Lee, to try to pick off the shooter from the air. But as they got close to the tower, the heat rising from all of the pavement and concrete buildings created too much turbulence for Lee to get a clear shot. If he wasn't sure he could hit the shooter, he wasn't going to take a chance on injuring anyone else. Whitman fired two shots at the tiny plane that ripped through its fabric-covered sides.

Lee couldn't keep the UNSUB on the tower in his gun sight, but he and Boutwell still provided an invaluable service by keeping Whitman's attention focused above him. Not only were some on the ground able to flee to safety, but two Austin police officers,

Ramiro Martinez, a twenty-nine-year-old father of twin five-year-old girls, and Houston McCoy, twenty-six, led a small assault team of police and civilian volunteers up the tower and onto the observation deck. Approaching from around the corner onto the north side of the walkway, the two officers spotted Whitman. Martinez opened fire with his revolver. Whitman turned on him and began shooting the carbine, but his aim was obscured by the dust and debris created by bullets hitting the limestone walls. This gave McCoy, who had come up right behind Martinez, a clearer view of the shooter. Aiming at the white headband Whitman was wearing, McCoy squeezed the trigger of his shotgun and hit Whitman right across the eyes and nose. He flopped to the ground. Taking no chances, Martinez grabbed McCoy's shotgun and pumped another round into the still-moving body.

It was 1:24 P.M., just slightly more than an hour and a half since the first shots had rung out from the tower.

In the United States of 1966, a crime like this hadn't yet taken on the status of "the latest outrage" and still had the capacity to shock nearly everyone. Less than a month before, Richard Speck had butchered eight student nurses in Chicago while burglarizing their apartment. It was as if the nation had suddenly and inexplicably entered a new era of random horror, and as far as crime was concerned, America had lost its innocence. Everyone wanted to know why. There were plenty of possible answers once the inevitable investigation began, but none of them seemed adequate for such an act.

Charles Whitman was a mass murderer—along with Speck, the first one many people remember. But in trying to comprehend the crime and the motivation for it, it is important to understand Whitman in terms of what we in my unit came to call the "assassin personality." Though most of the subjects would probably disagree with this assessment, the fact that the end result is a senseless act of mass killing rather than a targeted assassination of a political figure or celebrity is less significant than the process that got them to one or the other crime in the first place.

Let's take a look at what we're talking about here and see how it applies to people like Charles Whitman.

From our study, much of it coordinated with the work of other experts such as Ken Baker, the behavioral guru at the Secret Service whom I've worked with closely throughout my FBI career, we've identified certain characteristics and motivators of this personality type that remain pretty consistent. Assassin personalities tend to be white male loners with self-esteem problems—no surprises there, since that describes a huge chunk of the violent predator population. More specifically, they tend to be functional paranoiacs. They shouldn't be confused with paranoid schizophrenics, who have a serious psychosis often described as a shattered personality. The people we're dealing with may be delusional, but they're not hallucinatory. Rather, their paranoia may be described as a highly organized or methodical delusional system that may be convincing if you accept the basic premise. In other words, if you accept the basic (but delusional) premise that everyone is out to get a particular individual and is ready and able to do him harm, then it becomes a convincing argument that this individual should strike out and neutralize these enemies before they can act against him.

Sometimes the delusional system will be based on a kernel of truth, but there will be no correlation between the defined problem and the action taken to deal with it. For example, I interviewed Lynette "Squeaky" Fromme, Manson family member and would-be assassin of President Gerald Ford, in the federal penitentiary in Alderson, West Virginia. She described for me all of the problems Charles Manson had pointed out having to do with pollution and corruption of the environment, among other things, and I had little beef with that. But what had that got to do with trying to kill the president? Sure, she could say she was "calling attention" to the problems, though there are many more-effective ways to do it than that. But by no stretch of the imagination would the act of assassination improve the situation that Fromme claimed to be so concerned about. Rather, the need to act out in this way betrays a deeper emotional issue. The political component, in most cases, is just window dressing to justify the violent behavior.

Obviously, Squeaky is unusual for an assassin type in that she's female. But in certain other respects, she fits the mold. One of the most important of these is the subordination of her own personality and judgment to a larger group and the following of an authoritative leader. Assassins are generally not leaders, and one of the reasons they are attracted to strong, charismatic personalities is to compensate for what they see, either consciously or subconsciously, as their own emotional shortcomings. Like serial killers, most of them come from troubled childhoods.

A lot of times they try to compensate in other ways, too. One of the most common ways, as you might suspect, is gun fetishism. Often they're initially introduced to guns and hunting by their fathers, but as they grow up, the fascination with guns increases and they begin to stockpile weapons and ammunition. The gun is a means of empowering this inadequate personality, ensuring them that when they want to, they can attain our three old standbys of manipulation, domination, and control.

Another telling characteristic is the way assassins tend to express themselves. A very large number of them will keep diaries or journals, recording not just events that happened or the way they're feeling on a particular day as most people would, but also every slight done to them and imagined conspiracies, as well as detailed plans for what to do about them. Since they don't have any close friends or trusted confidants, these social isolates express themselves *to* themselves in these detailed secret communications. In many cases, they actually use this journal writing to program themselves to commit the crime.

Arthur Bremer—who tried to assassinate Alabama governor and presidential candidate George Wallace in Laurel, Maryland, in 1972—had kept a detailed diary. So had Sirhan Sirhan, who murdered Senator Robert Kennedy in Los Angeles in 1968. Bremer had no particular beef against Governor Wallace. In fact, he'd first planned to assassinate President Richard Nixon, which would have given him greater glory and bigger press play. But the president's security was too tight for Bremer to get close enough. After the attack, the FBI found a detailed diary belonging to Bremer that revealed an individual with deep feelings of inadequacy, who didn't date and had no close friends. He wrote of his fantasy of robbing a Milwaukee bank, then fleeing to a bridge over the river. The police would confront him there, at which point he'd jump off the bridge and shoot himself in the head on the way down. Instead, for the first time in his life, he figured out a way to do something spectacular.

Was Charles Whitman an assassin personality? Let's take a look.

To all outward appearances, Whitman seemed to be the all-American boy. He was handsome and could be charming; he had a beautiful blond wife with a promising teaching career ahead of her; he was a former Marine and about to go on to his own career in engineering. But the disturbing element was what had been going on in him below the surface.

Charles Joseph Whitman was born on June 24, 1941, the oldest of three brothers. His family moved at least eight times by the time he was six, before finally settling in Lake Worth, Florida. He went to Catholic schools through high school and graduated seventh in his high school class of seventy-two in West Palm

Beach. The Catholic education was due to his devout mother, Margaret, who was described as elegant and gracious by virtually everyone who knew her. At one time, her son Charlie was the youngest Eagle Scout in the world. He was an accomplished pianist and a gun fanatic from an early age.

His father, Charles Adolphus Whitman, known as C.A., worked his way up from a tough childhood, much of it spent in an orphanage in Georgia, to become a busy plumbing contractor and successful businessman. What C.A. lacked in formal education, he made up for with determination and hard work. He also frequently beat Margaret and demanded strict discipline, backed by harsh physical punishments, from his three children. Years later, the elder Whitman would admit his shameful treatment of his wife but chalked up his behavior to a bad temper and Margaret's stubbornness, while he professed undying love for her.

As far as his treatment of his children, he looked back on that as being okay. As he told *Newsweek* shortly after his son's massacre, "With all three of my sons it was 'yes, sir' and 'no, sir.' They minded me. The way I looked at it, I am not ashamed of any spankings. I don't think I spanked enough, if you want to know the truth about it. I think they should have been punished more than they were punished."

That may be the way C.A. saw it, but right around Charlie's eighteenth birthday, he went out drinking with friends and came home noticeably drunk. His father pummeled him severely, then threw him into the backyard swimming pool. According to some accounts, Charlie nearly drowned. This was the last straw for him. He abandoned his plans to attend Georgia Tech and instead enlisted in the Marine Corps, where he'd show his father he was tough enough to handle anything.

In one respect, because of his father, Charlie had an advantage upon entering the Corps. C.A. described himself as fanatic about guns and "a great hunter," and with the experiences he imparted to his son, Charlie wasn't long in the Marines before earning a sharpshooter rating and becoming a proficient sniper. In the service, just as in civilian life, he took great pride in his weapons.

We can interpret Whitman's motivations in joining the Marine Corps in somewhat the same way as we see Squeaky Fromme's involvement with the Manson family. Both attempted to derive some personal meaning and direction from something larger and more together than themselves. But Charlie's relationship with the Marines became as troubled as his relationship with his father had been.

He had scored high enough on his tests to win a Navy and Marine Corps scholarship, which would give him a college education and make him eligible to become a commissioned officer. He entered the University of Texas as an engineering major on September 15, 1961. So far, so good, but there were already indications of some alarming personality traits. He was a frequent poker player but often refused to make good on his debts. He hunted illegally in a state that considered poaching a serious matter. He physically assaulted a Saudi Arabian student who'd mistakenly sat in his seat in one classroom. He threatened other motorists with his guns. He once commented to a friend that the University of Texas tower would be a good place to hold off an entire army while you shot people. Just as the serial sexual predator's crimes begin in fantasy, so Whitman's did as well, and the fantasy could be reinforced every time he walked across the campus and looked up at the tower.

During the summer after his first year, in August of 1962, he married his love, Kathy Leissner, of Needville, Texas. She was able to mitigate his behavior to a certain extent. Certainly they seemed a wonderful and attractive couple.

But things continued to go downhill for Whitman. His grades weren't very good, and the Marines lifted his scholarship and sent him back to active duty at Camp Lejeune, North Carolina. Kathy stayed behind in Austin to finish her degree. And in November 1963, Whitman was court-martialed on a variety of charges, including threatening another Marine and illegal weapons possession. He was sentenced to ninety days' hard labor, thirty days of confinement, and reduction in rank from corporal back to private. It was during this period that Whitman kept a detailed diary—another of our assassin-like traits. In it he recorded his new hatred for the Marine Corps (had it become another punishing father?) and how his love for Kathy was sometimes the only thing that kept him from exploding. He called his journal "The Daily Record of Charles J. Whitman."

He was discharged from the Marines in December 1964 and reenrolled at the University of Texas in 1965. He was as relentless and obsessive in his new school career as he had been in so many other aspects of his life, using the prescription amphetamine Dexedrine to remain awake for many days at a time.

Then came what, in retrospect, seems another clear precipitating stressor in Whitman's life. In the spring of 1966, his parents separated. Margaret was finally fed up with C.A.'s behavior toward her. Charlie drove to Florida to get her and bring her back to Austin, genuinely afraid his father might try to kill her. Almost immediately, C.A. was calling, pleading with her to come back, promising never to lay a hand on her again. Charlie was having none of that, though. It was as if his mother's action had finally liberated him to face his own scary feelings, and he confessed to one of his professors that he wanted to kill his father. A campus psychiatrist he visited once later described him as "oozing with hostility."

Not surprising, his grades slipped during all of this turmoil, and Whitman was once again concerned about flunking out. On top of all this, he was starting to repeat his father's despised behavior. On at least two occasions during arguments he struck Kathy. At one point she reportedly told the landlady she was afraid of removing one of his guns for safekeeping because if she did, "He'll beat me again." She confided to her parents she was afraid his explosive temper might take hold of him and that he could kill her, mirroring Charlie's concerns about his father regarding his mother.

Instantly remorseful, Charlie pledged to do better and communicated that pledge in the one way he felt comfortable: through journal-like entries that he wrote to himself on index cards. One, released after his death by the Austin Police Department, was headed GOOD POINTS TO REMEMBER WITH KATHY and listed the following tips: "1. Don't nag 2. Don't try to make your partner over 3. Don't criticize 4. Give honest appreciation 5. *Pay little attentions* 6. Be courteous 7. *BE GENTLE.*"

And so, when Charles Whitman was planning the final act that would define him and assure his place in history, it is perhaps not surprising that he left a written communication. It began, "I don't quite understand what it is that compels me to type this letter. Perhaps it is to leave some vague reason for the actions I have recently performed."

After a long first paragraph in which he described all the stresses he was under, he began his second paragraph:

It was after much thought that I decided to kill my wife, Kathy, tonight after I pick her up from work at the telephone company. I love her dearly, and she has been as fine a wife to me as any man could ever hope to have. I cannot rationaly [*sic*] pinpoint any specific reason for doing this. I don't know whether it is selfishness, or if I don't want her to have to face the embrassment [*sic*] my actions would surely cause her. At this time, though, the p rominent [*sic*] reason in my mind is that I truly do not consider this world worth living in, and am prepared to die, and I do not want to leave her to suffer alone in it. I intend to kill her as painlessly as possible.

I can think of more painless ways to die than multiple bayonet wounds to the chest. I guess the considerate part was that he stabbed her while she was sleeping. It's also interesting to note that the victims he knew, he did up close and personal. The strangers were mainly killed from a depersonalized distance. But this is a guy who's rationalizing his own selfishness and narcissism in terms of what's "best." Shades of John List. The main difference is that Whitman knew he was going to go, too, after taking out his wife and mother. And that is what the third paragraph in the communication describes—the similar reasons for which he is killing his mother.

The letter was left in his house for the police to find along with Kathy's body.

Unlike the political assassins, Charles Whitman found no particular focused target for his rage or obsession, and that is why all of those people died that hot August afternoon. The motive, I think, was to make the statement about himself and the people around him he'd been trying to make unsuccessfully for many years.

Texas governor John Connally, who, less than three years earlier, himself had nearly been killed in the assassination of President John Kennedy, appointed a commission to try to get some answers to the question of *Why?* But in the end, a distinguished panel of psychiatrists and scientists concluded, "Without a recent psychiatric evaluation of Charles J. Whitman, the task force finds it impossible to make a formal psychiatric diagnosis."

There was one more factor that has been pointed to as a possible motivator for Whitman's action. When a full autopsy was conducted on his body the day after the massacre, pathologist Dr. Coleman de Chenar described a small tumor that he discovered, as he wrote, "in the middle part of the brain, above the red nucleus, in the white matter below the gray center thalamus."

The significance, if any, of this brain tumor has been the subject of endless speculation in the last thirty-odd years and speaks directly to the debate on where violent antisocial behavior comes from. Those who believe in the organic, physiological origins of violence cite this as the explanation for why Whitman "suddenly" took it upon himself to kill so many innocent strangers.

We may never solve this issue to everyone's satisfaction, but my own opinion, based largely on the work of experts in a field in which I have no expertise, is that the tumor is merely an incidental finding and that the real answers go back to this particular personality type we've been describing.

Dr. Richard Restak, clinical professor of neurology at the George Washington University Medical Center, is one of the country's leading neuropsychiatrists. He has frequently consulted with my unit in Quantico and has done a lot of work in this field. He edited a special issue of the journal *Seminars in Clinical Neuropsychiatry,* published in July 1996, that had as its topic "Brain Damage and Legal Responsibility." Based on the size, location, and characteristics of this slow-growing tumor, Restak discounts its significance in Whitman's behavior.

"Lesions in the frontal lobe have been associated with psychopathological responses," he explains, "but this tumor near the midbrain could not be considered a frontally mediated psychopathy. Nor is it the kind that would affect the control of impulses or planning. In this case, there would be more than a couple of synapses between the stimulus and response, and the more of these we have, the more possibility we have of self-reflection before considering any action."

And in this regard, the facts of the case speak for themselves. Whitman planned his final days meticulously; there was nothing spontaneous or impulsive about the entire operation. He had scouted out the location more than a week beforehand, he heavily armed himself, provided enough food, water, and supplies to hold out for days or weeks if it came to that. He methodically bought himself the time he wanted before discovery by placing the note on his mother's apartment door and calling Kathy's boss at work. But unlike a guy like Brad Bishop, or even John List, Whitman wasn't trying to get away. He just wanted to be able to complete his program.

If organically induced impulsivity had been his problem, it's doubtful Whitman would have refrained from shooting at the many cars that came into his target range. He was interested only in people. And his motor control was not affected in the slightest, either. He was every bit as effective with human targets as he had been with artificial targets in sniper training in the Marine Corps. He hit one man crossing a street five hundred yards away.

As Restak says, "A certain number of people are going to have brain tumors. But they don't go up in towers and start shooting because of it."

In other words, the mere finding of a small, slow-growing brain tumor does not imply a particular kind of aberrant behavior any more than a broken leg or diabetic condition does. It was an incidental physical finding. It's always comforting to have some kind of concrete explanation, but here, as in so many of the subjects I've dealt with, such an attempt would be grossly inadequate.

Even in terms of straight mental illness, our research has shown us that people laboring under severe psychoses are seldom so effective in carrying out their crimes.

In Restak's journal issue, mentioned earlier, Stephen J. Morse, Ph.D., an attorney and professor at the University of Pennsylvania Law School, has an interesting and insightful take on causality and responsibility, in an article titled "Brain and Blame." Morse writes:

> If Whitman believed, for example, that mass murder of innocents would produce eternal peace on earth, then he should be excused, whether the delusional belief was a product of a brain pathological condition, childhood trauma, or whatever. But if Whitman was simply an angry person who believed that life had dealt him a raw deal and that he was going to go out in a blaze of glory that would give his miserable life meaning, then he is unfortunate but responsible, whether his anger and beliefs were a product of the tumor, childhood trauma, an unfortunate character, or whatever.

Like the vast majority of the other violent offenders we've dealt with, Charles Whitman chose to do what he did fully mindful of the consequences and moral implications.

Just after 1 P.M. on the afternoon of April 27, 1979, 300,000 spectators lined the streets of San Antonio, Texas, in anticipation of the start of the Fiesta Battle of Flowers parade. The parade had been a tradition since 1891, when President Benjamin Harrison visited the city. He was to be greeted with a staged "battle" of people throwing flowers at one another, in imitation of similar events held in France. That first parade was marred by rain. Even so, it became a yearly event, a tribute to Texans who died for the state. This year, the parade would be marred by something far more serious than rain.

Suddenly, approximately five thousand people who had gathered around the intersection of Grayson Street and Broadway were forced to dive for cover as a gunman, described as "heavily armed," began firing into the crowd from his motor home, a green-and-white Winnebago parked nearby, at the beginning of the parade route. Two women died and about fifty more people were injured—at least thirty by gunshot, the rest while trying to escape the carnage. As far as victimology, the first targets were six police officers posted at an intersection. Then the gunman went after the parade spectators. Unlike Charles Whitman, who carefully selected his targets, this one, according to one witness, shot "at anything that moved."

As he began firing at the police from inside his motor home, the sniper shouted, "Traitors, traitors, traitors!"

A woman, her daughter, and the daughter's boyfriend, carrying the woman's young son on his shoulders, were running by the Winnebago. The sniper tried to pull the boy inside, but his relatives were able to wrestle him away.

The gunfire lasted about a half hour. At 1:45, fifteen minutes after the abruptly canceled parade had been set to begin, a San Antonio police SWAT team fired bullets and tear gas into the motor home from a neighboring rooftop. When they stormed the motor home, they found the body of Ira Attebury, sixty-four years of age, dead of a self-inflicted gunshot wound to the right ear from a .38 caliber revolver. They also found fifteen weapons, including a double-barreled shotgun, a semiautomatic pistol, nine rifles, and four .38 caliber revolvers.

One of the officers told reporters, "He had enough ammunition to start a war."

The dead victims were identified as Ida Long, twenty-six years of age, and Amalia Castillo, forty-eight. Mrs. Castillo had thrown herself on top of her six-year-old granddaughter to protect her from the bullets. Two of Mrs. Castillo's children, ages eight and eleven, were wounded but recovered.

Here was another senseless, shocking mass murder, and like Charles Whitman, Ira Attebury very much represents the paranoid assassin personality—so classically, in fact, that I used this case frequently in my teaching at Quantico. It was brought to me in one of my classes by a National Academy student who was a San Antonio police officer.

Ira Attebury, it was learned just after his death, was a retired independent truck driver—an inherently solitary profession—though he hadn't worked regularly for years, according to his brother Roy, fourteen years his junior. Ira was overweight and had a heart condition for which he was drawing disability checks. He had served in the Coast Guard during World War II. Besides hunting, though, Roy said Ira had no special training in firearms; his family was shocked to learn of the number of weapons he owned. He had never married.

His brother described him as always having been headstrong and temperamental, frequently fighting with their father, dropping out of high school to pursue the nomadic life of a trucker. About a year before the attack, Attebury had been forced to leave one trailer park because of his paranoid behavior. He claimed the police were always watching him and that neighbors were stealing from him. He suspected one of taking the battery from his car. He also suspected the police of poisoning his water supply. Roy described him as growing increasingly paranoid over the last few years.

His last landlord characterized him as a quiet loner who always paid his rent in cash because he was afraid of banks. He also kept his windows covered so no one could see inside. He told the landlord he'd be away for a while after the parade.

As with Whitman, there was evidence of planning. A week before, he'd asked permission from a tire store to park his motor home in their parking lot near the parade's starting point. He washed the Winnebago the day before. When the staging for the parade began, spectators who noticed the recreational vehicle thought it odd that someone who'd obviously gone to such effort to secure such a good viewing spot would leave all his window shades down.

Attebury grew up on a farm in Missouri, near the Arkansas state line, one of seven boys and two girls. Fifteen years before the attack, he'd been involved in an accident in Ohio in which two women were killed. It was determined to be their fault—they ran a red light and his truck plowed into their car—but he was pinned in his truck, afraid it would burst into flames. He spent months in a Veterans Administration hospital but remained in poor health. The accident effectively ended his trucking career, but he remained financially self-sufficient from a combination of savings, pension, his disability checks, and a share of the rental income from the family farm. Attebury traded the nomadic life of a trucker for that of a retiree living in a motor home. He was probably okay as long as he felt his life had meaning and direction, but once he could no longer work, his paranoid tendencies would have time to expand and take over all of his waking thoughts. In 1975, he bought himself a grave marker.

"Things have been different since that wreck," his brother Howard told the Associated Press. "He imagined things that weren't quite true."

Do we have a situation similar to Whitman's brain tumor here? Could the accident have caused some physiological change? That could certainly be a theory, although it's not as if this were some outgoing, people-oriented guy whose personality suddenly changed. But even if it did, even if he became delusional about people being out to get him, there is absolutely no evidence that he did not understand the consequences of his actions or the difference between right and wrong.

Here we have so many of the elements of the classic paranoid loner: no spouse or friends, solitary lifestyle, lots of guns. He even lived in a home he could take with him so his possessions never had to be out of his sight. It was reported that he refused to answer his own door and would speak to callers only from behind the curtained window.

Why did Attebury choose a crowd of strangers rather than a particular famous figure to vent his paranoid rage on and make his name? It might have been because he wasn't sophisticated enough to create the intellectual overlay of a "cause." Or it could have been because he was at least sufficiently in touch with his own feelings and motivations that he didn't feel that need.

It's difficult to interview this type, even in prison. They don't want to make eye contact or look at you. They're very distrustful, particularly of someone like me who represented the FBI, which could easily be part of their delusional system. When you do interview a guy like this, you quickly see how difficult it would be for him to work in a group. It would be virtually impossible for him to participate in a conspiracy because he doesn't trust anyone. Conversely, no one's going to trust him, because he seems so weird. When I interviewed Arthur Bremer, I didn't get a whole lot out of him because he was so suspicious of me and was convinced I had some ulterior motive. Like most assassin types, he wouldn't look directly at me and was noticeably uncomfortable when I looked directly at him. Ironically, in the years right after the assassination attempt on the then-segregationist George Wallace, Bremer became something of a hero to many of the black inmates in the penitentiary. So even though he'd be incarcerated for the rest of his life, he did briefly attain a measure of the status he so desperately yearned for.

The problem with this type from a law enforcement perspective is, how do you monitor someone like this? The mere fact that someone keeps to himself doesn't mean he's going to be an assassin personality. But without having anyone around to observe him, you don't know if and when he might become dangerous. People like Ira Attebury have become one of the unpredictable hazards of modern life.

If this type is married or in a more structured work or social situation, you have a better chance, although often that chance is missed.

James Huberty complained about the Communist threat, he complained about Soviet spies, he complained about the fact that the CIA was following him and that the military kept him from getting jobs. He had complained about President Jimmy Carter, and then he complained about President Ronald Reagan. Neighbors worried about his temper and confrontational style, and they worried about the arsenal of guns he kept and shot behind his locked doors, drawn blinds, and No Trespassing and Beware of the Dog signs.

Around four o'clock on the afternoon of Wednesday, July 18, 1984, the forty-one-year-old James Oliver Huberty, dressed in combat camouflage pants, walked into the McDonald's restaurant a block from his apartment in San Ysidro, California, in southernmost San Diego County, just north of the Mexican border from Tijuana, and opened fire with a Winchester pump-action twelve-gauge shotgun. When he missed with that weapon, he fired point-blank at the manager, twenty-two-year-old Neva Caine, with a nine-millimeter Uzi submachine gun. She died minutes later. In addition to the Winchester and the Uzi, Huberty carried a nine-millimeter Browning semiautomatic pistol. In a massacre that lasted for about an hour and a quarter, Huberty killed twenty-one people and wounded another nineteen until he committed suicide by cop and died of a SWAT team shooter's clean shot through his chest.

The investigation produced a grimly familiar-sounding set of details. Like so many other assassins, James Huberty never could seem to get it right. He was born in October of 1942 in Canton, Ohio. His father, Earl, was an inspector at a roller bearing factory but really wanted to be a farmer. When Jim was seven, Earl finally realized his dream and bought a farm about twenty miles outside of town, while he continued working at the factory. But there was a steep domestic price to pay. Earl's wife, Icle, refused to move away from town and wanted nothing to do with the farm. She decided her own future lay in preaching, and she left to become a missionary on Indian reservations out west, leaving Earl to take care of Jim and his older sister, Ruth. Young Jim, who had already had to battle polio and wear braces on his legs that made his classmates laugh at him, couldn't understand what kind of a God would cause such pain and take his mother away from the household.

Huberty grew up lonely and withdrawn, and his polio left him with a strange way of walking that always made him stand out. He discovered guns, and for the first time in his life he felt empowered. As he grew, his love of guns increased. He got so that he could even produce his own ammunition loads.

After Waynesdale High School in Apple Creek, Ohio, he began at Malone College in Canton but dropped out and decided to attend mortuary school in Pennsylvania, with the idea of opening his own funeral home. He married Etna Markland, whom he met at Malone, and got a job at a funeral home back in Canton. Within two years, Huberty was fired. He was fine with the work, but he had no live-people skills and made families and other mourners very uncomfortable. We need not spend much time analyzing the significance of someone feeling more comfortable with the dead than the living, but his next career choice, as a welder, was one in which he could retreat behind a metal mask and essentially tune out the rest of the world.

Huberty did all right in that field for a while, getting a job at a public utility plant. He was an obsessive worker and pulled down a lot of overtime. When he did speak to others, it was often to spout his conspiracy theories. He and Etna bought an old house about ten miles outside of town. The few people permitted inside reported seeing guns everywhere they looked, all loaded.

The Hubertys had two daughters, Zelia and Cassandra (whom they called Bobbi). Sometimes Jim's temper flared and he hit Etna or the girls. Etna tried to manage their lives in such a way as to avoid as much stress to her husband as she could. While not keeping a diary, Huberty kept meticulous records on what he called "debts": any perceived offense or slight against him or his family. He called the police frequently with complaints about the neighbors. He also threatened neighbors directly when he couldn't get any other satisfaction.

In 1982, the utility that employed Huberty shut down, and after thirteen years on the job, Huberty was out of work. With this type, when whatever it is that is giving them stability is suddenly yanked away (another example would be if Etna had left him), these guys start to decompensate. In fact, he told another laid-off worker that if he couldn't support his family any longer, he was going to kill himself and take a lot of other people with him. He managed to get another job, but in a little more than a month that plant closed, too. Clearly, in Huberty's mind, people were out to get him.

Then the following August, Huberty was involved in an automobile accident in which his car was rear-ended. The collision exacerbated his existing physical problems and made his hands shake. Like Attebury's accident, this was to prove crucial, and Huberty worried that he wouldn't be able to work as a welder any longer. He contemplated suicide, though Etna was able to talk him out of it. They sold the house for a disappointing amount, which only reinforced his perception of conspiracies against him.

He decided they should move to Mexico, where the cost of living would be cheaper. There is also evidence he thought that by going somewhere far away and exotic, he could make a lot of money and show up all the people who'd done him wrong. The family moved to Tijuana. Zelia and Bobbi went to an American school in San Ysidro. Etna drove them back and forth over the border every day. But after three months, Huberty decided the living arrangement wasn't working out. He didn't speak Spanish and he wasn't making a lot of money.

So they moved back north across the border, into a two-bedroom apartment on Cottonwood Road in San Ysidro. They were the only non-Hispanics in the apartment complex. Jim shot his guns from the balcony at night, waking and alarming the neighbors. He applied for a job with a security company, but after the interview the owner thought he was unstable and probably lying on his application and told his staff in no uncertain terms that this man was not to be hired. Finally he got a job as a night guard at a condominium complex. He became obsessed with the military and from a magazine ordered the camouflage pants he was wearing on the last day of his life.

Then he lost his job when his supervisors decided he was too unstable, just as the previous potential employer had. Huberty got the idea that the Defense Department was behind the firing.

He had a brief flicker of personal insight and called a psychiatric clinic, but since his problem was judged to be noncrisis, he was told he'd be called back within a few days. Had he mentioned that he had weapons or given any indication that he was in crisis, the clinic director later stated, he would have been seen right away.

On Wednesday morning, July 18, Huberty had to appear in traffic court, but the judge let him off with a warning. He and Etna had lunch at a downtown McDonald's, after which they walked around the zoo. Among the things she remembers him telling her was that "society had their chance."

They went home, and while Etna prepared lunch for the girls, Jim changed into his camouflage pants and a maroon short-sleeved shirt. "I want to kiss you good-bye," he said to his wife.

His message to twelve-year-old Zelia was even more ominous. "Good-bye," he said as he kissed her. "I won't be back." He was carrying something long and narrow wrapped up in a blue-and-white blanket. He could easily have walked, but had too much to carry, so he put it in his old black Mercury Marquis. Police determined that Huberty fired at least 250 rounds inside the McDonald's. His youngest victim was eight months old, the oldest seventy-four.

When the horror was complete, the San Diego medical examiner was asked to do a full autopsy, as had been done on Charles Whitman, to try to determine what in his brain had caused this outburst. In this case, the pathologist found nothing. Others had their own theories. His father, Earl, speculated that Jim's physical problems as a child finally caused him to snap. Etna filed an unsuccessful suit against McDonald's, claiming that her husband's rampage was caused by eating too many hamburgers and Chicken McNuggets—that the high levels of monosodium glutamate they contained interacted with the lead and cadmium he had built up in his system during his years as a welder. I don't know of any other cases of welders going berserk and killing innocent men, women, and children. Former San Francisco supervisor and police officer Dan White, who killed Mayor George Moscone and supervisor Harvey Milk in 1978, got off on a diminished capacity plea after claiming his mental capacity had been adversely affected by consuming too much high-sugar junk food—the famous "Twinkie defense." Ultimately, White ironically righted the legal mistake by committing suicide in October of 1985, a year and a half after he was released from prison.

Everyone's got something you can point to, but when you go searching for evil, it's pretty tough to pinpoint it on a map. It all leads me to once again pose the question I keep asking over and over again: *Isn't anyone responsible for anything anymore?*

If we look at victimology, while it was arbitrary who happened to be at the wrong place at the wrong time, I think the general victimology and the target were highly symbolic. The president of the United States, an understandably popular target in any era, represents the nation—all that's good and bad about it—in the assassin's mind. So does something like McDonald's. Like Coca-Cola and Disneyland and the U.S. Capitol building (site of a fatal shooting of two police officers in 1998, as well as the Trump-supporting mob riot of 2021), McDonald's is a national symbol and landmark. Huberty would go in there and see families enjoying themselves, togetherness, good times—all the things he had come to resent and mistrust. He, on the other hand, was living in reduced circumstances, surrounded by "foreigners" he didn't trust, being persecuted by everyone. In a way, he was like Thomas Hamilton in Dunblane. If he couldn't have what was his due, he'd take out the innocents, the children, in this restaurant, another child-oriented environment. Just as if he were trying to kill the president, in his mind Huberty was striking out at the heart of America. The reason he chose this particular McDonald's was that this was the one closest to his home, the one he had scouted most completely, the one where his comfort level was the highest.

McDonald's closed the restaurant in San Ysidro and made a contribution of a million dollars to a fund for survivors. Then they tore down the building and donated the land to the city of San Diego to become a public park.

James Huberty was old for an assassin. Most of them go active in their mid-to-late twenties, when it becomes inescapable that their lives are going nowhere and something spectacular has to be done to give them some meaning and recognition. When they're older, like Huberty and Attebury, it's usually because something has suddenly come apart.

Samuel Joseph Byck was well known to the Secret Service, which was concerned about his potential as a presidential assassin. In 1972, he had written to President Nixon with his list of grievances and threatened to take action if they were not met. The following year he was committed for psychiatric evaluation after two arrests by the U.S. Park Police for picketing in front of the White House without a permit, demanding that the government return his constitutional rights. He came back again on Christmas Eve of 1973, this time wearing a Santa Claus suit. He told reporters, "I want to see if they have the guts to arrest Santa Claus."

Despite these aberrant and paranoid tendencies, Byck was functional as long as there was some structure to his world: a wife, a home life, a job. But by February of 1974, his world was coming apart. His marriage had broken up the previous year, he lost his salesman job, he was being treated for depression, and at forty-three, he'd reached that stage when it didn't look like things were going to get any better.

Unlike Whitman or Huberty or even Attebury, Byck had no experience or familiarity with guns. But that didn't stop him from procuring a .22 caliber pistol and driving out to Baltimore-Washington International Airport early on the morning of February 22. He figured he knew how to handle a weapon just from watching television shows. He had also rigged up a simple bomb consisting of two gallons of gasoline wired to a triggering device, concealed in the attaché case he was carrying. When he approached the security checkpoint, he aimed the gun at the head of the guard, George Ramsburg, and fired. Ramsburg died almost instantly. Byck then rushed the entryway of Delta flight 523, a DC-9 scheduled to depart for Atlanta at 7:15 A.M.

Eight passengers were already on the plane when Byck charged into the cabin waving his pistol. He ordered the door secured, then went into the cockpit and directed the pilot, Captain Douglas Reese Lofton, "Fly this plane out of here!" Lofton explained that the wheels were still chocked, so they couldn't move anywhere until the chocks were removed. Not satisfied with this response, Byck went back into the passenger cabin and grabbed a woman as a hostage, presumably to force the pilot to comply.

Back in the cockpit, Lofton once again explained that he couldn't move the plane. Byck then shot and wounded both him and the copilot, First Officer Fred Jones. He then went back again to the passenger compartment and exchanged his female hostage for a second woman, whom he then brought back to the cockpit. He repeated his order, and Lofton and Jones again explained that it was out of their control to move the airplane with the wheels still chocked. Byck then shot them both again, and this time he killed Jones and critically wounded Lofton.

Meanwhile, police officer Charles Troyer, who had responded to the shooting of Ramsburg, was out on the tarmac trying to shoot out the DC-9's tires with his .38 caliber revolver. When that didn't work, he took Ramsburg's .357 magnum and tried again. With the more powerful weapon, he succeeded. His main target, however, was the hijacker himself, and as soon as Byck presented a clear target through the cockpit window, Troyer drew aim and fired, hitting Byck in the chest and abdomen. These shots would have proved fatal within a minute or so, but as soon as he was hit, Byck turned his own weapon on himself and shot himself through the temple. He died instantly.

Now, this case presents some very interesting dynamics. There is strong evidence that this crime was not a spontaneous response to despair; rather, it had been planned for at least six months. According to investigative columnist Jack Anderson, who received a tape recording from Byck, the subject intended to fly the plane to Washington and crash it into the White House. This would be the ultimate blaze of glory.

But contrast this to his behavior in the plane, in which he goes back and forth repeatedly between the cockpit and passenger cabin, changing hostages for no apparent reason. Far more significant, what does he think he's going to be able to do once he shoots the only people who can fly the plane? This is a man who is essentially disintegrating before everyone's eyes. He's still fixed on the mission, but he's lost all sense of practicality.

A profound insight into his mind-set can be had from another tape recording he made, this one while sitting in his car in the airport parking lot that morning. He titled the tape "Pandora's Box." The tape shows that he'd thought out the whole thing, though his intention was to shoot only the copilot if necessary to get the pilot to do what he wanted. He would not actually shoot the pilot until it was time to force the aircraft down onto the White House.

But just as profound are the insights he gives into himself and his motivation for the crime. He says that he feels like a single grain of sand on a beach with billions and billions of grains. He also frets about the fact that he's parked in the expensive lot, rather than the more economical long-term one. He realizes the ludicrousness of this concern, since he knows he's not going to have to pay the fee, or ever come back for the car, for that matter. But he still remains very uncomfortable with where he's opted to park. He also notes that he doesn't have any identification on him.

I think this seemingly silly anomaly is tremendously significant, because what he's essentially saying is, "I don't belong here with all the wealthy, important people who park here and then go fly places on airplanes. I'm just a grain of sand on a beach. I'm not as worthy as anyone else. I'm just an inadequate nobody, and the only way I can become important is by some great act that affects all those important people." Like McDonald's, jet planes are a symbol of modern life. A guy like Byck would perceive that this is how successful people travel. And if he can take over one, then he's successful, too. The fact that he doesn't have any ID on him, likewise, is a subconscious way of saying to himself that he's a nobody, a person without identity.

And finally, he goes on to wrap his mission in the trappings of a cause, saying this is "a job I feel has to be done for mankind."

He sees himself as a real-life Lone Ranger or Shane. "I think a tombstone that I would like to have is that 'He didn't like what he saw and he decided to do something about it.'"

But at the same time he worries, "I just wish that I don't get to be known as a maniac or madman," explaining that his motive derives from "being robbed and cheated out of my dignity and seeing my country being raped and ravished almost before my very eyes, and I won't stand idly by and allow it to happen."

Whether this type of personality evolves into an assassin or a mass murderer, whether he goes after the president of the United States or a legendary rock star—all of this will be determined by both the individual details of that person's emotional development and the skills and interests he develops. Someone like Charles Whitman, who had exceptional skills as a sniper, is going to fantasize his crime based on that ability. Someone like Attebury, who had no such skills, has to plan to put himself right in the middle of the action to be effective. A Sam Byck wouldn't have to go through the elaborate plan of hijacking an airplane if he could figure out how to get physically close enough to the president to shoot at him.

But here's the point I want to make: regardless of the specifics of the crime, regardless of the so-called cause, the violent act is the result of a deep-seated feeling of inadequacy on the part of the assassin. I could conceive of rare instances in which there might be a higher, even an altruistic purpose, such as the various attempts to assassinate Adolf Hitler. By the same token, you occasionally come across someone who's so out-and-out delusional that he's lost touch with reality. Richard Lawrence, who tried unsuccessfully to assassinate President Andrew Jackson, believed Jackson to be the king of England. But these cases are so rare that they need not really concern us here.

No matter who we look at, we're going to find an individual—overwhelmingly, a white male in his twenties—who does not feel good about himself and never has. In some way, he sees the violent act as the solution to his problem.

When two CIA employees were gunned down in their cars as they arrived for work at the Agency's Langley, Virginia, headquarters, it appeared to be a politically motivated crime, striking at the heart of American imperialism. And the American intelligence and law enforcement establishments, including the FBI, moved heaven and earth to hunt down the suspect, thirty-three-year-old Mir Aimal Kasi, to his native Pakistan, where he had fled. When he finally made a statement about his crime, he claimed it was in response to America's "wrong policy toward Islamic countries." But I submit that just like Bremer's attempt on the life of Governor Wallace, this was the work of an inadequate little nobody who wanted to become a hero for the sake of his own self-worth. The cause was a convenient justification.

Perhaps the ultimate examples of assassination (or attempted assassination) based on the inadequacies of the shooter are Mark David Chapman's murder of John Lennon and John Hinckley Jr.'s attempt on the life of President Reagan.

Mark Chapman idolized John Lennon and tried to pattern himself after the former Beatle in every way he could think of, even to the point of seeking out Asian women to be his girlfriends since Lennon had married Yoko Ono. The woman he did marry, four years his senior, was Japanese. Chapman wanted *to be* Lennon but reached a point where that possibility became clearly unrealizable and his own inadequacy became overwhelming. He had attempted suicide while working in Hawaii and had been hospitalized as a result. He told his wife, Gloria, that he intended to kill Lennon, but she didn't take him seriously. When he shot Lennon outside the musician's home at the Dakota apartment building in Manhattan on December 8, 1980, Chapman could then have easily turned the gun on himself, now that he didn't have this impossible role model to look up to. In fact, he admitted as much to my Secret Service colleague Ken Baker when Ken interviewed him in prison. In a strange but internally logical way, Chapman perceived he could solve his own problem by eliminating Lennon. Once he had squeezed the trigger and Lennon had fallen, Chapman was no longer a nobody. His name would be forever linked with his hero's.

Interestingly, Chapman had an alternative plan if he wasn't able to kill John Lennon during his New York trip. Instead, he would go to the top of the Statue of Liberty and shoot himself in the head. From prison he commented, "No one else had killed themselves there before. I wanted to go out in a blaze of glory." Here we have another highly symbolic American icon, and we have that phrase "blaze of glory," which is at the heart of each of these endgame scenarios.

Another interesting observation came from Gloria, who said Mark was uncharacteristically calm before the trip. This squares with the emotions of so many others, including Huberty and Whitman. Once they decide on their course of action, stress and conflict are lifted.

But not quite. After hanging out at the Dakota for many hours, Chapman met Lennon, who was extremely gracious and autographed a record album for him. Chapman started thinking to himself that maybe this was enough. He had the autograph, something from Lennon, so maybe he should just go home. Yet the mission was prime in his mind, so much so that he waited around many more hours until Lennon came home again from a recording session and got out of his limousine. It was then that Mark David Chapman squeezed the trigger of his Charter Arms .38 and pumped five bullets into John Lennon's body. The only thing going through his mind at the time, he later reported, was how gratified he was that the gun was working so well.

In addition to the fact that they were both pathetic white male losers in their twenties, Chapman and John Hinckley Jr. had something else in common: a preoccupation with J. D. Salinger's landmark novel of disillusioned youth, *The Catcher in the Rye*. In fact, Hinckley picked it up from what he knew about Chapman, who, in a sense, became a role model. It's as if the book somehow justified them and, through the main character, Holden Caulfield, gave them both a persona—gave their lives some definition and meaning. Even though he attacked Reagan on March 30, 1981, as the new president was leaving the Washington Hilton hotel after a speech, Hinckley's crime had no more political component than Chapman's. Rather, as we all know, he wanted to impress the object of his obsession, actress Jodie Foster. Now, in real life, a rich, beautiful, famous actress is unlikely to have much to do with a nonentity like Hinckley, who essentially has accomplished nothing in his life. Retrospectively, the fact that she took his phone calls at Yale was a mistake. In trying to be gracious, Foster inadvertently encouraged him in his fantasy that if he played his cards right, she would be attainable. If he could just do something really dramatic, he thought, she would be his.

Obviously, that didn't happen. Foster went on to a brilliant career as an actress and director, twice winning Academy Awards. I was pleased to advise her on the practices of my unit during the filming of *The Silence of the Lambs*. Hinckley, on the other hand, has spent nearly twenty years cooling his heels at St. Elizabeth's mental hospital in Washington, D.C., after being found not guilty by reason of insanity for the shooting of Reagan, press secretary Jim Brady, and others. But on one level his plan succeeded. This boy never got the girl, but he was no longer an obscure nobody. Like Chapman's, his name remains associated with the object of his obsession.

Not all of these guys are completely inadequate in every way. Joseph Paul Franklin probably could have continued making a good living as a bank robber for many years if that was all he was interested in; he was that good at it. But like other assassin personalities, Franklin had other items on his agenda.

Franklin has killed, sniper/assassin-style, throughout much of the United States, primarily in the South and Midwest, although he's "worked" as far west as Utah and as far northeast as Pennsylvania. Many of his crimes have been against blacks, for whom he professes a pathological hate. In August 1977, he killed an interracial couple in Madison, Wisconsin. Two months later, he killed a Jewish man leaving a synagogue in Richmond Heights, Missouri, while the victim's two daughters looked on in horror. In July 1978, he killed another interracial couple as they left a Pizza Hut restaurant in Chattanooga, Tennessee. In August 1979, he killed the black manager of a Burger King restaurant in Falls Church, Virginia. In January 1980, he killed a black man waiting in line at a Church's Fried Chicken restaurant in Indianapolis. Two days later, he killed another black man at a market in the same city. In April of that year, still in Indianapolis, he shot and wounded another interracial couple. In May, he picked up a female hitchhiker and killed her in a state park in Wisconsin. In June, he killed two black youths as they walked along a road in Bond Hill in Cincinnati. In August, he killed two black joggers running through a park with white women in Salt Lake City. And that same year, in Lewisburg, West Virginia, he killed two white women who were hitchhiking. And these are only the attacks he has been convicted of or admitted to. There are plenty more in which he is a suspect or where charges are pending. Even he is not sure how many people he's killed, and unlike a lot of the up-close-and-personal serial killers, he doesn't get emotionally involved with his victims.

But perhaps Franklin's two most notorious assassination attempts were ones in which he failed to kill his target. On March 6, 1978, Franklin shot *Hustler* magazine publisher Larry Flynt in Lawrenceville, Georgia, leaving the champion of pornography permanently paralyzed below the waist and in constant pain. According to a 1997 interview with *Gallery* magazine, he now regrets that shooting. On May 29, 1980, he shot and wounded Vernon Jordan, the prominent attorney, civil rights leader, and president of the Urban League outside Jordan's hotel in Fort Wayne, Indiana. In each case he had stalked his target for about a year. He had tried to shoot former Georgia state legislator and civil rights activist Julian Bond before going after Jordan, but no one was ever home when he went to Bond's house. The motive for the killing of the two black youths in Cincinnati, by the way, was that Franklin was unhappy that the media were discounting the idea that the attempt on Jordan's life had been a racially motivated crime.

Joseph Paul Franklin was executed by lethal injection at the Eastern Reception, Diagnostic and Correctional Center at Bonne Terre, Missouri, on November 20, 2013. One of the things that really annoyed him while on death row was that he wasn't as famous as some other serial killers and assassins, whom he didn't consider nearly as accomplished as himself.

He had been arrested in September 1980, but after five and a half hours of interrogation, managed to slip out a police station window.

On October 15, FBI Civil Rights Section chief Dave Kohl, who was a good friend of mine throughout my years in the Bureau, asked me to do a fugitive assessment on Franklin. I went up to headquarters in Washington and reviewed the entire file.

He was born in Mobile, Alabama, in 1950, and was named James Clayton Vaughan Jr. He claimed he was abused by his alcoholic father and hated his overly strict mother. He did poorly in school and was considered disruptive. He dropped out of high school. As a teen, in an attempt to escape the hold of his family, he changed his name to Joseph Paul Franklin. The "Joseph Paul" was in honor of Nazi propaganda minister Paul Joseph Goebbels. The "Franklin" was in honor of Benjamin Franklin. Was this guy kind of mixed up and conflicted? I'd say there was a pretty good chance.

He wore a swastika on his clothing and joined such white supremacist groups as the National Socialist White People's Party and the Ku Klux Klan. Even within those groups, though, he remained essentially a loner. He didn't think most of the members were serious. While he was ready to start acting for the cause, all most of them seemed to want to do was talk. He was also concerned that both groups had been infiltrated by FBI informers.

He began bombing synagogues and Jewish leaders. But what he was really adept at was sniping. This is significant because as the result of an injury, he had lost the vision in one eye. His expert marksmanship was a means of compensating for this handicap. In fact, if we look at everything in Franklin's background—the marksmanship, changing his name, joining hate groups—it's all about compensation for his own perceived inadequacies. Inadequate people have to try to feel worthy, and one way to feel worthy is to find someone else unworthy or inferior. If you can't find many people less worthy than yourself on individual merits, then you have to find them inferior by race or creed. Blacks and Jews have always been favorite targets for that. Evidently, and this squares with my analysis, Franklin targeted Larry Flynt after he saw an interracial photo spread in *Hustler* and decided it was up to him to uphold the honor of his race.

The thinking went that if he murdered enough blacks, other white people would follow his example and take up the fight themselves. He claimed he got the idea from Charles Manson's ideas of "Helter-Skelter." Franklin married twice, for about a year each time. It had been reported that he abused both wives.

All the while he was carrying out his assassinations, Franklin was supporting himself by robbing banks and convenience stores. He knew it took a lot of thinking and planning, and Franklin was willing to put in the effort. It became clear to me that he felt comfortable only in situations he could control completely. Because his murders were of the sniping variety, in which he would hide and wait, I thought that when he was caught, there could be a good chance of suicide rather than the type of physical confrontation he would be unable to control. I thought also that there was a chance he might return to see his young teenage wife and daughter, since they were all he really had in life, and I thought he might try to boost his own ego by bragging about his criminal exploits.

I believed there was a good chance he would go back to Mobile, where he would feel comfortable. I didn't know if he'd stay put, since he would be pretty sophisticated at this point about police matters and knew he was a very wanted man. But I thought he would probably stay somewhere along the Gulf Coast, particularly while it was cold up north.

He turned up on October 28 in a blood bank in Lakeland,

Florida, to donate plasma for money. Nurses there recognized him from his tattoos; investigators had blanketed the area with photos since President Carter was coming to town and Franklin had threatened Carter in the past. The nurses called the FBI, who arrested him at a nearby store he had gone into to cash the check. He denied his identity, but he was identified through fingerprints. He was brought to the FBI field office in Tampa. While agents interrogated him, they asked if he wanted anything to eat or drink. Franklin replied that he would like to have a hamburger, but only if they could make sure that it had not been prepared or handled by "niggers." Though he wouldn't admit anything to the agents, the next day he bragged and confessed to nearly all of his crimes to his cellmate in the U.S. Marshal's Office.

In early November, Franklin was to be transported back to Salt Lake City to be charged with the crimes there. We figured if he was sent by private plane rather than a commercial flight, this would be a good time to try to talk to him. We also knew he wasn't crazy about flying, so his stress level would be up and he might look for emotional support from whoever was accompanying him. The Tampa Field Office once again contacted me for advice on conducting another interview. I suggested they use only a very senior, authoritative agent, wearing the complete FBI uniform—crisp white shirt, black suit, the whole cliché—and that they not initiate anything, but let him start running his mouth. Once he started talking, I thought, it would be a good idea to stroke his ego and build up his "place in history." The strategy worked well. Special Agent Robert H. Dwyer was dressed to the nines in a three-piece suit, with a bunch of case material, including articles about Franklin, on his lap. When Franklin did initiate the conversation and asked to see the articles, Dwyer let him. When Franklin wanted to continue talking, Dwyer said he would have to turn on the tape recorder and advise him of his rights. Franklin agreed.

During the course of the flight, he gave Dwyer chapter and verse on his techniques and disguises and even placed himself in various cities at times when crimes had occurred. Dwyer was amazed by his obsession with blacks, and at one point Franklin said how much he disliked Mississippi because it was such a "nigger-loving state." He wouldn't drive Cadillacs or Lincolns, because they were "nigger cars." He went on to describe the conspiracy through which Jews controlled both the American and Soviet governments. The only crime he wouldn't react to at all was the Vernon Jordan shooting. In thinking about it, we felt that he was probably upset that he hadn't "succeeded," that he'd only wounded Jordan. His place in history was suspect.

Seeing how he had reacted to the stress of the first interview by spilling to his cellmate, I thought if we could put enough pressure and stress on him in this interview, more could be gotten out of him within twenty-four hours after the flight. So as the charter plane flew over the easily recognizable Utah State Penitentiary, the FBI agent pointed out that this was where Gary Gilmore had faced the firing squad. The autopsy showed that four bullets had pulverized Gilmore's heart. It was pointed out that if Franklin was found guilty and given the death sentence, that was where it would be carried out. Within twenty-four hours Franklin did, in fact, spill to several individuals in the Salt Lake City jail.

In the early 1990s, Ken Baker and I interviewed Franklin in Marion Federal Penitentiary in Illinois as part of a joint Secret Service–FBI project studying assassination. He was in the prison's protective wing because it was feared he'd quickly be killed for his racist views if he were released into the general convict population. Initially, his affect was quite low and he was generally unresponsive. He wore thick glasses, and his eyes darted back and forth between Ken and me, trying to read us. After some considerable time, we were able to make clear to him how much we knew about his background and crimes, and then he became more responsive and animated. He's not a superbright guy or a deep thinker by any means, but he was cooperative and articulate, and at that point, I sensed he just wanted to get proper credit and have us be impressed with him. He never indicated any remorse or sense of contrition. It was all kind of matter-of-fact.

In no way could we relate to Franklin's views or outlook on life. But we appreciated his candor and willingness to work with us, and we learned a lot from him. In our interview and in other material on him since then, he's articulate, forthright, and courageous in expressing his wildly unpopular ideas. In fact, while he seems very much concerned with his reputation and with setting the record straight about his deeds, he seems totally unconcerned with being "popular" or with what anyone thinks about him, which, interestingly enough, is fairly unusual for a repeat killer.

When I asked him about the Vernon Jordan shooting, he just smiled and said, "What do you think? I'll just say that justice was done." At that point he hadn't admitted that one yet, but his ego couldn't bring him to deny it, either.

He was willing to speak about other crimes freely. He described how he was driving in Madison, Wisconsin, when he thought another car had cut him off. He went after it and saw that it carried a young black man and a young white woman. Franklin became enraged and followed the car until it turned into a shopping center parking lot. The couple noticed him and got out of the car, possibly to exchange words. By that point, Franklin had decided he was going to kill them. As soon as they got close enough, he blew them away.

He implied that he was often cruising around, looking. It was like hunting. He described for us how, once he decided he was going to kill, he would plan meticulously, down to what kind of clothing he would wear to blend in with the site he had chosen.

He would secrete the weapon there the night before, its serial number carefully filed off, and knew that as soon as the crime was completed, that weapon would be abandoned. Everything would be wiped down, and he would wear gloves when handling potential evidence. Sometimes he would steal a bicycle to take him from the scene to his car so that witnesses would not be able to identify it. He had a police scanner so he could monitor their communications frequencies. Depending on the situation, he might get a thick seven-inch nail from a hardware store, drive it partway into a telephone pole, wrap it with cloth, and use it to stabilize his aim. As with hunting, he might shoot whatever struck his fancy. If it was a deer rather than a human being, that was okay, too. With Franklin, it was always open season.

If any subject of conversation was going to be able to get to Franklin on an emotional level, I figured it would be his daughter. And when we brought up her name, he grew quite despondent over the fact that his ex-wife had restricted the girl's communication with him. We had a camera with us, and he asked if we'd take some photos of him and send them to her. We agreed, and he proceeded through a series of martial arts poses—very serious, very macho, the whole bit. Remember, this was for his daughter, but this is the way he wanted to portray himself.

Unlike an Arthur Bremer, a guy like Joseph Paul Franklin never expected to be caught in his assassination attempts. But he was still out for the personal satisfaction, to vent the rage, and to make a name for himself. When that didn't come, he felt extremely frustrated.

This is not without precedent. John Wilkes Booth, this country's first celebrity assassin, kept a diary after the assassination of President Lincoln in which he expressed shock and dismay that he hadn't been made into a hero for his act. And I predicted correctly that when he came to Washington, John Hinckley would have visited Ford's Theater to commune with this great role model of the past. I suspect nothing would have pleased Joseph Paul Franklin more than to receive the accolades denied these other two, even if it meant facing execution to achieve it. And one other thing I wonder. Despite Booth's political feelings about Lincoln, would he have planned and carried out the assassination had he been as successful and famous and fulfilled an actor as his older brother, Edwin?

So, with what we've observed about assassins, is there anything meaningful we can say about the one crime that has haunted the nation since the moment it occurred? And that, of course, is the murder of President John Kennedy in Dallas on the afternoon of November 22, 1963. Well, I know I'm going to disappoint or dissatisfy a lot of readers when I say that by my analysis, despite a deeply flawed investigation, the significant evidence—behavioral and forensic—points to Lee Harvey Oswald as the lone assassin. Ken Baker, who has researched this subject extensively in his capacity in the Secret Service, agrees with me. And if you make the argument that a Secret Service agent wouldn't come clean with what he knew, then the first thing I'd say is that you don't know Ken, who is a man of towering integrity, and you've come up with just one more conspiracy theory.

On one level or another, we're all drawn to conspiracy theories. In a strange way, they make the world seem comprehensible. They explain what otherwise seems random and chaotic. It would make much more sense that it took a network of powerful, sophisticated, and evil people to change the course of history, rather than one misguided schlepp who couldn't hold down a decent job. But that isn't what the evidence points to. The fact of the matter is that Oswald conforms pretty classically to the assassin profile we've come up with. He was a paranoid individual who didn't fit in with any group he tried to become part of.

As for a large *government* conspiracy, that, I think, is laughable. I know I'm trying to prove a negative, which is inherently impossible, but anyone who's worked in the government, even in the intelligence community, will tell you that *nothing* that big or well publicized stays secret for long. The big bureaucracy is fundamentally incapable of carrying out a conspiracy and keeping it under wraps.

Oswald's not the kind of person you'd bring into a conspiracy, even as a dupe, because you couldn't trust him. If you're an agent of some sort, you're not going to try to develop someone like Oswald. He's too unreliable, too unpredictable, too much of a flake. He's got too many personal problems, plus he's not that smart. I don't believe that any secret evil cabal could have known enough about behavioral psychology back in 1963 to choose someone who so perfectly conformed to the lone assassin profile to be their front man. So, what else would you hire him for—just to be a shooter? Well, maybe, but one of the prime arguments against him is that he wasn't a good enough shooter to get off the requisite number of shots.

I disagree with this point, too, though. Oswald was trained in the Marine Corps, and though not the best, he was a decent shooter. Sure, you'd have to be lucky to be that accurate in that short a period of time. But the feat is possible, and I submit that there is no way to re-create the actual situation in simulations after the fact. Any successful assassin has to get lucky. Oswald was lucky in many ways, among them that Kennedy directed that the clear bubble top not be placed on the presidential limousine. Another was that the president was wearing a brace for his bad back. Had he not been, he might have been thrown forward by the first bullet and out of the critical line of fire.

It's always a confluence of unrelated coincidences. Gavrilo Princip was the nineteen-year-old Serb who assassinated Austrian archduke Francis Ferdinand and his wife, Sophie, in the Bosnian capital of Sarajevo on June 28, 1914, and effectively plunged Europe into World War I. Six previous conspirators had failed to kill Francis Ferdinand that same day for a variety of reasons, and when the archduke's route was changed and Princip could no longer gain the access he felt he needed, Princip despaired of accomplishing his self-appointed mission. He repaired to a local bar and was shocked when the archduke's carriage came right by on the way to a hospital Francis Ferdinand decided he wanted to visit. Princip climbed onto the carriage, and history was changed.

I won't go into all the details of the so-called "magic bullet theory" of the Kennedy assassination, but our ballistics guys and the ones who work for the Secret Service have analyzed many, many bullets, and there is nothing terribly unusual about the way this one deformed and traveled through soft tissue before finally coming to a stop.

No—though I don't expect to convince anyone in this short a discussion (how many forests have fallen to provide paper on this very point?)—I believe that Lee Harvey Oswald was just another paranoid loser who went from job to job, group to group, cause to cause, looking for something to believe in, something to make him significant. And unfortunately for all of us, when he climbed to his perch on the sixth floor of the Texas School Book Depository and aimed his 6.5-millimeter, bolt-action, clip-fed, Italian-made Mannlicher-Carcano rifle at the motorcade turning the corner into Dealey Plaza and passing a short distance below, he caught up with, then overtook, history. A few days later, Jack Ruby, another paranoid loser who thought with one bold act that he could become a hero, took his own shot at immortality.

## CHAPTER EIGHT

# RANDOM ACTS OF VIOLENCE

*To know the artist, study his art.*

I've used that phrase a lot in my career, but up to now we've been speaking metaphorically, as we've analyzed cases in terms of the offender's behavior before, during, and after commission of his crime. Now we move into the world of the bomber, where the concept takes on a more literal meaning.

Just as the way a man murders his family gives us insight into his makeup, the way a bomb is constructed—meticulously, carefully, consuming a lot of time, or sloppily, with errant fingerprints left by the bomb maker—as well as how it is delivered are keys to who the bomber is.

Case in point:

In 1989, my unit was called in to assist in the investigation of a series of mail bombs throughout the South. There had already been two deaths, and a third person was badly injured—and this despite the fact that two bombs were discovered and disarmed before they had a chance to explode. The FBI was involved because the devices were sent through the mail. We were asked to consult with the multiagency task force (FBI, ATF, postal inspectors, local police from the four cities involved, U.S. marshals, and more) and develop a profile of the UNSUB.

The first in a cluster of cases occurred around two o'clock on the afternoon of Saturday, December 16, 1989, when fifty-eight-year-old U.S. Circuit Court of Appeals judge Robert S. Vance began opening the mail in the kitchen of his home near Birmingham, Alabama. Helen, his wife of twenty-seven years, was nearby, taking a break from wrapping Christmas gifts. The return address on one package they received that day indicated it came from another judge, and as Vance started to open it, he remarked to Helen that it likely contained more horse magazines, reflecting an interest he and the presumed sender shared.

But this was not a package of magazines. From where Helen sat, about four feet across from her husband at the kitchen table, the ensuing blast was enough to knock her to the floor and inflict injuries so severe she spent two weeks in the hospital recovering from damage to a lung and her liver caused by a nail planted in the bomb as additional shrapnel. Her husband wasn't so lucky. The bomb ripped into his midsection; he was dead by the time help arrived.

Within hours, word went out to all U.S. marshals to warn everyone in any way connected with the judicial system to beware of, and report, any suspicious packages. Judge Vance hadn't received any threats recently and wasn't a sufficiently controversial figure to explain his being targeted for such a vicious attack. So while it could have been an isolated, random incident, the presumption had to be that more bombs could be out there.

The following Monday, a security officer X-raying mail at the U.S. Eleventh Circuit Court of Appeals in Atlanta (where Judge Vance had been seated) spotted another bomb. In a truly heroic operation, authorities were able to evacuate the building, remove the package from the heart of downtown, and disarm it without anyone getting hurt. I say heroic because instead of just blowing it up out at the Atlanta Police Department's bomb range, techs from the FBI, the police department, and ATF went to great lengths—at great personal risk—to disassemble the device so it could be analyzed as evidence. The lab can do a lot with debris, but you get much more out of the "artwork" in its original form.

Late in the afternoon that same day, black attorney and city alderman Robert "Robbie" Robinson was opening his mail in his downtown Savannah office. He didn't know that the package in the brown paper wrapper with the red-and-white, neatly typed address label and stamps featuring Old Glory waving over Yosemite National Park and looking from the outside just like two other packages would prove to contain lethal devices. Immediately following the blast, the forty-one-year-old victim was left kneeling in front of what was once a large cherry desk. The walls around him were covered with embedded nails and pieces of his flesh.

Dr. Emerson Brown, an optometrist whose office was nearby and who ran to aid Robinson after he heard the blast, was in the Army reserves and trained in combat casualty care, but the scene was overwhelming: Robinson bled profusely from what was left of his right arm—blown off around the elbow—and from his left wrist, which was now connected to his hand just by mangled skin. His chest was ripped open on the right side, and he had a hole in his thigh where it looked like a chunk of bomb cut right through. It was apparent that some of the debris on the wall was actually Robinson's hair and bone fragments.

Remarkably, he was not only still alive but capable of fighting on some primitive level, screaming as emergency personnel took him off to the hospital. He was brought into emergency surgery accompanied by FBI special agent Frank Bennett, assigned to stay with Robinson to maintain the chain of custody over evidence ranging from pieces of shrapnel removed in the O.R. to clothing shreds to Robinson's severed arm and, finally, to the victim's body itself. Robinson passed away around 8:30 P.M., nearly three and a half hours after the blast.

That same day, another tragedy was averted by a series of everyday aggravations that kept a potential victim from opening her own mail. A package was delivered to the Jacksonville office of the NAACP, where sixty-four-year-old branch president Willye Dennis would have opened it had fate not intervened. After a press conference, she had car trouble; then problems getting a tow truck kept her from returning to her office. Before she went in the next day, a close friend and fellow NAACP member called with a warning. He'd seen reports on the news about the other bombs. Just to be on the safe side, Dennis contacted the sheriff's office.

Their bomb tech, John Sheddan, got in touch with the ATF in Atlanta for a description of the bombs. What he heard convinced him they had a live one. At least with the one from the Eleventh Circuit courthouse already disarmed, he had an idea what he was looking at, although that didn't make his job of rendering harmless the one in front of him any safer.

He was able to successfully disarm the device, a job made a bit easier by the fact that the exterior of the packages weren't the only parts of the bombs that were consistent: the devices inside all had the signature of the man who put them together. These were pipe bombs, but unlike any others most of the investigators had ever seen. For one thing, the UNSUB had painstakingly attached nails to the pipe using rubber bands, ensuring that there'd be plenty of cutting shrapnel for maximum damage. And this "artist" took great pains to optimize the explosive force. While traditional pipe bombs are essentially what their name suggests—pipes full of explosive powder, closed at each end with commercially available screw-on caps—these were reinforced on the ends with metal plates that were actually welded to the pipe. On top of that, a metal rod was inserted through holes in the plates and bolted in place. These slight deviations in basic pipe bomb design may not sound like much to the layperson, but they served to strengthen the structure of the bomb, delaying the explosion after detonation for milliseconds, making it all the more powerful when it came, and rendering the device even more deadly for the individuals who opened the packages.

It also made construction tremendously risky for the bomber. If he wasn't careful, it would be easy for him to set off his own bomb while putting it together—which could result in his being classified among the victims of the crime, depending on what evidence might be nearby.

When we talk about signature elements here, we mean the things the bomb maker does that aren't necessary to the commission of his crime but are important for him to get emotional satisfaction out of the deed. In this case it would be the carefully wrapped nails, threaded rods, and welded ends of these pipe bombs. The devices would likely have been deadly without these signature elements, but he wanted to make sure, and that told us a lot about his level of anger, resentment, and hatred. He didn't want to scare people and make a political statement. He didn't even want to harm. He wanted to kill, or at the very least painfully maim and destroy his victims.

I mentioned that *most* veteran investigators from the FBI, ATF, and other agencies involved had never seen pipe bombs like these before. But as it turned out, the bomb design was so unusual, the signature so distinctive, that it revealed the UNSUB to several local investigators who recognized these unusual elements from a bomb case they'd seen years earlier. That device made such an impression on one ATF bomb specialist that he was able to draw a sketch of it just off the top of his head. This is a guy who'd seen thousands of bombs over the years, but his recollection of this one was so vivid in detail—and so like the current bombs—that agents shown the diagram after one of the first meetings of the task force mistook it for one of those.

Back in 1972, a young woman named Hazel Moody had been badly injured when she opened a package she found in her home. It was addressed to an automobile dealer who'd repossessed an MG she and her husband had bought and nearly paid off, but she thought it contained parts for a model airplane her husband was working on. Instead it held a dangerous explosive device. The blast, which set her hair on fire, left Hazel with first- and second-degree burns to her face, neck, and left arm. Her left eye was damaged badly, her right hand mangled. It took the doctor considerable time and effort to remove the gunpowder from her eyes. Hazel's husband, Walter Leroy Moody Jr., known as Roy, was ultimately convicted and sentenced to five years in prison. More than a decade after his sentence was over, Moody was still appealing the case. His most recent setback was a June 1989 ruling against him—in the Eleventh Circuit Court of Appeals.

Now, in 1989, many in Georgia believed the UNSUB had to be Moody, or someone who spent time with him in jail learning his technique. But the latter option was unlikely: these bombs demanded such a high degree of skill, workmanship in construction, and real understanding of the chemistry and engineering behind their design that it wasn't a technique the average con could pick up.

And this is one reason why a lot of bomb experts and profilers alike didn't buy into one early, incorrect, but painfully persistent theory in the case. There had been an explosion of a tear gas grenade in a package at the Southeastern regional office of the NAACP in Atlanta back in August, four months before the recent bombings. The device was untraceable—no DNA or fingerprints left anywhere, just as with the later bombs, although this one was not lethal—and at the time it struck some investigators as perhaps a warm-up by someone looking to perfect his technique and to test screening and defense at this civil rights group target.

Around the same time, copies of a strange letter were received by television stations from Philadelphia, Pennsylvania, to St. Paul, Minnesota, to Little Rock, Arkansas, to Atlanta. The letter was titled "DECLARATION OF WAR" but read less like a challenge to the NAACP (could the timing be coincidental?) and more against the Eleventh Circuit Court, with the American public as scapegoat. The author railed against injustice and "the court's failure to render impartial and equitable judgments . . . due to rank bias and the mistaken belief its victims can not effectively retaliate." This guy was now apparently ready to retaliate, threatening poison gas attacks on populated areas "until widespread terror forces the court to addopt [sic] the impartial and equitable treatment of all as its highest priority."

No tear-gas-type attacks were forthcoming, fortunately, but now leadership of the different investigating agencies in Washington took a look at the victimology and decided the emphasis should be on checking out the Ku Klux Klan and other white supremacist hate groups. There'd been two NAACP offices affected, a judge who'd ruled on civil rights cases (although not known as particularly controversial) and a black lawyer who'd done some legal work for the NAACP. It seemed likely to some that we were dealing with a person or persons holding a grudge against blacks.

In any high-profile case like this—especially one where so many investigating agencies shared jurisdiction—dueling agendas can arise to complicate things, and this case was no exception. Fueling the white-supremacist-hate-group camp's position were additional communiqués received from the bomber, including letters enclosed in the package with the safely defused Jacksonville bomb and one sent to a popular anchorwoman at the CBS affiliate in Atlanta. The sender now purported to be part of a group, Americans for a Competent Federal Judicial System, which spoke out simultaneously against the U.S. court system and black leadership, who were warned: "If you want to live, you shall take that action required to prevent black men from raping white women." The letter to the anchorwoman, in particular, had racist undertones, as it referenced a well-known, controversial rape-murder case of a white woman victimized by a group of black men. The letter demanded the anchorwoman air parts of the letter outlining the group's complaints about that case or face "assassination."

There were a couple of reasons why this didn't strike many of us as the immediate validation of the hate-group-as-bomber theory it seemed on its face. For one thing, the black offenders in the rape-murder case mentioned in the letter weren't identified and arrested until after the original tear gas bombing at the NAACP in Atlanta. Also, as in most extortion and threat cases, when you look at a communiqué like this, you should read "we" as "I." These offenders are not typically guys who got notes on their report cards in elementary school saying, "Works well with others." In most cases, they're loners. And when you do find a group of hate- and rhetoric-filled losers banded together, it's usually to talk about their gripes, not to act on them. Experts on groups like the KKK in the cities where the bombs went off didn't see them as organized enough, or possessing enough skills, to pull off this kind of crime. Plus, if they could, they wouldn't be able to keep quiet about it. Here, no one was beating on his chest and providing any juicy details about his "accomplishments." It was more likely that this was one lone guy with a grudge against the court system, using the racist stuff as a smoke screen to keep us from identifying him, to provide rationalization for his actions, or even to try to win over some of the public to his cause.

Whether it was a hate group or not, though, wasn't as important as keeping an open mind, I thought. So many times I'd seen investigations derailed, arrests and convictions delayed, further crimes not prevented, because someone in command contracted a bad case of tunnel vision early on. Remember, the original assumption was that the Atlanta child killer was a white redneck or a Klan-like group.

So I sent Bill Hagmaier down to Atlanta for on-site consultation and to act as liaison. From time to time he'd return to Quantico or phone in for consultation that involved not just the ISU but also the people from the arson and bombing programs. I was grateful that Dave Icove and Gus Gary brought in their particular expertise to the mix. Gus also went to meet with one of the local investigators.

Based on what we knew about the bombings, the profile was of a white male, age forty-five to fifty, probably living and working on his own, although he might have another person he could confide in. The UNSUB was neat, clean, disciplined, and paid careful attention to detail, as reflected in the construction of his bombs. From the wording in his letters and what we know of bombers in general (not the kind of guys who can confront someone face-to-face with a knife or even a gun), he would seem somewhat soft, or "feminine." The UNSUB had some college education—maybe even beyond—and would feel that his job was beneath him. A social outcast, we wouldn't expect him to be a member of a group like the Klan. But he would have his own ideology that he very much wanted others to understand, hence the communiqués. The letter sent to the anchorwoman referencing the racial crime seemed hurried, as if the subject didn't like the press he was getting and needed to put something out to try to generate public sympathy for his cause. And to round things out, his vehicle was profiled as a pickup truck or four-door sedan, dark in color.

Bill presented the profile formally two weeks into the investigation as part of the first multiagency, multijurisdictional meeting on the bombings, held at the Richard Russell Federal Building in Atlanta. Afterward, many there expressed surprise at how eerily the profile matched Roy Moody. Moody was in his mid-fifties, a loner who lived with his second, much younger wife, Susan. He had attended college, reportedly planning to be a neurosurgeon, but didn't do well there, and also went to law school—but the 1972 felony conviction would prevent him from practicing law. Rather than holding a steady job, he tended to live off the income of the woman in his life at the time, while pursuing moneymaking schemes, including a mail-order business repeatedly under investigation by the Postal Service. He definitely had his own sense of how things should be run, filing numerous lawsuits against defendants ranging from his own siblings and his ex-wife to a bank he did business with. And he was reportedly dangerous; in 1983, he was accused of the attempted murder of employees on whom he had taken out "key man" insurance. The charges were dismissed, though, after a hung jury. In 1989, as investigators began interviewing people who'd known him over the years, they encountered many who spoke only on the condition that their whereabouts or the fact that they talked to the authorities not be revealed to Moody, from whom they feared legal and/or physical retaliation.

So Moody's signature devices immediately made him a suspect with locals, whose suspicions were bolstered by our profile. We assisted in interview and prosecution strategies, and the guy was arrested. End of story, right? Hardly. Unfortunately, investigations are rarely quite that simple or cut-and-dried, and this was no exception. Over about the next year, law enforcement agents gathered tremendous circumstantial evidence against Moody; for example, witnesses placed him at stores buying materials like those used in the bombs. And as to motive, he had professed his anger against the courts repeatedly, and the Eleventh Circuit in particular had recently denied his appeal. But the pieces didn't really come together until his young wife, Susan McBride Moody, felt safe enough—that is, protected from him—to tell what she knew.

Susan, about half her husband's age at the time of the bombings and diagnosed as suffering from Battered Woman Syndrome, was granted a deal where, in exchange for the dropping of charges against her (including obstruction of justice and contempt), she would testify against him. Then, in addition to telling the court how he beat her and controlled her, separating her from her family, doing all the classic things the dominant offender does with and to a compliant victim, she described how he worked for hours in a bedroom he kept sealed off from her, sending her out to buy items like those found in the deadly bombs. He told her how to disguise herself when shopping, to wear gloves and use phony names, and to drive to stores far away for her purchases. She told of mailing items for him without looking at them. And she told of hearing a bang once from inside that room he would not let her enter, the same room where he worked on a chemical project that he abandoned. (Perhaps that was why the threatened gas attacks were never carried out.) And she described how her husband redecorated his room in December 1989, getting rid of the old carpeting, replacing the subflooring and carpet and repainting the walls. Her testimony was a treasure trove of details.

The story of Moody's trial is as multilayered as his background, with twists and turns built in as he alternately "helped" and destroyed his own defense, refusing to allow an insanity defense to be considered. My colleague Park Dietz interviewed him several times and diagnosed a paranoid personality disorder, but didn't classify him as delusional. Or, as one psychiatrist who analyzed him put it, "Mr. Moody is not the kind of man to say that the judge has two heads. He is the kind of man to say that the judge is out to get him."

In February of 1997, Moody was sentenced in Alabama to death in the electric chair for his murder of Judge Vance. He was already serving seven sentences of life without parole for federal convictions related to the bombings.

Walter Leroy Moody Jr.'s story well illustrates how the "artist" can be undone by his art. We could tell from the bombing subject's device design, delivery method, letter writing and media campaign, and victim choice that he was smart and motivated by hate. And when we learned more about Moody, we saw that our evaluation was confirmed.

Moody's IQ has been estimated at around 130; lawyers and judges have found some of his more cogent legal work compelling; and obviously, he could design and build a heck of an explosive device. But he was not the master manipulator, dominator, controller, litigator, or bomb maker he would have liked to believe. After all, in the end he was done in because he lost control—over his subservient wife, over his insisted-upon courtroom strategy, and ultimately over his own devices. He gave himself up in his work.

If you accept the premise that we Americans lost our national idealism with President Kennedy's assassination on November 22, 1963, that we lost our naiveté about the potential for mass, spontaneous violence always lurking in our midst with Charles Whitman on August 1, 1966, then you'll probably agree that we certainly lost our complacency regarding the threat of terrorism within our own borders on April 19, 1995. That was the day a bomb ripped through the Alfred P. Murrah Federal Building in Oklahoma City at 9:02 in the morning, killing 168 and wounding more than 500, including twenty-one children under five. Like those previous traumas and a couple of others, this event was a watershed, after which nothing, and none of us, would ever be exactly the same again.

And yet, after the dust had settled, after the living had been rescued and the dead buried and mourned, after all the recrimination and soul-searching, what did the specifics of this monumental tragedy turn out to be?

The perpetrator of this crime—the costliest and most devastating in human terms in all of American history—was a scrawny, pissed-off young hick driving an easily traceable rental truck carrying more than four thousand pounds of fuel oil and doctored-up cow shit. Talk about the banality of evil.

Like arsonists and certain types of assassins, bombers are cowards. They wreak their destruction without the need for direct confrontation. Not only can the victim or victims be totally random; there may never have been any direct contact between them and the offender. In many cases, offenders never place themselves in harm's way. If they take risks at all, it is in the assembly of certain types of inherently unstable devices; and that detail can often serve as a signature element, as we saw with Moody. But though they are all cowards, there are important distinctions and differences within this vile species.

Timothy J. McVeigh, the twenty-seven-year-old man convicted and sentenced to death for the Murrah Building bombing, is one of the most basic and straightforward types.

He was strong on motive—strong on hatred and resentment, strong enough to set a bomb he had to know would kill and maim many people. What he was weak on was technique—basic criminal sophistication. He was arrested an hour and a half after the bombing, about seventy-five miles away, near Billings, Oklahoma, when a state trooper stopped him because the battered 1977 Mercury he was driving had no license plate. Peering into the car, the trooper noticed a gun and arrested him, then took him to jail in Perry, Oklahoma. This is the equivalent of picking up the guy driving the bank robbers' getaway car around the corner from the bank because he's double-parked.

Remember, at this point, a foreign terrorist group was the prevailing theory of the case, so McVeigh wouldn't have even been the profile they were looking for. Only the most talented and experienced observers, people like terrorism expert Louis R. Mizell Jr., immediately understood the significance of the date: Patriots Day (the anniversary of the Revolutionary War Battle of Concord, a commemoration the militia movement holds dear) and the second anniversary of the fiery end of the Branch Davidian siege in Waco, Texas. Meanwhile, the FBI recovered the vehicle identification number from the wreckage of the Ryder truck used to deliver the bomb and traced it back to the location from which it had been rented. The clerks there gave them a description of the renter, which FBI artists transformed into a sketch and circulated throughout the area. The owner of the Dreamland Motel in Junction City recognized the sketched face and gave agents McVeigh's name. They ran it through the National Crime Information computer and learned that he was being held in Perry—and about to be released—on an unrelated charge. When McVeigh's clothing was subsequently examined, traces of residue from the detonation cord were found on his shirt.

So, who is this guy, and what made him tick? That's certainly what thousands of tormented, grieving, and enraged survivors, family members, and friends demanded to know. It comes down to our old question: What kind of person could do such a thing?

Tim McVeigh's background is going to have haunting overtones of Oswald's, Whitman's, Franklin's, and other assassin types, and that should give us some insight into his motivation throughout his life. He was born April 23, 1968, a middle child between two sisters. He grew up in an all-white neighborhood in

Pendleton, New York, in the Buffalo–Niagara Falls corner of the state. McVeigh's father, Bill, worked in a plant that made heating and air-conditioning systems for General Motors, and enjoyed bowling and gardening. The *Dallas Morning News* reported a co-worker and fellow bowler of Bill McVeigh's as saying he never even knew Bill had a son until Tim was arrested in the bombing. Bill was described as an extremely nice guy, but he never talked about his children.

That same newspaper story related that when FBI agents came to search Bill's home in Pendleton, looking for potential evidence, he sat in the living room calmly reading a bowling magazine.

In 1978—when Tim was ten; his older sister, Patricia, twelve; and his younger sister, Jennifer, four—their mother, Mildred, left the family, apparently bored by life with Bill. Two years later she moved to Texas and took Jennifer with her. Patricia took much of the responsibility for caring for her brother, who resented his mother from then on. When he got to the Army years later, he referred to her as "that no-good whore," one Army buddy recalled.

Tim was small and thin, a decent student who hardly ever talked to anyone. No one remembers him ever having a date during high school. But then, as is true of so many of these guys, a lot of his fellow students and even teachers don't remember him at all. He already fit the angry, paranoid profile: asocial, asexual, broken family, underachiever, pervasive feelings of inadequacy, combined with a desire to get back at others who ignored him and to one day "prove" himself.

His parents finally divorced the same month he graduated from Star Point Central High School in Lockport, New York, in 1986. Still living with his father, Tim enrolled in Niagara Community College, but lasted only a few weeks—the first of a number of endeavors that just didn't work out. He got a job at a local Burger King, then the following year got a firearms permit and went to Buffalo, where he got a job as an armored car guard. His love of guns grew, and he kept adding to his collection as he got money to buy them.

In 1988, McVeigh enlisted in the Army, and for the first time in his life felt as if he'd found a home. He loved the discipline and order, the classes on military tactics, and, of course, the guns. His dream was to become a member of the Special Forces. During basic training at Fort Benning, Georgia, he met two other men who were to become critical to his life and crime: Terry Nichols and Michael Fortier, both of whom participated in the bombing plot. Nichols was another loner from an emotionally needy background. He and McVeigh would come to feed off each other's inadequacies.

After basic training, the unit went to the Army's First Infantry Division ("The Big Red One") at Fort Riley, Kansas. McVeigh was assigned to be a gunner on a Bradley Fighting Vehicle. Again, no one remembered ever seeing McVeigh with a woman. Few recall ever seeing him laugh or smile, which is typical of paranoid types.

During this time, McVeigh became enamored of a book titled *The Turner Diaries,* by William L. Pierce, published in 1978. Presented as a novel, the book is a racist, anti-Semitic, antigovernment story about a soldier in an underground army who uses a home-made fertilizer-and-fuel-oil bomb packed in a truck to blow up a federal building in Washington, D.C. Which one? you may ask. Why, the FBI building, of course. The bomb kills seven hundred people. Earl Turner knows that noncombatants will be killed but accepts the fact that this is a consequence of war and hopes it will inspire others to strike out against a government trying to outlaw the private ownership of firearms. *The Turner Diaries* became something of a bible for McVeigh. He recommended it to others. Some people reported that he idolized Hitler.

Late in 1990, McVeigh was accepted into a program to evaluate his potential for Special Forces, but then in January 1991, the First Infantry Division was shipped out to the Persian Gulf for service in Desert Storm. McVeigh went with his unit, served with distinction, and won a Bronze Star. As long as he was in such a structured environment and was appreciated for what he was doing, he was relatively stable. This is like the phenomenon we see with many offenders who "rehabilitate" in a carefully regulated prison situation. I would expect McVeigh to be described as a model prisoner now for this same reason.

He left the Persian Gulf in March and went to Fort Bragg, North Carolina, for another shot at Special Forces. He took all the IQ and aptitude tests but dropped out after a few days of tough marches and maneuvers, saying he wasn't physically prepared. In failing to achieve his goal of becoming a Green Beret, McVeigh might have felt he had given up his stake in the system; the other side of his personality—the disenfranchised, lonely, paranoid side—could now be given free rein. If he couldn't be a hero to one group, he'd be a hero for another.

He had re-upped before leaving for the Persian Gulf, but after the Special Forces dream dissolved, he seemed to lose interest in military life. In the fall of 1991, at twenty-four, he accepted the Army's offer for an early out. Nichols had already left the service on a hardship discharge when his wife divorced him and left him to take care of their seven-year-old son, Josh—a situation paralleling McVeigh's own childhood experience. McVeigh moved back in with his father and got a job as a security guard. His supervisor at the Niagara Falls Convention Center reported that she'd had to post him at the back door because his ability to handle people and relate to them was so poor.

He started writing angry letters to the local newspaper, complaining about race relations, taxation, gun control, crime, and political corruption. Without the structure of military life, he had to find another group to give him the same order and organization, or revert to his own tightly rigid personality to get by. And after a while, that rigidity becomes exhausting.

In January 1993, McVeigh left home and began drifting around the United States, all his possessions jammed into an old car. For a while he stayed with Army buddy Michael Fortier in Kingman, Arizona. He spent more time with Terry Nichols and Terry's brother James at James's farmhouse in Decker, Michigan. Despite his extreme-right, survivalist-oriented politics, McVeigh was not formally a member of any groups other than the National Rifle Association and the Republican Party, something else we'd expect in the paranoid individual. And McVeigh's obsession with gun magazines can be likened to the sexual serial killer's obsession with S&M pornography.

His favorite movie, according to published reports, was *Red Dawn,* a 1984 John Milius film featuring Patrick Swayze and Charlie Sheen, about a group of small-town high schoolers who transform themselves into guerrilla fighters to resist the commie commandos who have invaded their community. Guys like McVeigh can compensate for a while by "talking the talk," but then—generally toward the late twenties, as we've noted—they look in the mirror and realize they're going nowhere fast. That's when you have to worry: when they start fantasizing about becoming Rambo. McVeigh wore camouflage fatigues and black combat boots. He resigned from the NRA because it wasn't strong enough in opposing the ban on assault weapons. Though not as rabid as a Joseph Paul Franklin, he considered blacks inferior and Jews a natural enemy. He warned his sister Jennifer—who shared many of his views—that the FBI was tapping their phones and told other people that the Army had secretly planted a computer chip in his butt so they could control him.

In March 1993, McVeigh traveled to Waco during the government standoff with self-proclaimed prophet David Koresh's cult. While he was there, he was interviewed and photographed by a college journalism student who went on to a career in broadcast journalism. Photographs show him selling bumper stickers with slogans such as "Fear the Government That Fears Your Guns," "Ban Guns—Make the Streets Safe for a Government Take-Over," and "A Man with a Gun Is a Citizen. A Man without a Gun Is a Subject."

Waco, it turned out, would be McVeigh's trigger, his rationale and excuse to vent his anger and frustration. He could lash out, and it would be getting back at the real enemy. He could commit violence, but someone else would be responsible. Someone else provoked him beyond the point of acquiescence. Waco was a banner under which he hoped to be able to get others to follow him.

In September of that year, at one of the frequent gun shows he attended, McVeigh was overheard by a detective as he was explaining to someone how a flare gun could be modified to "shoot down an ATF helicopter." It was the Bureau of Alcohol, Tobacco and Firearms that staged the initial raid on Koresh's compound. McVeigh was already passionately angry over the FBI's shooting of white separatist poster boy Randy Weaver's wife, Vicki, and son, Samuel, during the standoff at Ruby Ridge, Idaho, in August of 1992, and by the passage of the Brady gun control act. When Congress passed the Omnibus Crime Bill in August of 1994, outlawing nineteen types of assault weapons, McVeigh felt that the feared New World Order was gaining unacceptable strength.

It was then that McVeigh and Terry Nichols started putting together their plan to make a huge bomb in the mold of *The Turner Diaries*. Using ammonium nitrate and a manure-based fertilizer as the key ingredients, they could construct a large, simple, relatively inexpensive bomb that would truly give them the most bang for the buck—enough bang to take out the kind of building described in *Turner.* Unlike other types of bombers, they did not consider the explosive device itself to be important. The only thing that mattered was the "mission."

Keep in mind that McVeigh and Nichols weren't operating in a vacuum. The same events that moved them to action—Ruby Ridge, Waco, the Brady law, and other apparent manifestations of the New World Order—were energizing militia and survivalist movements, and hate groups like the Klan and neo-Nazis, in their various pockets and under their various rocks throughout the country. The Michigan Militia, for example, one of the more organized groups, was sending out a catalogue with information on starting up paramilitary groups, survival techniques, and weapons acquisition.

But here's where we separate the talkers from the doers. At McVeigh's trial, his younger sister testified that five months before the bombing, he told her he was no longer in the "propaganda stage" but had moved to the "action stage." We saw this same kind of behavior in Joseph Paul Franklin, who had no patience with the racists who merely talk about white superiority when he was ready to do something about it.

In both cases, you've got a player who's all fired up by the rhetoric, and now he wants to get into the big game on Sunday. But then he realizes the rhetoric is all there is; there isn't going to be a big game on Sunday. Well, if this isn't going to be a team effort, he'll play solo and make a name for himself that way. We saw a similar type of phenomenon with the Manson family. Charles Manson gave his disciples all this bullshit about Helter-Skelter and the coming war. But after interviewing him, I became convinced he was willing to keep on talking as long as he could maintain his audience. It was when his follower Tex Watson decided to start implementing Charlie's vision that all the shit suddenly hit the fan. It's the same mind-set that led us to conclude that one of these groups was not responsible for the 1989 mail bombs.

As the bombing plan took on more and more critical mass, as Tim McVeigh sat all alone all day long in his motel room in Kingman, Arizona, with the blinds drawn, Nichols and Fortier started backing off. But McVeigh kept moving forward. He finally left the motel April 12, having already purchased two fifty-pound bags of ammonium nitrate fertilizer from a TrueValue hardware store to use as a test. On Easter Sunday, April 16, he and Nichols checked out their target site and got the lay of the land. But Nichols, a timid, go-fer, follower type, would go no farther. That didn't deter McVeigh. On April 17, using an assumed name since he had no intention of returning the vehicle, McVeigh rented a twenty-foot Ryder truck in Kansas capable of carrying a five-thousand-pound load. He purchased the fertilizer in McPherson, Kansas. And on April 19, he parked that truck in front of the Murrah Building and set the fuse. He left a note on the vehicle saying it had a bad battery so the police wouldn't tow it away. Like his fictional hero Earl Turner, he was willing to accept the casualties. The fact that the rest of us were not, the fact that some children would never grow up and others would be deprived of mothers or fathers because of his actions—none of this was of any concern to him. In fact, it wasn't even the kind of thing he could relate to.

Once arrested, he called himself a prisoner of war. It was the ultimate unwillingness to take upon himself responsibility for what he had done.

Had Timothy McVeigh not delivered himself into police hands, solving the crime would obviously have been considerably more difficult. But that's like speculating what would have happened if Moody had designed a device totally different from his 1972 bomb. In both cases, we still would have had a profiling start based on the significance of the target, the type of explosive device, and the fact that the perpetrator or perpetrators clearly wanted and intended to get away rather than go out in a blaze of glory with their victims. Add to this McVeigh's choice of date. Then, since people with little or no bomb-making experience have to try out their devices before the real crime, there will have been a test somewhere, generally outside of town, that someone will have noticed.

We begin any investigation into a bombing by considering three essentials: the motivation of the bomber, his traits and characteristics, and the crime analysis.

Motivation for bombing runs the gamut of our negative human impulses. Power, as it is for the arsonist, is one of the primary motives. We have the strictly mission-oriented people, who are thrilled by the act of constructing and placing the bomb and come up with some overarching cause as an excuse. We have the technician, whose gratification comes from the elegance of the design. There is criminal enterprise, involving the extortionist, or profit-oriented bomber. We have bombs set in political, religious, racial, or labor disputes, just as we do with fire setting. We have those who set bombs for revenge. And there are those who use bombs as a dramatic means of suicide. Of course, we can have mixed motives, too. Timothy McVeigh could easily fit into the power, mission-oriented, political, and revenge classifications. Essentially, we want to know—as with every other crime we've discussed—*why* this bomb was made, set, and exploded.

The bomber's personal traits and characteristics often have to be inferred, since there are often no witnesses and he has little or no direct contact with his victims. But from our research, study, and interviews, we start out with some basic assumptions, which we then alter as the situation or investigation warrants. The bomber tends to be a white male of average or above-average IQ (one of the key ways in which he differs from, say, the assassin); he's an underachiever but a meticulous plotter and planner; he's cowardly (even more so than the assassin) and nonconfrontational, nonathletic, a loner with a self-perceived inadequate personality or social skills.

If we look at someone like McVeigh, we see that this profile fits pretty well. Though McVeigh was certainly athletic in his younger days and in the service, in his last few years he had let his military fitness lapse. And though he had a number of episodes in which he lashed out with an explosive temper, once he was out of the Army, he pretty much kept to himself. So we see that as he moved closer and closer to his actual bomb making, he conformed more and more closely to our established profile.

The final key investigative consideration is the crime analysis, and this includes the critical evaluation of the explosive device itself. What level of expertise or training does it suggest? Are there any unique components, workmanship, or design elements? Was it a time-set, remote-controlled, or booby-trap explosive? When we correlate the device and the crime, does it appear that the bomb builder and the bomb setter are one and the same, or is there implication of a conspiracy of two or more individuals? Evaluation of the device helps us determine, as an example, whether the UNSUB is merely a former childhood fire starter who grew up to have military explosives experience or someone much "stranger" than that.

What about victimology? Is the victim (or victims) accidental, or targeted? Random, or predictable? What was the risk factor for the victim being in this particular place at this particular time? And how big a risk is the UNSUB taking by constructing or placing this bomb? Compare the danger for Moody in assembling his device versus McVeigh driving around with a truck full of manure.

Is the physical property that was targeted easily accessible, or remote? Is it individually owned, community owned, corporately owned, or government owned? Was the bomb set off at a time of day when it would be reasonable to expect that there would (or would not) be victims on the premises? Is this a single incident, or part of a series?

All of these questions will help us determine *Who?* and *Why?*

On November 1, 1955, United Airlines flight 629, a DC-6B en route to Portland, Oregon, exploded out of a clear northern Colorado sky eleven minutes after takeoff from Denver's Stapleton Airport, killing all thirty-nine passengers and five crew members. Aviation terrorism, as we know it, was unheard of in those days, which left three possible causes for Federal Aviation Administration and FBI investigators: mechanical failure, pilot error, or some form of sabotage, although sabotage had never been practiced before against an American civilian aircraft.

At the still-smoldering wreckage site, though, agents found evidence that confirmed their worst suspicions: tiny metal fragments containing deposits of sodium carbonate along with small traces of nitrate and sulfur—by-products of a dynamite explosion. Lab analysis also detected traces of manganese dioxide from the battery used to detonate the dynamite. This was the first time the FBI lab ever used residues to identify explosive substances.

Investigators combed the passenger manifest and looked for motives. One passenger, Mrs. Daisie King, was carrying $37,000 worth of travel insurance policies for this trip, taken out by the twenty-three-year-old son who had put her on the plane in Denver. John (known as Jack) Gilbert Graham had specified himself as the beneficiary. When FBI agents searched Graham's home, they found in a shirt pocket a piece of copper wire with yellow insulation identical to wire used in the bomb's detonator found at the crash site. A store clerk recalled selling him dynamite and blasting caps and his wife, Gloria, remembered him putting a

312 JOHN DOUGLAS AND MARK OLSHAKER

small wrapped gift into his mother's luggage for her to find when she unpacked.

Graham confessed, then later recanted his confession. He was found guilty of first-degree murder, and fourteen months after the crash, he was executed in the Colorado State Penitentiary gas chamber.

This was a landmark case: the first of a type, but unfortunately far from the last. The motive the prosecution presented and the jury accepted was pretty straightforward—greed. It was the essential criminal enterprise offense. But as it turned out, it was probably another case of mixed motive—because after Graham's execution, the psychiatrists who had examined him at the Colorado Psychopathic Hospital to determine his sanity revealed their discovery of the relationship between Graham and the woman he killed, along with all her fellow passengers, for money.

Graham's father died when Jack was only a boy. Daisie remarried, but rather than taking him with her in her new life and relationship, she shipped him off to Clayton College for Boys, a charity home in Denver. Jack never got over this rejection. After her second husband died, Daisie's attitude toward her son was said to be domineering. The month of the bombing, he told her he wanted her to spend Thanksgiving with him and Gloria and their two babies. She said she was going to Alaska instead. This one final rejection symbolized all the others for Jack. He decided he'd had enough.

For more than a decade, the most-wanted serial killer in the United States was one that none of his victims—alive or dead— had ever laid eyes on, an individual so mysterious and elusive that he was known only by the case code name the FBI had given him: Unabomber, since his early bombings were directed at universities and airlines. Unlike the one big, crude blast of Tim McVeigh and his cohorts, unlike the scattered but nearly simultaneous explosions set by Moody, these bombings were spaced apart; this guy could wait, act over time. He was more specifically directed. He was clever, he was diabolical, and his motive was wrapped in layers of mystery.

I was called into the case after the fourth bombing in the series, in the spring of 1980. Tom Barrett, who had been a new agent with me in Detroit and was now working out of the Chicago Field Office, called me at Quantico. "We've had a bombing in Lake Forest," he explained. "June tenth. Percy Wood, the president of United Airlines, was injured opening a package addressed to him at his home." Tom was reasonably convinced that this was not the first bombing, but the fourth in a series.

I asked if the airline had gotten any threat communications.

"No," Tom replied. "No ransom demands or anything like that. There's no apparent motive. I know you're doing a lot of work and research in sexual homicide and trying to profile the offenders. Do you think you could do anything on this type of guy?"

By this point in our research, I'd already made the connection in my own mind between arsonists and assassins, and soon, it would turn out, I'd be folding in product tamperers as well. Since bombing was another crime carried out without direct contact with the victims, I thought we could probably make some headway there, too.

There was another consideration, which affected me on at least a subliminal level. Though we hadn't done much work on the subject, it was a series of bombings that had been indirectly responsible for creating the discipline of profiling within the FBI. From the late 1940s through the mid-1950s, New York City was rocked by more than thirty bombings of public buildings, including Grand Central, Pennsylvania Station, and Radio City Music Hall. As a kid growing up in Brooklyn at the time, I remember well the criminal the papers were calling "the Mad Bomber."

Not knowing what else to do, in 1957 the police turned to a Greenwich Village psychiatrist by the name of Dr. James A. Brussel. He studied photos of the bomb scenes, analyzed the bomber's taunting letters to newspapers, and came to a number of conclusions that now might seem rather tame and straightforward but at the time represented a tremendous breakthrough in behavioral science. Brussel concluded that the UNSUB was a paranoiac who hated his father, was obsessed with his mother, and was a disgruntled employee or former employee of the city's public utility, Consolidated Edison, the target of much of his written vitriol. He also concluded that the Mad Bomber lived in Connecticut and had a serious heart condition. He ended his advice to police with the now-famous statement: "Look for a heavy man. Middle-aged. Foreign born. Roman Catholic. Single. Lives with a brother or sister. When you find him, chances are he'll be wearing a double-breasted suit. Buttoned."

Going through the voluminous Con Ed records, investigators happened on the name of George Metesky, who thought he had a claim against the company for an injury that doctors didn't find to be as permanent as he did. At any rate, when police went to see the single, heavyset, middle-aged, foreign-born Roman Catholic with a heart condition at the house in Waterbury, Connecticut, where he lived with his two unmarried sisters, they found him in his pajamas. They asked him to get dressed, and when he came back to them several minutes later he was in a double-breasted suit that was, of course, buttoned.

Howard Teten, one of the pioneering instructors in behavioral science at the FBI Academy, sought out Dr. Brussel and started applying his principles to crime solving on an informal basis. That's where the original serial killer study and I come into the story.

And looking back, that probably had a lot to do with why I

told my old friend Tom Barrett that this bombing he had on his hands was something we might be able to help on.

There are many ways the UNABOM story can be told, and many interesting details that could fill up many volumes. We could easily show it from the task force's perspective, or the subject's. But for our investigation of motive here, I think the most enlightening and succinct way to approach the case is to follow how we dealt with it at Quantico—as a progression of incidents in which our knowledge, understanding, and ability to interpret grew in incremental stages. Eventually, others would become involved, both within my unit and on the task force, and they would add new and updated analyses. But I continued to consult and to take an active interest in the case up until the time I left the Bureau, when the Unabomber still remained a dangerous UNSUB.

The case file Barrett gave me showed that Percy A. Wood, the president of United Airlines, was injured on his hands, face, and thighs while opening a package sent to his home. In addition to the bomb, the package contained a novel titled *Ice Brothers*.

I tried to correlate the information between that and the first three crimes. The first occurred May 26, 1978, at Northwestern University, in the northern Chicago suburb of Evanston, and was rather intriguing. A package addressed to an engineering professor at Rensselaer Polytechnic Institute in Troy, New York, had been found the day before in the parking lot of the engineering department of the University of Illinois, Chicago. It was then brought to the individual on the return address, Professor Buckley Crist, at Northwestern's Technological Institute. Crist said he hadn't sent it, and turned it over to the university police. It exploded when they opened it, slightly injuring campus police officer Terry Marker. The device was a pipe bomb constructed of match heads and packed in a carved wooden box. We assumed Professor Crist was the intended target, which first of all gave us some respect for the cleverness of an UNSUB who'd deliver his bomb with this kind of "double reverse," and also got us wondering what it was about this distinguished scholar (without any known enemies) that would make someone want to blow him up.

The second bomb was more direct: a cigar box, taped shut and left on a table between study cubicles on the second floor of Northwestern's Technological Institute. A civil engineering graduate student, John G. Harris, opened the box. It blew up, and he sustained relatively minor cuts and burns. The debris suggested a device composed of match heads, wires, and flashlight batteries—another simple, crude bomb. This time, however, there was no evidence the bomber had a specific victim in mind.

The third case shifted targets. On November 15, 1979, American Airlines flight 444 from Chicago to Washington, D.C., was forced to make an emergency landing at Dulles International Airport in Virginia after smoke filled the cabin. Twelve aboard the Boeing 727 were treated for smoke inhalation. A bomb was hidden in a package mailed from Chicago and was rigged to detonate when cabin pressure reached a certain level. The explosion was not powerful enough to blow a hole through the airplane, but it did start a fire in the cargo hold. The fire burned the address on the package, so investigators couldn't tell who the target was. But like the first bomb, that could have been a ruse anyway, since the device was carefully constructed to go off in midair.

So now we had someone who was escalating not only in his level of technical sophistication but also in his targets. This device wasn't intended merely to maim, or blow the hands or arms off, some unfortunate professor or engineering student. The UNSUB had graduated to the big time. Like Jack Graham almost exactly twenty-four years before, this guy wanted to take out an entire airliner. He just hadn't perfected his technique.

In addition to a basic profile of an obsessive-compulsive white male loner in his late twenties to early thirties with above-average intelligence and all that, the evolution of the bombs and the escalation of the viciousness of their intent suggested someone with a high degree of technical ability and criminal sophistication. There was no reason to believe this evolution would not continue. On the contrary, we'd expect him to get better and better the more experience he had. I saw no reason to change my basic belief from other types of serial crimes, that the earliest ones tell you the most—before the offender gets too good at what he's doing. I felt the UNSUB would stage his initial offenses in a place where he had some level of comfort and familiarity. To me, this said the offender was from the Chicago area and was an academic or had something to do with a university. It might not be Northwestern—that could merely be a convenient, close-by symbol—but the Chicago and academic connections I was pretty sure about.

With the shift of target and the increasing sophistication of the bombs themselves, some investigators started thinking that the airlines figured in more strongly. Perhaps we were dealing with a disgruntled airline employee—probably a mechanic—who was "practicing" when he sent his earliest bombs. He could not have known that his package would end up on an American Airlines plane, so that bomb was probably generic—against the industry—while the fourth one, mailed directly to the United chief executive, would have been more telling. Personally, I wasn't sure why Mr. Wood got the bomb, but I was sticking with my idea about the academic connection.

It was after this fourth bombing that a task force was formed and the FBI assigned the major case code name: UNABOM.

The next bomb didn't show up for more than a year. A package bomb placed in a business classroom at the University of Utah in Salt Lake City was defused without injuries. I'd stopped thinking much about UNABOM since I had so many other active cases to deal with. But when this happened and I reviewed the facts, I became more convinced than ever that the UNSUB must have some sort of academic background and orientation. This attempted bombing also showed the subject was mobile and felt comfortable moving outside his primary zone, the Chicago area. Mobility tends to add some years to the profile age estimate, because along with the means to get around the UNSUB has the criminal sophistication and increased confidence to feel secure doing so.

And I was starting to get a feel for motive. The target was non-specific again here, but clearly directed at a university. The bomber's anger was directed at authority: institutions of higher learning in general, a professor, a classroom, and an airline executive in particular. But the point is, though the bomber had ventured out of his comfort zone in Chicago, the university setting represented another type of comfort zone. This is a guy who feels comfortable walking around classrooms while he places his bombs. He blends in there, and even though he's likely a pretty intense paranoid, he isn't self-conscious or worried about being singled out there. In my opinion, this was not a disgruntled airline mechanic. It would have been much easier for an intelligent guy like this to learn how to make bombs than it would be for a blue-collar, technically oriented guy to move in these intellectual circles.

Our bomb experts told me that the devices were still relatively unsophisticated, but the bomber was clearly taking time assembling them. You don't just wake up one morning and say, "I think I'll be a bomber." You have to experiment, you have to practice. I was convinced that if we could make people in and around Chicago aware of this guy's preoffense type of behavior and the fact that someone has been exploding bombs for practice, someone could tell us something. I also thought that this type of offender would probably conform to behaviors characteristic of other violent serial criminals, in that he would now be following, and trying to affect, his own press.

The following spring—May 5, 1982—a package addressed to Professor Patrick Fischer at Pennsylvania State University, forwarded to his office at Vanderbilt University in Nashville, Tennessee, exploded when his secretary, Janet Smith, opened it. She sustained some serious lacerations and had to be taken to Vanderbilt Hospital. Like some of the others, this was a pipe bomb in a wooden box. The pipe was filled with smokeless powder and match heads. Fischer had moved to Vanderbilt two years before, but it was possible that his name and address were just a guise, and that the sender wanted to get the package sent back to the return address, since the stamps were already canceled when the package was put in the mail at Provo, Utah, on April 23. The return address was that of LeRoy Bearnson, a professor of electrical engineering at Brigham Young.

But we were starting to think about something else. It was a little far-fetched, but it couldn't be ignored. Professor Bearnson's middle name was Wood, the same as the United Airlines president's last name. The bomb containers were made of wood. Could this be a clue? we wondered.

The UNSUB was showing us he was flexible enough to change his M.O., his method of delivery—by going back to the mails. Perhaps last time was a close call when he placed the bomb personally. And we had to have some respect for his technical ability. These bombs needed to be stable enough to travel through the mail without accidentally detonating.

There would also be more opportunities to be proactive, I felt. Since he mailed this device, presumably he was not in the area where it exploded. But for his own satisfaction, he'd want to follow media accounts. A small explosion in a university would probably be carried only by local papers, which means he'd need access to out-of-town press. I thought we ought to start checking libraries around Chicago that carried such papers, just as we did with our Tylenol suspect.

On July 2, less than two months after the last incident, he struck again. This time, Diogenes Angelakos, professor of electrical engineering and computer sciences, noticed a can of some type, perhaps left by a student or construction worker, in the fourth-floor faculty lounge of Cory Hall at the University of California, Berkeley. It exploded when he picked it up. Professor Angelakos was seriously injured.

It was another small metal pipe bomb, and this one was personally placed, not mailed. So the UNSUB was on the move again, and he felt comfortable operating around here. We had another nonspecific target, but again directed at a university technology department. This bomb was more dangerous, and we doubted the UNSUB would now go backward in this respect.

Then there was an almost three-year interval when nothing happened. We figured the bomber might have committed suicide, accidentally blown himself up, or was on ice somewhere for some other crime. But on May 15, 1985, there was another explosion at Cory Hall at Berkeley. A bomb was left in a computer room in a stack of three-ring binders. John E. Hauser, an engineering graduate student and pilot, picked it up. The explosion severed two arteries in his right hand and destroyed parts of several fingers. He also lost partial vision in one eye. This bomb was more powerful than previous ones, containing a mixture of ammonium nitrate and aluminum powder.

Less than a month later, on June 13, a mail bomb sent from Oakland, California, turned up at the Boeing Aircraft Fabrication Division in Auburn, Washington. It had actually been mailed before the last Berkeley bomb, but was lost in Boeing's internal mail system. This one was successfully disarmed by the bomb squad without injury. Since this bomb was sent around the same time the last one was left, we wondered if it was not part of the Unabomber's proactive program to confuse the issue—he'd know we would clearly be focusing on Berkeley. But there was still a Bay Area connection, so we knew where he felt comfortable.

That November 15, a package bomb was mailed to University of Michigan psychology professor James V. McConnell's home outside Ann Arbor. A one-page letter postmarked Salt Lake City was taped to the outside and read, "I'd like you to read this book . . . Everybody in your position should read this book." McConnell and his young assistant, Nicklaus Suino, were both injured when Suino opened the package in McConnell's kitchen. Suino had shrapnel wounds and powder burns on his arms and legs. McConnell lost some of his hearing.

Here we had another specific target, a man known widely in the academic community for his views on behavior modification. And the UNSUB was spreading his university net even wider. The shift to the home target again showed that he was adaptable, able to evolve and stay ahead of the investigation.

Less than a month later, the stakes grew enormously. On December 11, 1985, Hugh Campbell Scrutton, the owner of a computer store in Sacramento, California, picked up a paper bag he thought might be some construction debris from the parking lot in back of his store. It was filled with pieces of nails and killed him when he touched it, as the shrapnel ripped through his chest to his heart. The Unabomber had gone back to personal delivery with an even more deadly type of bomb, and now he was a murderer. He was moving around, and felt comfortable being out here in broad daylight. I thought the computer store could still be an academic connection, since computers have to do with education and figure heavily at universities.

The next target—the twelfth—was another computer store, and the crime had a similar M.O., though it didn't occur until February 20, 1987, this time back in Salt Lake City. Gary Wright, the owner of Caams Computer Store, was injured in the store parking lot when he tried to move out of the way a stack of wood debris with nails sticking out from some two-by-fours. But this time, a witness saw someone leaving wood in the lot about an hour before the explosion. Police developed what became the famous Unabomber composite.

He was still working familiar areas, only this time he might have slipped up. If he realized this, if he knew that someone might have seen him, then being the coward he was, we'd expect him to lie low for a while. But during that time, he'd be experimenting with more powerful and sophisticated devices. He'd already killed, and he'd come back for more. He'd made no demands and hadn't tried to communicate. So, sooner or later, if he wasn't neutralized, he'd be back. He wasn't going to stop on his own.

As we predicted, there was a long gap in which we heard nothing from the Unabomber. There was hope that for one of the reasons speculated about during earlier gaps, he might finally be out of business. But on June 22, 1993, a package bomb postmarked Sacramento, California, arrived at the Tiburon home of Dr. Charles Epstein, a geneticist at the University of California, San Francisco. Dr. Epstein was seriously injured when he attempted to open the package.

The more the crimes evolved, the more we saw patterns that had worked in the past repeated, and techniques that proved riskier abandoned. Now the Unabomber was back to the safety and anonymity of the mail, sticking with professorial targets within his geographical sphere of comfort.

Some of us thought there might be another reason the Unabomber decided to get back in the game when he did. This guy clearly felt quite pleased with himself, and his ability to thwart national and local law enforcement for all these years must have been doing a good job of compensating for all of his personal deficiencies and disappointments in life. Though he might be known only to himself, he was a someone, the biggest bombing deal there had ever been. Then someone stole his thunder. On February 26, 1993, Islamic terrorists attempted to blow up the gigantic World Trade Center twin towers in lower Manhattan, killing six and injuring more than a thousand. Suddenly, the Unabomber wasn't the big kid on the block any longer.

At any rate, just two days after the last Unabomber crime, on June 24, Yale University computer scientist David J. Gelernter received a package bomb at his New Haven, Connecticut, office. The blast seriously wounded him in the abdomen and chest, tore off part of his right hand, and robbed him of his sight in one eye and hearing in one ear.

Our bomb people were telling us the devices were now of such a level of complexity and sophistication that they would each have required about a hundred hours of careful assembly. This guy had to be pretty bright and pretty dedicated, with a lot of time in which he didn't have to account to anyone.

Around this same time, the government established a million-dollar reward for information leading to the arrest and prosecution of the Unabomber. The task force's twenty-four-hour toll-free hotline, 1-800-701-BOMB, would ultimately handle more than twenty thousand tips.

On December 10, 1994, Thomas Mosser, vice president and general manager of the Young & Rubicam advertising agency, was killed instantly when a package bomb exploded at his residence in North Caldwell, New Jersey. The parcel, about the size of a videocassette, was sent from the San Francisco Bay Area. The return address was that of a fictitious professor at San Francisco

State. As in the crime against Professor Patrick Fischer, in this case the UNSUB was behind the times, and addressed Mosser in his old position with the Burson-Marsteller public relations firm, a job he'd left more than a year before. The shift of the bombing campaign to New Jersey seemed yet another attempt to disrupt an investigation that was centered in Chicago and San Francisco.

There was no clear motive for this one until the following April 24, when the *New York Times* received a letter explaining that Mosser's agency was targeted for "manipulating people's attitudes." The bomber had established this elaborate antitechnological ideology, but I saw this as an intellectual smoke screen for his rage and frustration. Once he'd begun communicating, I knew it was only a matter of time before we got him.

What turned out to be the final crime took place the same day letters were received by the *New York Times* and Professor David Gelernter, who had been severely injured in 1993. This was outrageous, of course, but it meant the Unabomber was continuing to communicate, and that was very good news.

In the letters, the UNSUB railed against computers for a variety of problems, ranging from invasion of privacy to "environmental degradation through excessive economic growth," and then took off on genetic engineering.

Perhaps the most insulting, and telling, part of the letter to Gelernter was this: "People with advanced degrees aren't as smart as they think they are. If you'd had any brains you would have realized that there are a lot of people out there who resent bitterly the way technonerds like you are changing the world and you wouldn't have been dumb enough to open an unexpected package from an unknown source."

The letter to the *Times* went on for pages and, in explaining the killing of Mosser, tried the old ploy of claiming the killer was part of a political group, but "for security reasons we won't reveal the number of members of our group." As with Moody, though, we knew the "we" was bullshit.

But that same day, there was more hell to pay. Gilbert P. Murray, president of the California Forestry Association, was killed when he opened a mail bomb in the association's headquarters in Sacramento. Here we had another strong "wood" connection. Murray was a victim of opportunity. The package was addressed to his predecessor, William Dennison.

We felt quite strongly that the timing was far from coincidental. Just five days before, the Murrah Federal Building in Oklahoma City had been destroyed, along with massive casualties, with a very crude bomb, but in a crime that dwarfed anything the Unabomber had done. And yet, the Unabomber must have seen himself as more artistic, more committed, more successful. After all, he'd been doing this for more than a decade and hadn't been caught. Losing center stage was an intolerable situation to him, we were sure, and he had to grab back the limelight in the only way he knew how—writing outrageous letters and killing people. And now we knew with reasonable certainty that he could be undone by his ego.

He next communicated on June 27, this time to Jerry Roberts, the editorial page editor of the *San Francisco Chronicle,* warning that his terrorist group, which he had previously identified as FC, would blow up an airliner out of Los Angeles International Airport within the next six days. He never delivered on this, nor did we feel he would, but this threw civil aviation in the United States into turmoil with the need for increased security over the Fourth of July holiday. This was just what he must have wanted. He later admitted it was a hoax in a letter to the *Times.* The return address on that letter, by the way, was Frederick Benjamin Isaac Wood, 549 Wood Street, Woodlake, California. (Get it? *F. B. I. Wood.*)

From that point on, the Unabomber communicated rather

regularly with the *New York Times,* the *Washington Post,* and another Berkeley professor. Then he came up with his ultimate demand. He would stop his bombings if the big papers in the country, particularly the *New York Times* and the *Washington Post,* would publish his thirty-five-thousand-word "Manifesto," which set out his gripes about modern technocratic society in an extremely tedious, academic way. He graciously waived the copyright on this work, allowing anyone who wanted to publish it.

The Manifesto confirmed my earlier beliefs that this was a messed-up, very bright, failed academic who was taking out his rage on society in general and the university world in particular behind this cloak of an antitechnology cause. Despite the fact that many in the task force had steadfastly adhered to the idea that it would take a technical person to construct the bombs, which meant to them the airline mechanic, this document pretty well spoke to what, if not who, our offender was.

Throughout the document he reveals telling aspects of his personality. Over and over again we see his need to depersonalize everyone—his perceived enemies, society in general, in fact every one but himself—to justify his terrorism and destruction. This guy is so inadequate, and so resentful of everyone who isn't inadequate, that unless he depersonalizes everyone else, he is nothing by comparison.

He speaks in the document of our powerlessness to rein in technology. What he is really talking about is his own feelings of powerlessness. From the very first bombs, he had been expressing his anger and hostility, striking out. The rest of it, with all the antitechnology trappings and the disdain for modern values— that would have been developed as he went along, to justify his actions.

There was a tremendous amount of agonizing debate over whether the newspapers should accept this extortion and give in to his vanity. There is no easy answer to this question, but most of us on the behavioral side (I was retired from the FBI by this point and so not part of the discussions) felt that the more this guy showed his hand, the more chance there was of someone knowing him.

And that, of course, is what happened. After the *Post* and *Times* ran special sections devoted to the Manifesto in mid-September, David Kaczynski, a social worker in upstate New York, was haunted by the similarity of the Manifesto to certain ideas and phrases put forth by his strange and estranged older brother, Theodore, almost fifty-five years of age, a failed academic who had been living as a hermit in a tiny cabin without electricity outside of Lincoln, Montana. David was struck not only by the offbeat philosophy but by certain turns of phrase that were uniquely Ted's, things like, "You can't eat your cake and have it too." He checked the printed Manifesto against some letters of Ted's he'd retrieved when their mother, Wanda, sold her house in Chicago to move nearer David and his wife, Linda. Everything he saw made him more and more nervous.

David contacted Ted and said he wanted to come see him. Ted refused. David and Linda then consulted an old friend of hers, Susan Swanson, now a private investigator. She looked at the evidence and shared David's alarm, but she wanted another expert opinion. So she called Clint Van Zandt, a retired FBI agent with a specialty in hostage negotiations, who had finished out his Bureau career working in my unit in Quantico as a profiler. Clint compared the letters with the Manifesto and concluded there was at least a 60 percent probability that both were written by the same individual. He then asked another expert to confirm or contradict his work, and when the second expert came back even more sure than he was, Clint told Swanson that if she or the people she represented weren't willing to go to the FBI, he felt morally compelled to.

David then made what must have been the hardest judgment of his life, a courageous choice that led to lives saved just as surely as his brother's choice had led to lives lost and shattered. I cannot overstate my admiration for David and Linda Kaczynski. Faced with conflicting loyalties, they made the difficult and heroic decision and, in so doing, became role models of morality and citizenship.

I think it is important here to say a few words about how, at long last, Theodore Kaczynski was identified as the Unabomber and brought to justice. The FBI, and law enforcement in general, came under a lot of criticism to the effect that, in the end, nothing they did for all those years really "mattered," that Kaczynski was caught on a "fluke." I must say that I completely disagree, and take strong issue with this premise—*This is exactly the way we want to catch criminals.* If I have any criticism of the course the investigation took—and I do—it is that not nearly enough was done on a proactive basis early enough. That might have led to a similar conclusion years earlier.

With a bomber, unless you happen to have a previous exemplar of his work and know who did it, as with Roy Moody, then it is extremely difficult to close a case strictly from forensic evidence. The only other exception to this would be an actual eyewitness to the planting of the bomb or prints left at the scene. So your best chance for catching the guy is always going to be enlisting the help of the public. More than most other types of violent offenders, bombers leave a trail of behavior. What I kept urging the Bureau to do was get the story on this guy out, describe the type of behavior we expected, describe the types of academic situations we imagined, and see if anyone recognized them.

Could we have predicted that the Unabomber would be living in a little cabin tucked away in Montana? Absolutely not. But could we have predicted that he would be from the Chicago area, a brilliant academic type in one of the scientific or techni-cal fields, without any close friends or attachments to women, who would have dropped out of the university world at some point and walked away from a promising future? Indeed we did. Ted Kaczynski came in contact with a lot of people before and during the course of his Unabomber career. If we'd gotten to one of those, we might have had him a lot earlier.

FBI agents and members of the elite Hostage Rescue Team began pouring into the rural Lincoln, Montana, area where Ted Kaczynski lived. They secured the perimeter around his cabin. On Wednesday, April 3, 1996, Special Agent Donald Sachtelben and a Justice Department lawyer went before a federal judge in Helena with a written request for a search warrant. After obtain-ing it, they drove the twenty or so miles back to Lincoln. Sachtel-ben and a team of agents approached the cabin and knocked on the door. When Kaczynski answered, they quickly subdued him. An explosives team swept the tiny but crammed room to make sure it wasn't booby-trapped.

It took days to fully examine and catalogue everything in the cabin. Among the items the agents found were notebooks filled with detailed sketches of explosive devices, handwritten notes describing chemical compounds that could be used to create ex-plosive charges, logs of previous experiments, pipes for making pipe bombs, containers of bomb-making chemicals, batteries and wiring, a complete array of tools, drafts of the Manifesto, a type-writer, and other communication linking Kaczynski with the Un-abomber. He also had a partially completed pipe bomb ready to send, along with a list of targets. So much for his pledge not to bomb anymore if his Manifesto was published.

He was taken to the jail in Sacramento, California, site of the Scrutton and Murray murders, and kept in an isolation cell. The en-suing investigation established positive links to many of the crimes as Kaczynski's whereabouts over the years were charted. The evidence continued to mount. Triggering emotional events in his life were correlated. And all the while, Ted continued to refuse to have anything to do with David or his mother.

Theodore Kaczynski turned out to be pretty much what we would have expected, only brighter. He'd been a withdrawn and lonely child. He had no normal relationships with women. He'd gone to Harvard and faced a promising career as a professor of mathematics at Berkeley. Then, at a certain point, unable to deal with the pressure of normal life, he just dropped out.

If we compare Theodore Kaczynski with someone like Timothy McVeigh or Joseph Paul Franklin, what we see is someone with a very different background and intellectual capabilities, combined with similar emotional problems. This helps explain why they each became involved in violent, terroristic-type crimes, but in varying ways. All three were withdrawn and asocial growing up. Neither Ted nor Tim ever had a girlfriend. Both were unmemorable in school. Ted was even unmemorable at Harvard. After his arrest, many people in his class racked their brains wondering why they couldn't even place him.

Franklin and McVeigh both got their solace and feeling of empowerment from guns; Kaczynski, like Moody, from bombs. Moody had many of the external trappings of a successful life: a young, attractive wife, cars, airplanes, nice home, successful business. But these would mean little to an offender such as Moody without total control over every aspect of his life, and the U.S. court system, like the car dealership he targeted before that, refused to acknowledge his dominance, his intellectual superiority, his right to set things as he felt they should be, without regard to the laws governing other people. Compared with the others, Ted was too intellectually sophisticated for racial or religious bigotry. He had to couch his resentment in terms of technocratic society at large, in some ways akin to McVeigh's paranoid fear of the New World Order. McVeigh and Moody were very meticulous. Kaczynski, from all reports, was something of a pig in his personal life and habits, but was very meticulous in his intellectual life (the realm where McVeigh and Franklin were far sloppier), more like Moody, whose mind was tightly wrapped around his own legal rhetoric, which only sometimes made sense. One extreme but still representative example involves a letter Ted wrote his brother in which he consented to have David send him a book as a gift for his birthday. But, Ted sternly warned, the book's width must not exceed seven inches, because that would necessitate a separate trip to the post office. Also, David must agree that Ted would be free to trade it for a different book if he so desired.

Ted imposed a special system of marking envelopes from his family in the unlikely event that they had to get in touch with him in a hurry. Otherwise, he might not deal with the letter for weeks or months. When David used the system to inform him that their father had died, Ted chastised him for misusing the system for something that didn't warrant it.

Kaczynski kept a journal in which he detailed what he did with his bombs and what the results had been. In 1985, for instance, he wrote of the device left behind the Sacramento computer store, "Planted bomb disguised to look like scrap of lumber," then matter-of-factly reported the result that the store owner was "blown to bits." Nowhere in any of this journal-keeping is there the slightest hint of remorse or a focus on anyone other than himself. An entry from 1980 reads, "After complicated preparations I succeeded in injuring the Pres of United A.L. but he was only one of a vast army of people who directly or indirectly are responsible for the jets."

In terms of motive, Ted Kaczynski simply had a desire to kill and maim and make other people as unhappy as he was. "My motive for doing what I am going to do is simply personal revenge," he wrote in 1971. He also had enough self-awareness to admit, "Of course, if my crime . . . gets any public attention, it may help to stimulate public interest in the technology question . . . [but] I certainly don't claim to be an altruist or to be acting for the good (whatever that is) of the human race. I act merely from a desire for revenge."

When he was a grad student at the University of Michigan in 1966, he was already thinking about this. As he wrote in his journal, "My first thought was to kill somebody I hated and then kill myself before the cops could get me." But then he decided he "was not ready to relinquish life so easily. So I thought, I will kill, but I will make at least some effort to avoid detection, so that I can kill again."

His infrequent communications with his family were equally telling. During the summer of 1991, he wrote to his mother, "Suppose that for a period of years whenever you touched—let us say—a banana, you got a severe electric shock. After that you would always be nervous around bananas, even if you knew they weren't wired to shock you. Well, in the same way, the many rejections, humiliations and other painful influences that I underwent during adolescence at home, in high school, and at Harvard have conditioned me to be afraid of people."

As with so many of these guys, the deep-seated feelings of inadequacy competed inside him with equally strong feelings of grandiosity and superiority, of being better and more deserving than everyone else. He admitted to himself that he was "superior to most of the rest of the human race. . . . It just came to me as naturally as breathing to feel that I was someone special."

He went on to say, "I am tormented by bitter regret at never having had the opportunity to experience the love of a woman," then closed by blaming his mother for not nurturing him in a way that would allow him to relate to people. He said he hated her, "because the harm you did me can never be undone."

By the way, there is no evidence of any abuse or neglect on the part of Ted's parents, Wanda and Theodore R. Kaczynski. They raised two sons, one of whom went on to become a notorious criminal, the other of whom became a social worker and helper of those around him. In fact, in 1970, before he had become as embittered as he eventually became, Ted wrote to his parents that they were the best that anybody could ask for.

Unlike McVeigh, who in some ways was a model soldier, finding a replacement family in the military, the Unabomber would never have been profiled to have a military background, even though that would have been a logical place to acquire an expertise in explosives. A guy like this would have had a real tough time in the service. He would not have fit in, he would have ended up with a dishonorable or general discharge, and he would have been pegged earlier. Also, his preoccupation with wood is not what we would have expected from someone in the military. We would have been looking for something much more functional, possibly some form of plastique as the explosive.

On December 22, 1997, five weeks of jury selection ended in Sacramento. Kaczynski faced ten counts in connection with four UNABOM cases. On January 5, 1998, he agreed not to fire his attorneys and serve as his own counsel. Just afterward, he attempted to hang himself in his cell. He was placed on suicide watch.

During the second week of January, he was examined by court-appointed psychiatrist Dr. Sally C. Johnson, who found him competent to stand trial in spite of various mental illnesses. Again Kaczynski requested that he be able to represent himself after disagreeing with his attorneys' strategy of hinging their defense on an insanity plea. After going back and forth with U.S.

District Court judge Garland E. Burrell Jr., he finally won the right to represent himself the day before opening statements in the trial were scheduled to begin.

The suicide attempt, the legal wrangling, the refusal and then agreement to submit to a psychological exam—all of these, in my mind, were simply ongoing attempts at manipulation, domination, and control.

On January 22, 1998, as the jury waited to begin hearing the case, Theodore John Kaczynski pled guilty to the ten-count indictment in Sacramento and a three-count indictment in New Jersey under an agreement with the Justice Department that let him be spared the death penalty and face a life in prison without the possibility of parole.

The courtroom provided the first occasion for Ted and David Kaczynski to see each other in more than a decade. It had been sixteen years since Ted had had any contact with his mother. It called to mind a letter of Ted's to his parents that David mentioned to FBI agents who had interviewed him. It read, in part, "I can't wait until you die so I can spit on your corpse."

# CHAPTER NINE

# YOU MAKE THE CALL

It's often been said that criminal behavioral profiling is an instance of life imitating art—that the concept began not with real-life experts but with such past masters of fiction as Edgar Allan Poe, Wilkie Collins, and Arthur Conan Doyle. Also, throughout my profiling career, I've often been asked to analyze some of the famous real-life murder cases of the past. Not surprisingly, the two requests that come up most frequently concern Jack the Ripper and Lizzie Borden, though I've been referred back as far as Richard III's alleged murder of his two nephew princes in the Tower of London in 1483, and we've even knocked around the idea of taking up the Cain and Abel case.

Once I retired from the Bureau, profiling finally came full circle for me. For the first time I was asked to analyze a murder that never happened—one that arose from the imagination of the greatest master of them all.

I don't have much background in classical literature or drama. Growing up, I always wanted to be a veterinarian. In the Air Force and in college, I didn't know what I wanted to be. And then I wanted to be a G-Man. So that's where most of my education and training have been directed. But my coauthor Mark Olshaker does have that kind of literary background and interest. In fact, he's passionate about the theater and intrigued me early in our relationship with his observation that actors and detectives were very similar in what they did: both came to a "scene" and tried to figure out what was really happening between the "characters" in that scene. Detectives call that clues or evidence. Actors call it subtext.

Patrick Stewart is an accomplished and celebrated British actor who has enjoyed a successful career as a member of the Royal Shakespeare Company, as Captain Jean-Luc Picard in *Star Trek: The Next Generation,* and in a variety of challenging modern roles. He's a good friend of Mark's, and narrated the film on my unit Mark wrote and produced for PBS's *Nova* series, *Mind of a Serial Killer.* So when Stewart came to our area in the fall of 1997 to star in the title role of Washington, D.C.'s, Shakespeare Theatre production of *Othello,* Mark asked me to meet with him and give him some character perspective based on my experience investigating and studying domestic violence, since that is what the play ultimately hinges on. Stewart wanted to know what would cause a man to murder the wife he apparently loves with all his heart.

I said I'd be happy to meet with such a distinguished actor, but that I wasn't sure how much help I could be because I had to admit I really didn't know much about the play. Mark said that was actually better, because then I could approach the situation objectively, as if it were a real case.

Mark filled me in a little on the play. Othello, a Moor from Africa, is a war hero and high-ranking military officer in medieval Venice, who falls in love with and marries Desdemona, the beautiful daughter of one of the city's gentry. In the course of the play, Othello is led further and further by his ensign and supposedly close friend, Iago, to believe that Desdemona is cheating on him with Iago's superior officer, Michael Cassio. In the end, Othello, consumed with jealousy and grief, murders her in her bedroom. I was struck with the evident parallels to the O. J. Simpson case, for whose civil trial I had consulted with the Goldman family's attorney Daniel Petrocelli.

That was basically what I knew about the play when I met with the actor over lunch at Mark's house. Stewart was warm and charming, both intellectual and visceral at the same time, anxious to unravel the mystery of character as he had done so many times before. As I talked, he took notes in the back of his copy of the play. I told him I would talk to him as if he were a local detective bringing me the facts of a case.

The first thing that occurred to me in thinking about the "case" was that this guy Iago must want Othello's gorgeous wife for himself, but Patrick and Mark both said no.

"So what is his motive?" I asked.

"He's brimming with rage that Othello has given to Cassio the promotion he thinks he deserves," Patrick replied. "And so he sets out to destroy Othello by carrying out this plot to make him think his wife is being unfaithful."

We talked about the stages Othello would have to go through in convincing himself that destroying the wife he adored was his only course.

Patrick asked what I thought was the key behavioral question: "John, how would Othello feel hearing these things about his wife? Would he believe them? Would he try to defend her honor?"

From what I understood about the character from Patrick and Mark, I explained that rather than Othello being outraged at this slur on his wife's honor and integrity, his own insecurities and feelings of inadequacy and unworthiness would be brought out by Iago's charges. Of course his wife would be unfaithful to him, because deep down he worries he's not good enough for her.

Her father was passionately against the marriage, and maybe he was right. Othello has compensated for being a foreigner and a racial minority and someone not considered part of the Venetian elite by being this great warrior who everyone has to admire because they're depending on him to protect them. But Iago, like many predatory personalities, is a pretty good profiler himself and understands how to get to his boss.

When Patrick asked me what Othello would be thinking about as the play went forward—in other words, his preoffense mind-set and behavior—I told him Othello would be preparing for the event in his own mind, getting emotionally comfortable with it. Ultimately, before he can go through with it, he will have to come to the classic acceptance of "If I can't have her, nobody else will."

"Tell me about the crime scene," I said.

"Desdemona's bedchamber in the castle," Patrick replied.

"How's he going to kill her?"

"Strangles her in bed. In our production, Desdemona is a very beautiful and diminutive woman, much smaller than I am, and I straddle her waist and press down on her neck."

Manual strangulation sounded "reasonable." This was a domestic personal-cause homicide, and this type of direct, face-to-face murder would tend to indicate to an investigator that the offender and the victim knew each other well. I told Patrick, for example, that to carry this off, someone like Othello would have to depersonalize her at this moment, to set himself apart emotionally. Therefore, I suggested that when he strangled her, he close his eyes and look away. We'd call this a "soft kill."

Someone in this situation would try, at least initially, to cover up the crime and get away with it, because he had convinced himself of the rightness and the justice of his actions. This would be the same, I explained, as the belief I'd voiced to Petrocelli that O. J. Simpson would probably pass a polygraph, since I believed he had convinced himself that he "had" to kill his wife.

I came away from that afternoon with a profound respect for Shakespeare's ability as a profiler. Everything that I'd seen real, contemporary offenders do in similar circumstances, the playwright had anticipated by more than four hundred years.

"Is he found out?" I asked.

They told me how Desdemona's maid, Emilia, who is also Iago's wife, comes upon them just after Othello has strangled his wife. Then Iago and some of the Venetian officials show up at the crime scene after Emilia starts screaming about the murder of her mistress. It is at that point that the dimensions of Iago's plot become clear, both to Othello and to the others.

I "warned" them that emotionally, this would be a very precarious place for Othello to be. Perhaps Othello's strongest bond is with his troops, and now he will have lost face, lost moral authority with Cassio and the others. His whole life has been the military, and now, through his subordinate Iago, he's been betrayed by what he believes in the most.

"You'd have a real suicide threat here," I said.

Patrick brightened. "That's exactly what happens!" After Othello is disarmed, he stabs himself with a dagger he's hidden in the room. Someone like Othello must stay in control, even in death.

Part of my task as a criminal investigative analyst is to put myself in the frame of mind where I can visualize the murder, where I can imagine what the victim must have been going through as they realized they were being killed. And so it was an interesting and moving experience a couple of weeks later when I sat in the theater audience with my wife and children and, for the first time, watched the play, culminating in the murder scene that

I had already visualized that afternoon at Mark's house. And it was particularly fascinating to see how brilliantly Patrick Stewart translated criminal investigative analysis into action, and made theory come alive.

Now that you've seen some of the ways we think and work in my business, and have delved into the anatomy of motive, let's try out a few cases. In the same way that a distinguished actor brought this Shakespearean murder case to me, I'm going to bring some "cases" to you, as if you were the profiler at Quantico. Of course, in this limited amount of space, I can give only simple fact patterns, but in each one there will be one or more elements that would lead the profiler to make certain conclusions about the motive and/or identity of the offender.

## CASE #1

A call comes in from a detective with the Atlanta Police Department about a product tampering.

Harry Ellison, the store manager of a local Fresh Faire supermarket, received an anonymous letter saying that a jar of baby food had been poisoned and that another product would be poisoned next week. To prove that the writer was serious and capable of doing what he threatened, the letter said, the jar could be identified by a red $X$ on the bottom. A duplicate copy of the letter was received by the anchorwoman of the local ABC station.

Immediately upon receiving the letter, Ellison had the baby food section sealed off, instructed his checkout clerks to remove baby food jars from the grocery cart of anyone currently in the checkout line, and called the Atlanta police and the regional manager of the grocery store chain.

When police officers arrived and began going through the shelves under Ellison's supervision, they found a jar of strained peaches at the very back of one shelf marked with the red $X$ mentioned in the threat letter. By this time, the television station had arrived and began shooting video. The story made the six o'clock news and began a mini hysteria, with hundreds of parents returning all sorts and brands of baby food to various stores in the area.

Examination of the affected jar indicated that the vacuum seal had been broken. The entire remainder of the stock on the shelves and in the storeroom was also scrupulously examined, but no other adulterated products were found. The regional manager instructed the rest of the stores in the chain to examine all existing stock, but again, no other problems were discovered.

Laboratory analysis of the tampered-with jar showed that it had been adulterated with rat poison pellets. The pellets were distinguishable from the food with which they were mixed. The particular poison product was available in the same supermarket.

So far, no one has been injured, but the extortionist has threatened to poison another product next week, and the community is in a state of fear.

Who could have done this? you are asked. Why is it being done? And how dangerous do you think the perpetrator is?

The threat letter was written to the store manager, you confirm.

"Yes, that's right. Even his middle initial, K," says the detective working the case.

Is the name posted anywhere in the store?

"I don't think so, not that I recall. But I'll take a look and get back to you." When he calls back, he states that Mr. Ellison's name is not posted.

In this case, you tell the detective, profiling cannot identify the UNSUB, but it can probably tell you what kind of person did this, why, where to find him, and how serious a threat he poses.

Let's take the final consideration first. The jar was marked just as the letter said it would be; the store and the media were warned ahead of time; and the product—just one unit—was placed at the very back of the shelf. This tells us that unlike, say, the Tylenol poisoner, this UNSUB does not want to hurt anyone. He has gone to fairly great lengths to make sure no one walks off with this particular jar. Also, this is in no way a sophisticated poisoning. Most mothers and fathers of babies are used to opening several of these jars a day and would notice that the top felt different when it was unscrewed. If for any reason they missed that step, as soon as they stuck a spoon into the jar they would notice the foreign pellets. And so, even though the food was adulterated to the point where it could prove fatal to a baby who ingested it, the chances of actually getting to that point are slight.

There is no money demand in the letter, which speaks against a product tampering for profit. Even if the letter is just to show that the UNSUB is serious and capable, the threat of further poisonings should have been tied to some demands. Just as significant is the fact that the letter is sent not to the supermarket chain but to an individual store. And more specifically even than that, it is directed to an individual manager whose name is not known to the public. The fact that it is addressed to him, to the extent of including his middle initial, strongly indicates that the UNSUB has a grudge against this particular store and this particular manager.

His motive? He doesn't want to hurt innocent people. He doesn't want money. What he wants is satisfaction. He wants to disrupt the operations of this particular retail outlet. He wants to embarrass Mr. Ellison, to show that he cannot control his own store. He wants to punish him for something by making him look bad, and possibly lose his job. That's why the UNSUB made sure the television station was on hand for greatest exposure.

What the police want to do, you tell the detective, is to question Ellison about any personnel problems he has experienced recently. The UNSUB will probably be someone who perceives he was adversely affected by those problems, or somehow got a raw deal in the process. In fact, there is a good chance that the subject will make it his business to visit the store after the publicity, to come up to Ellison to say hello and graciously ask him how he's doing. He may say something to the effect of, "You look tired," or "Are you feeling okay?" To make his scheme satisfying, he will have to evaluate the effect he's having on his target.

When the detective follows up, he reports that Ellison said there was a recent staff reduction at that particular location because the regional office felt it did not need so many employees on a shift for the volume of business the store was doing. Three employees from each shift were transferred. Ellison was instructed to make the selection himself. The one who complained most vociferously about the move had, in fact, stopped by the store and greeted Harry Ellison. He was questioned by the police and soon confessed to the crime.

## CASE #2

A detective from the Cincinnati Police Department calls with what appears to be a particularly senseless hate crime. Frederick and Marsha Dorling came home one night to find their house brutally vandalized: furniture and clothing ripped, debris all over the floor of the living room, drawers pulled out and strewn around the bedroom, and anti-Jewish and antiblack slogans written with Magic Marker on the walls. Fred is black, Marsha is Jewish, and they are the only racially mixed couple in the neighborhood. They have no children. Their dog, a male rottweiler named Max, was out with them at the time of the crime, which would suggest that whoever did this knew details about their household and watched their comings and goings. The case has gotten some minor media attention, but enough that the "gold shields" upstairs are anxious for a solution.

Where exactly were these slurs written? you ask.

"Mostly on the walls of the bedroom, but also on a large mirror as you come in the front hall."

Any outside?

"Apparently not."

And what did the damage consist of?

"Furniture upholstery was ripped with a kitchen knife, as were some of Mr. Dorling's suits and Mrs. Dorling's dresses. The large television in the den was knocked over onto the floor and smashed. In the same room, a rack stereo system had been thrown to the floor piece by piece. They were lucky that some old family pictures on the wall of the same room were left alone."

Was anything taken?

"As closely as they've been able to determine, some jewelry and a couple of watches are missing, and some cash—less than five hundred dollars. Oh, and a video camera. That part didn't upset them too much. Marsha said the only thing she really cared about was a set of antique silver from her mother. And even though it was dumped on the dining room floor from the china cabinet where they kept it, none of the pieces seem to be missing."

You may feel a little awkward, but you have to ask the standard question about insurance.

"Their homeowners policy will take care of the cleanup and repair of the walls and furniture, but we checked: they don't stand to make any profit off this."

Okay, fine. You just had to ask. Had they received any threat communications, either written or over the phone?

"Nothing overt like that, no. But they did say they just never felt comfortable in the area. For example, they wouldn't be invited to neighborhood parties that everyone else on the block would be invited to. Or they'd feel like they were getting the cold shoulder whenever they'd see someone in the supermarket. You know, like nobody else approved of their marriage. They're really hoping this wasn't done by anyone in the neighborhood itself, but they're worried."

Well, how have they been treated since the incident?

"Much better, they say. Everyone they've talked to, and everyone I've talked to, for that matter, seems genuinely embarrassed that something like this could happen in their midst. Some of the neighbors have even instituted night patrols on their own initiative. It's very impressive."

You're glad to hear that. This is the kind of thing we encourage—everyone looking out for everyone else.

"So, from what I've told you, what type of individual or group do you think we ought to be looking for in this case?"

Before they go any further in their investigation, you advise, they'd better check out the Dorlings themselves.

"Okay," the detective says with surprise. "I'll get back to you."

Less than a week later, the detective calls back, even more surprised, to say that he got the Dorlings apart and questioned each of them for a considerable period of time. Ultimately, they confessed that they had staged the vandalism.

What was it about the description of the crime that made you suspect them?

Whenever I have to confront a case of vandalism or arson to a home, I first think about the victimology, and then I want to know about the crime scene: Specifically, what was taken, destroyed, or damaged? I was a little suspicious that a crime that is usually as impulsive as this—and often committed by teenagers—would happen to have been done when the dog was out of the house, and that there was no vandalism to the outside of the house. But the kicker for me was that with all the damage done, the two categories of items left intact were the family photos in the den and the antique silver service; in other words, the only things that had emotional value and could not be replaced for money.

The motive? It was quite clear that these people should be taken at their word that they did not feel comfortable among their neighbors. Having tried other, more traditional ways of gaining acceptance, they felt a need to resort to something dramatic: to embarrass the other folks in the community with the public and media spotlight of hate, to galvanize them into accepting them as they should have all along.

It's unfortunate and pathetic when you see cases like this, but you do see them.

## CASE #3

An ATF agent in California calls for consultation on a serial arson case at Pfeiffer–Big Sur State Park. Four fires have been set over the past three weeks. Luckily, all occurred in the early morning and were spotted and extinguished before getting out of control. But officials know the arsonist is not likely to stop, and they don't want to rely on luck to keep the wilderness—and visitors—safe. The agent is hoping for some guidance that will help lead them to the UNSUB, and this week they got a break she hopes will be helpful: it's been kept from the press, but park rangers found evidence of a fifth fire that failed to catch.

She reviews the case thus far. The first fire was set on a rocky hillside just outside some of the densest forests in the park. This actually saved the wooded area, she and the rangers believe, because there wasn't enough undergrowth for a fire to burn well or spread. The smoke was easily visible from the ranger tower.

"We don't think this guy's any too bright," the agent adds.

Why's that?

"Well, he didn't seem to learn much from that fire. The next was set in an area just as scruffy, although more of a dirt-and-sand mix than rocks. Not a real good place for a forest fire. And as you can imagine, there's plenty of dry timber around. Based on the location of this fire, the subject hiked right past some choice places to get a good fire going, but he made it hard on himself. He also could have gotten more bang for the buck if he waited until dusk, when it would be harder to spot smoke and there are fewer rangers on duty."

For the third and fourth fires, the arsonist appeared to be escalating in frequency: two in just the past week, three if you count the one that didn't catch.

"And it's a good thing he chose this week to get busy and not next," the agent added.

Why?

"Well, the General Assembly's considering cutting the park's budget, and it looks like some of the rangers are going to get the ax, no pun intended. The rangers are pretty up in arms about it. They resent that people think all they do is sit up in their towers, gazing at spotted owls through binoculars. Next week, to protest the cutbacks, there were threats of a sick-out. But now those plans have been put on hold."

What about the new evidence found this week?

Although the frequency of his crimes has escalated, the arsonist's M.O. has remained consistent, based on the time of day the fires are spotted and the debris found once the rangers reach them. And the device just found was completely intact. It was a small brown paper bag—like the kind kids take their lunches to school in—with a layer of sand on the bottom. Wedged in the sand, to keep it upright, was a candle, and there were small strips of paper all around the candle's base. The candle would burn down, set the paper strips on fire, and it would all go from there. It had worked four out of five times. And it probably would have worked again, but for a guy who happened to like hiking early in the morning, who smelled the candle just off the trail he was taking. "We checked this guy out—seeing as how he was, conveniently, alone at the time he found the device. But he just got back from two weeks doing business on the East Coast, so he wasn't around for the other fires.

"What we're really interested in is your take on this signature aspect," the agent stresses. "What do you see as the significance of the bag-and-candle setup? As you can imagine, with this many fires in just three weeks, and wildfires such a problem out here, this has become a pretty high-profile case. There's a lot of pressure to catch this guy. To give you an idea what it's like, after this evidence was found, one of the rangers came up with a theory that it's part of some bizarre religious ritual. He wants it reported so the other rangers can compare it with any reports of strange hikers they've had in the past few months."

But that's not the direction you'd take the investigation.

Why not?

You would focus on that concerned park ranger, for several reasons. Start with victimology, even though in this case the "victim" is nature. It's significant that the fires have all been set in areas where they were unlikely to do much damage. This UNSUB is not motivated to destroy the wilderness. Rather, he's going out of his way to do the least amount of damage. This is someone who cares about nature, is comfortable in and around it, not some guy getting a sexual thrill out of watching the devastation he's wrought.

The fire-setting method, too, tells us a lot about our UNSUB. He is methodical, organized, brings what he needs to the scene; he's no dummy. His device allows him enough time to get away and be with others when the fire is discovered, but doesn't let the fire spread in the interim. Even the time of day he sets the fires reveals his concern that he get what he needs (time to get out cleanly) but that the fire be spotted before there's any real threat. He is willing to use the forest to make his point—a point he feels is important—but not at the expense of the woods.

With the threat of budget cutbacks and frustration in the ranger ranks, a few "good" fires would show how important these people are, how potentially dangerous their job is. They'd only be more appreciated for putting the safety of the land and taxpayers ahead of their own job concerns by not calling in sick while this arsonist is still out there.

Finally, you know I'm often suspicious of people who inject themselves into an investigation, and ultimately, it would be this ranger's postoffense behavior that would raise red flags for me. This guy's giving himself away with his agitation. He doesn't think the arsonist is a religious nut any more than you or I do. He's thinking, "Shit, what if they find fingerprints on the candle?!" He's trying to get information from investigators—find out what they have—in a way that won't arouse suspicion.

Advising the agent from a behavioral standpoint, then, we'd give preoffense behavior we'd expect from this UNSUB: he would have been vocal and angry about the proposed budget cuts. Then, when the fires started, he would have made sure he was with someone each time one was spotted, and he would have responded with them, giving himself the opportunity to make sure all evidence that could link him to the scene was destroyed. Compare this with Eddie Lee Adams considering returning to Ola Temple's house to make sure it burned down enough to cover his tracks. Now that one of the UNSUB's fires was discovered too early, we would expect his concern to grow with each passing day. He would keep checking in, even to the point of hounding investigators.

Authorities call in the suspect ranger to talk over the case with them. They show him a map of the park, with red dots indicating where each of the fires occurred. Pictures of the last, intact device, taken from several angles and blown up to poster size, are hung all around the room. The interrogators give him a face-saving scenario ("We know you didn't really want to hurt the forest. After all, you've made it your life's work to protect it").

It doesn't take long for the enormity of the investigative effort to overwhelm him. After all, although he's a serial offender, he's not a career criminal. He didn't particularly enjoy what he was doing. He was out to save his job and make sure people didn't take him and his work for granted. Unlike the offender in Case #1, who is just unstable enough that I wouldn't want to trust him around the food service industry anymore, this guy can probably be "redeemed" with proper counseling and guidance. Even though he is a serial offender, I don't consider him a threat to repeat.

## CASE #4

The profile coordinator from the Portland, Oregon, FBI Field Office calls with reference to a kidnapping. These are always among the most difficult and emotionally searing cases for those of us in law enforcement. We can't help but project our fears for our own families onto the case.

It was a Sunday morning, the second week in January, and Nicole Singer, twenty-one years of age, had just bundled up her two-year-old, Elizabeth, known as Elsie, into her coat, hat, and mittens to visit Nicole's new boyfriend, Tommy Rowan, a twenty-eight-year-old successful construction contractor and avid sailor. As Nicole was passing by the kitchen of their garden apartment, she noticed a carving knife standing blade-up in the cutlery container on the drain board next to the sink. Fearing that if she didn't put the knife away properly, Elsie might get hold of it and seriously injure herself, Nicole reached for it to place it in a drawer. But just as she did, her hand slipped and the knife sliced across her palm.

The wound, while not deep, was a long cut and immediately

began bleeding noticeably. Nicole sharply told Elsie to go wait for her in the living room, then rushed into the bathroom to tend to the wound. Although she didn't lock the bathroom door, she closed it so that Elsie wouldn't see all the blood and become upset. At least twice while she was in the bathroom, Nicole called out to the little girl to ask if she was all right, and both times Elsie replied that she was, the last time complaining mildly that she was getting hot. Nicole told her to take off her hat and mittens and unbutton her coat, but not to take it off, because they were already running behind schedule.

By the time Nicole stopped the bleeding, cleaned the wound, and bandaged her hand, she figured about twenty to twenty-five minutes had gone by. She called Elsie but received no answer. She looked for her throughout the apartment. The child wasn't there. Now panic-stricken, she went out the door and ran down the hallway, first in one direction and then the other. She tried the stairwell and the lobby, but Elsie was nowhere to be found.

She raced back up the stairs to her apartment and dialed 911. She was bordering on hysterics when she told the operator that her "baby had been kidnapped." Despite Nicole's agitated state, the operator skillfully obtained the information she needed while attempting to calm her. Uniformed police officers were dispatched and arrived on the scene within six minutes of the call and immediately undertook their own search for the child, finding nothing. One of them noticed that the front door was ajar and asked Ms. Singer if the door had been closed or ajar, locked or unlocked, during the time the child was waiting for her mother to administer first aid to herself. Ms. Singer was still in an extremely agitated state, but said the door had definitely been in a locked mode, and that she thought the door was closed, but since she had then gone out and left it open behind her, she couldn't be sure. When the other officer suggested that either someone came into the apartment and took the child or Elsie became bored and wandered out on her own, Nicole again became hysterical. The officers drove her to the nearest hospital emergency room, where her hand wound was redressed and was closed with five stitches.

A large manhunt—composed of police and sheriff's officers and many volunteers—combed the area, but no trace of Elsie or any evidence was found. When the FBI was brought into the case the next day, agents advised the police to administer a polygraph test to Ms. Singer and to her boyfriend, Mr. Rowan. Both willingly agreed to undergo the examination. Mr. Rowan expressed deep concern for Ms. Singer's mental health, stating during the conversation with the FBI agent that he and Nicole had already started talking about marriage. Mr. Rowan had not been married previously. Both passed the polygraph, with Ms. Singer's examiner noting that she remained highly emotional throughout the test and clearly felt guilty about leaving the child alone for as long as she had.

Then on Wednesday, Nicole Singer called the detective assigned to the case. In that day's mail, a small package wrapped in brown paper had arrived. There was no return address. When Nicole opened the package, she found one of Elsie's mittens. When questioned by the detective and the FBI, she said she was absolutely certain the mitten belonged to Elsie and was not a duplicate or similar-looking one. She said she could tell because there was a snag in the fabric around the wrist and she had been meaning to repair it.

No note or communication of any kind was included with the mitten.

At that point, you tell the profile coordinator that he'd better go back and do another polygraph on Nicole Singer, because this is not a kidnapping. The little girl is dead and Nicole is the killer.

Why did you doubt her story?

There are a couple of elements that arouse suspicion. The first is that a mother left the child alone in an apartment that might or might not have been secured—but we'll give her the benefit of the doubt on that one. The second is that when she called 911, she told the operator her "baby had been kidnapped." This is such a horrible thing for parents even to contemplate that most of them will consciously or subconsciously suppress it as long as they can. Normally a parent under this kind of extreme stress will say something to the effect that her baby or child is missing, that she can't find her, that she's run off, that she's wandered away . . . anything not to confront the idea of kidnapping. As I say, this isn't ironclad, but it can get you thinking.

We'd also pay some attention to Ms. Singer's situation: she is a young single mother who is becoming increasingly involved with a single man without children.

But the element that really gives it away is the mitten sent through the mail. If you stop to think it through, it doesn't make any sense. There are really only three cases in which children are taken by strangers. The first is kidnapping for profit. The second is kidnapping by those who intend to do children harm for their own purposes, either for perverted sexual gratification or as a specific or general revenge. The third is kidnapping by unstable and pathetic people who wish to have a child of their own. The first of these three types of offenders will have to communicate with the parents to establish demands and make arrangements for payment. The second and third categories will want nothing whatever to do with the parents; only in the rarest of instances—when you have a truly insane or sadistic individual—would you see any attempt at communication. But that would be a real long shot, extremely unusual.

There is absolutely no reason for a child abductor to send the mitten back, except as proof that he has the child. And in that case, there would be some demand or mention of ransom. Kidnappers don't want to keep the hostage any longer than they have to.

What has happened here is that the mother has staged the crime according to how she thinks a real kidnapping would go down, yet she really has no idea, and this gives her away.

The polygraph is an imprecise and imperfect instrument and should never be accepted, one way or the other, without question. In this case, there are two solid reasons why the examiners' suspicions might not have been aroused. For one thing, if Nicole convinced herself that what she had done was "right" and "necessary," then she could do pretty well on the lie-detector test. An even more likely possibility is that the examiner interpreted her expressions of "guilt" as having to do with her acknowledged negligence in leaving the child alone.

When a second polygraph is administered, this time by an examiner aware of the different types of guilt he's looking for, the results are different. And when Nicole Singer is told that she's failed the test, is now the prime suspect, and is given her Miranda rights, she begins to break down. When the FBI agent gives her a way to "explain" herself without seeming like a cold-blooded murderer, she confesses—not only to strangling and burying Elsie, but also to intentionally cutting her own hand as part of the staging.

The motive? That grows out of the situation, and unfortunately isn't all that uncommon. She was a young, single mother, missing out on all the fun of her late teens because of the child. She had met Tommy Rowan, who told her he wanted to get married and start a family of their own. But either because of something he made clear, or because of her perception, she believed that he felt there was no room in their lives together for this child. So if Nicole was to achieve the kind of life she dreamed of, Elsie would have to go. Nicole is a pathetic offender, and what she has done may be psychologically explainable.

But that doesn't make it excusable.

Now, these cases are fairly simple, and if you've been paying attention throughout the book, you should have solved all of them. But you can only make your judgment based on the facts I've given you. Likewise, when we make our evaluations, they are only going to be as good as the information and input we're given or, in some cases, we can observe for ourselves.

If I've learned anything from my career as a profiler and mindhunter for the FBI, it is that we're all products of our own pasts—our experience on earth as well as whatever biological heritage and "hardwiring" went into making each of us the unique individuals we are. By studying these factors, we can begin to construct our profiles. That's why we can predict that one category of white male loner in their twenties will gravitate toward one type of crime, while another category that looks the same on the surface will gravitate toward another, or none at all. So what I've really learned from all this is that you can't make assessments based strictly on surface details. Human beings are far too complicated for that.

What we can say about each of us as human beings is that we establish patterns in our lives. We need them to reach the long term; we need them to get through the day. And if we break those patterns, there's a particular reason.

*Why* did it happen? *What* does the evidence tell you? *Who* could have done such a thing? That's what the anatomy of motive is all about.

# INDEX